THE FEAR OF BARBARIANS

THE FEAR OF BARBARIANS

BEYOND THE CLASH OF CIVILIZATIONS

Tzvetan Todorov

TRANSLATED BY
Andrew Brown

THE UNIVERSITY OF CHICAGO PRESS

Tzvetan Todorov was born in Bulgaria in 1939 and has lived in France since 1963. He is the author of fifteen books, most of which have been translated into English, most recently *Hope and Memory: Lessons from the Twentieth Century* and *The New World Disorder: Reflections of a European.*

Andrew Brown has translated numerous books from French, including several works on sociology and politics, such as Tzvetan Todorov's *The New World Disorder* and Jean-François Bayart's *Global Subjects: A Political Critique of Globalization.* He lives in Cambridge, U.K.

The University of Chicago Press, Chicago 60637
This English edition © Polity Press, 2010
All rights reserved. Published 2010
Printed in the United States of America

Originally published in French as
La peur des barbares © Editions Robert Laffont, 2008.

19 18 17 16 15 14 13 12 11 10   1 2 3 4 5
ISBN-13: 978-0-226-80575-7 (cloth)
ISBN-10: 0-226-80575-1 (cloth)

Library of Congress Cataloging-in-Publication Data

Todorov, Tzvetan, 1939–
[Peur des barbares. English]
The fear of barbarians : beyond the clash of civilizations / Tzvetan Todorov ; translated by Andrew Brown.
  p. cm.
Includes index.
ISBN-13: 978-0-226-80575-7 (cloth : alk. paper)
ISBN-10: 0-226-80575-1 (cloth : alk. paper) 1. East and West.
2. Civilization—Philosophy. 3. Islam and politics. 4. Islamic countries—Relations—Europe. 5. Europe—Relations—Islamic countries. 6. Democracy—Religious aspects—Islam. 7. Group identity—Europe. 8. Manichaeism. 9. World politics—1989– 10. Civilization, Modern—1950– I. Title.
CB251.T5913 2010
909'.09767—dc22

                                                2010009778

♾ The paper used in this publication meets the minimum requirements of the American National Standard for Information Sciences—Permanence of Paper for Printed Library Materials, ANSI Z39.48-1992.

In memory of
GERMAINE TILLION
and
EDWARD SAID

CONTENTS

ACKNOWLEDGMENTS

Thanks are due to all those who helped me think over the questions raised in this book, whether during conversations with friends or from my reading of their writings. More particularly, thanks go to (among the living): Antoine Audouard, Ulrich Beck, Ian Buruma, Anne Cheng, Régis Debray, François Flahault, Joseph Frank, Stephen Holmes, Nancy Huston, Annick Jacquet, Toshiaki Kozakaï, Amin Maalouf, Geert Mak, Abdelwahab Meddeb, Dominique Moïsi, Danny Postel, Olivier Roy, Amartya Sen, Richard Wolin, Elisabeth Young-Bruehl, Slimane Zeghidour; and also to Mohamed Charfi (d. 6 June 2008).

Introduction: Between Fear and Resentment

The twentieth century was dominated, in Europe, by the conflict between totalitarian regimes and liberal democracies. Following the Second World War, after the defeat of Nazism, this conflict took the shape of a global Cold War, intensified on the margins by various limited 'hot' confrontations. The actors in these were clearly identified. On the one side, the bloc of the Communist countries, extending from East Germany to North Korea, initially dominated by the Soviet Union. On the other side of the 'Iron Curtain' around these countries lay the West, the 'free world', essentially comprising the countries of Western Europe and North America, under the leadership of the United States. Outside this antagonism there was a third actor, a varied assortment of non-aligned countries, politically neutral, called the third world. The Earth was thus divided up on political criteria, even if other characteristics played a role too: the Third World was poor, the West rich, while in Communist countries the army was rich and the population poor (but not allowed to point out this discrepancy).

This situation lasted for over half a century. I was especially aware of it since I was born in Eastern Europe, in Bulgaria, where I grew up before going to live in France when I was twenty-four. It seemed to me that this division of the countries of the world would last forever – or at least until the end of my life. This may explain the joy I felt when, around 1990, the European Communist regimes collapsed one by one. There were no longer any reasons for setting East against West, or for competing in the struggle for world domination: and all hopes were permitted. The old dreams of the great liberal thinkers would finally come true. War would be replaced by negotiation; a new world order could be established, more peaceable than

1

the previous world of the Cold War. I do not think I was alone in placing my faith in this desirable development.

Only twenty or so years later, it has to be admitted that this hope was illusory; it does not seem that tension and violence between countries will disappear from world history. The great confrontation between East and West had relegated various kinds of hostility and opposition to the background: these soon started to re-emerge. Conflicts could not just vanish as if by magic, since the deep reasons for their existence were still there; indeed, they were quite possibly becoming even more influential. The world population is continuing to grow rapidly, while the territory on which it lives remains the same size as before, or, indeed, is shrinking, eroded by deserts and threatened by floods. Worse, vital resources – water, energy – are diminishing. In these circumstances, competition between countries is inevitable – and this implies that those who have less will become increasingly aggressive towards those who have more, and the latter will become increasingly worried about preserving and protecting their advantages.

These are permanent features of the landscape, but some new developments have also been occurring. Even though numerous hot spots are still found across the world, sometimes exploding into violence, their action remains limited in space, and no global conflict comparable to the Second World War has broken out for over sixty years. This absence of any major confrontation has enabled a veritable technological revolution to happen peacefully right in front of our eyes; and the latter, in turn, has greatly contributed to the strengthening of contacts between countries in the process known as globalization.

This technological shake-up has affected several different domains, but some advances have had a particularly strong impact on international relations. The most evident concerns communication, which has become incomparably more rapid than in the past, and is also taking many channels. Information is instantaneous, transmitted by both words and images, and it can reach the whole world. Television (and no longer just radio), mobile phones, email, the Internet: once we might have complained about being short of information, but now we are drowning in it. One of the consequences of this change is that the different populations on our planet are spending more time with each other. Words and images are making people more familiar with one another, standardized products circulate across the entire world, and people too are travelling more than ever before. The inhabitants of rich countries go to the lands of the poor to do business or enjoy

2

a holiday; the poor try to reach the lands of the rich to find work. If you have the means, travel has become much faster.

The intensity of communication and the ever-accelerating familiarity between countries and people have positive and negative effects; but one other technological innovation is a source of nothing but apprehension. This is the ease of access to weapons of destruction, in particular explosives. Anyone and everyone, it now seems, can procure them without difficulty. They can be miniaturized and carried around in your pocket; they are so sophisticated that they can kill tens, hundreds or thousands of people in a single instant. Bomb-making instructions are easily available on the Internet, the products needed to make them are sold in supermarkets, and a mobile phone is all you need to set off an explosion. This 'democratization' of weapons of destruction creates a completely new situation: it is no longer necessary to resort to the power of a state in order to inflict heavy losses on your enemy, since a few highly motivated individuals with even a minimum of financial resources are enough. 'Hostile forces' have completely changed their appearance.

These major technological achievements have had consequences for people's lifestyles, but they have not entailed the immediate disappearance of the old world – obviously, they could never have done so. What they *have* produced, however, is a juxtaposition of contrasts, in which the archaic is found cheek by jowl with the ultramodern. This simultaneous presence of opposites can be found within a single country, as well as between countries. The Russian or Chinese peasant is just as far removed from the way of life found in Moscow or Shanghai as the peasants of the Rif and Anatolia are from the inhabitants of Paris and London. The world of the former is dominated by a 'vertical' communication, ensuring the transmission of traditions; that of the latter, in contrast, is characterized by the force of 'horizontal' tradition, between contemporaries permanently linked to a network. What is striking here is the fact that the two worlds are not unaware of each other: images from both worlds circulate across the whole planet. And they do more than just see each other: ruined peasants leave their lands and make their way to cities in their own countries or, preferably, to cities in rich countries. Global metropolises, found in every continent, contain populations of different origins and, naturally, of extremely varied customs and manners. And thus it is that a *niqab* (veil covering the whole body) can be seen next to a G-string. (But both are forbidden in French schools!)

It is easy to guess at the results this collision between widely differing traditions might well lead to. In some people, it engenders envy, or rejection, or both at once; in others, it inspires contempt, or condescension, or compassion. The former have the superiority of numbers, and of a sense of anger, on their side; the latter have technology and sheer might on theirs. The mixture is explosive, and the number of conflicts is on the increase. The map of these conflicts, however, is not the same as that imposed just after the Second World War.

These days, we can separate out the world's countries into several groups, depending on the way they are reacting to these new circumstances. However, they can no longer be distinguished on the basis of political regime, as at the time of the confrontation between Communism and democracy; nor by big geographic divisions, as, for example, between North and South (since Australia is in the South and Mongolia in the North); nor between East and West (since China and Brazil often turn out to be similar); and even less between civilizations. In the eighteenth century, discussing the human passions that stir a society, Montesquieu introduced a notion that he called 'the principle of government': virtue in a republic, for instance, and honour in monarchies.[1] These days, too, a dominant passion or social attitude imbues government decisions as well as individual reactions.

I am fully aware of the risks one runs in schematizing things this way and freezing situations that are necessarily forever changing. Several social passions are always acting together at any one time, and none affects all the members of a population; their very identity is mobile and does not assume the same appearance from one country to another. In addition, the hierarchy between them is forever evolving, and one country can easily pass, in the space of just a few years, from one group to another. And yet their presence is undeniable. To describe this division, I will start out from a typology recently suggested by Dominique Moisi,[2] filling it out a little and adapting it for my own purposes, without forgetting the simplifications it will necessarily entail.

I will call the predominant passion of a first group of countries *appetite*. Their population often feels that, for various reasons, it has missed out on its share of wealth; today its time has come. The inhabitants want to benefit from globalization, consumption and leisure – and they will not skimp on the means needed to achieve this. It was Japan which, several decades ago, first went down this path, and it has been followed by several countries in South East Asia and, more recently, by China and India. Other countries, and other parts of the world, are now setting off down the same road: Brazil, and, possibly in a not too distant future, Mexico and South Africa. For several years, Russia seems to have been following the same route, turning its defeat in the Cold War into an advantage: its development no longer has to be reined in by ideology; nor does the enrichment of its citizens. The country no longer needs to take part in the competition for world hegemony.

The second group of countries is that in which *resentment* plays an essential role. This attitude results from a humiliation, real or imaginary, allegedly inflicted on it by the countries with the most wealth and power. It has spread, to various degrees, across a good part of the countries whose population is mainly Muslim, from Morocco to Pakistan. For some time, it has also been endemic in other Asian countries or in some countries in Latin America. The targets of this resentment are the old colonial countries of Europe and, increasingly, the United States, held responsible for private misery and public powerlessness. Resentment towards Japan is strong in China and Korea. Of course, it does not dominate everyone's minds or all activities; nonetheless, it helps to structure social life, since, like the other social passions, it characterizes an influential and highly active minority.

The third group of countries is distinguished by the place occupied in them by the feeling of *fear*. These are the countries that make up the West and that have dominated the world for several centuries. Their fear concerns the two previous groups, but it is not of the same nature. Western, and in particular European, countries fear the economic power of the 'countries of appetite', their ability to produce goods more cheaply and thus make a clean sweep of the markets – in short, they are afraid of being dominated economically. And they fear the physical threats that might come from the 'countries of resentment', the terrorist attacks and explosions of violence – and, in addition, the measures of retaliation these countries might be capable of when it comes to energy supplies, since the biggest oil reserves are found in these countries.

Finally, a fourth group of countries, spread across several continents, might be designated as that of *indecision*: a residual group whose members risk falling thrall, one day, to appetite or resentment, but who for the time being are not so affected by these passions. Meanwhile, the natural resources of these lands are being pillaged by nationals originally from the other groups of countries, with the active complicity of their own corrupt leaders; ethnic conflicts spread desolation among them. Certain strata of their population, often wretched, try to gain access to the 'countries of fear' which

5

are wealthier than their own, in order to enjoy a better standard of living.

I am not really competent to describe in detail each of these groups of countries. I live in France, within the European Union, so in the group designated as being dominated or in any case marked by fear; it is also the only one which I know from inside. I am going to restrict my subject even more, and limit myself to just one of the relations that can be observed here: the relation with countries and populations marked by resentment. My reason for attempting to analyse this particular passion is that it often seems to have disastrous results. The point that I would like to develop can be summed up in just a few words. Western countries have every right to defend themselves against any aggression and any attack on the values on which they have chosen to base their democratic regimes. In particular, they must fight every terrorist threat and every form of violence vigorously. But it is in their interest not to be dragged into a disproportionate, excessive and wrong-headed reaction, since this would produce the opposite results to those hoped for.

Fear becomes a danger for those who experience it, and this is why it must not be allowed to play the role of dominant passion. It is even the main justification for behaviour often described as 'inhuman'. The fear of death that menaces me or, even worse, menaces those who are dear to me, makes me capable of killing, mutilating and torturing. In the name of the protection of women and children (here at home), many men and women, elderly people and children have been massacred (abroad). Those people that it is tempting to describe as monsters have often acted out of fear for their dear ones and themselves. When you ask South African policemen and soldiers why, under apartheid, they killed or inflicted unspeakable sufferings, they reply: to protect ourselves from the menace to our community posed by the blacks (and the Communists). 'We did not enjoy doing this, we did not want to do this, but we had to stop them from killing innocent women and children.'[3] But once you have agreed to kill, you also consent to the next steps: you torture (to obtain information about 'terrorists'), you mutilate bodies (to disguise murders as attempted muggings or accidental explosions): all means are good when victory is the aim – and fear needs to be eliminated.

The fear of barbarians is what risks making us barbarian. And we will commit a worse evil than that which we initially feared. History teaches us this lesson: the cure can be worse than the disease. Totalitarian regimes presented themselves as a means for curing bourgeois

6

society of its failings; they created a more dangerous world than the one they were fighting against. The current situation is probably not as serious, but it remains disquieting; there is still time to change direction.

The excessive or badly targeted reaction of the countries of fear is manifested in two ways, depending on whether fear is produced on their own territory or on the territory of others. In the latter case, the countries of fear have yielded to the temptation of force and replied to physical aggression by deploying disproportionate military means and waging war. The United States is an exemplary embodiment of this reaction, following the attacks of 11 September 2001, when it intervened directly – or encouraged intervention – in countries such as Afghanistan, Iraq and Lebanon. European Union countries generally follow American policies but only reluctantly, grumbling and dragging their feet. These direct military interventions are complemented by what has been called the 'war on terror', responsible, among other things, for illegal detentions and acts of torture, as is now symbolized by the names Guantánamo, Abu Ghraib and Bagram.

Now, this policy leads to a twofold failure. It makes the enemy stronger, and it makes us weaker. This is first and foremost because the aggression to which it is a response is not a matter of states but of individuals (temporarily protected, admittedly, by the Afghan Taliban when the latter were in power) who cannot be reached by massive bombings or army occupation. But it is also because what we have here is a resentment and vengeance born of humiliation, which cannot be eliminated by inflicting a new military defeat on a country – quite the opposite. The American Army or its allies may destroy the enemy armies, but in so doing they merely stoke the resentment of the population, which is the real source of the initial aggression. The tortures inflicted also feed into the desire for vengeance. The individuals responsible for anti-Western attacks live with the feeling that their passions are just, and their ideas true; now, as Pascal said 350 years ago, 'violence and truth have no power over each other'.[4] In addition, this policy destroys the Western world from within, since, in order to defend the democratic values that we cherish, we are led to abandon them! How can we rejoice in our victory over a horrendous enemy if, in order to vanquish him, we have had to become like him?

When 'all is permitted' in the fight against terror, a counter-terrorist starts to become indistinguishable from the initial terrorist. Furthermore, all the terrorists in the world think they are counter-terrorists, merely responding to a prior act of terror. They are not the only ones: it is always possible, and easy, to find a prior violence that supposedly justifies our present violence. But, on this way of reckoning, war will never end.

These criticisms of the reaction of the American government to the aggressions its country has suffered do not proceed from any alleged anti-Americanism. On the contrary, they are part and parcel of a debate within the United States itself, and are motivated by the increasing gap between the ideals proclaimed and what actually happens in real life. On the political level, the decisions made by the United States are not all that different from those which many other countries would have made. However, they draw attention to themselves much more, and attract more criticism since, on the military level, the US occupies an altogether exceptional position. Its destructive arsenal is incomparably greater than all others, and there are fewer obstacles to its use: every other country fears the reaction of the United States. It is the high efficiency of US military technology that makes it the most dangerous country – for the others, but for itself as well: its nuclear weapons could endanger the life of the whole planet.

Inside Western and, in particular, European countries, where for several decades a significant minority of people from the 'countries of resentment' has lived, we also find situations that illustrate how the cure is worse than the malady. This minority practises a religion – Islam – different from that of the majority; and, above all, in the way its social life is organized, this minority gives religion a place it does not hold in contemporary liberal democracies of any stripe. The result, across a whole series of issues affecting everyday life, is friction between different sectors of the population. How can this friction be lessened? It is here that we encounter an unfortunate reaction, namely 'firmness', a euphemism for intolerance.

Nobody is entirely satisfied with the conditions in which he or she lives: we often have the impression that these conditions are getting worse. Whose fault is this? It is tempting to seek a simple answer and an easily identifiable guilty person or group: it is this temptation that produces populist movements and parties. The populism of the left replies: it's the fault of the rich; we need to get hold of their goods and distribute them to the poor. The populism of the right defends, not a social class, but a nation, and replies to the same question with the answer: it's all the foreigners' fault. Xenophobia constitutes the minimum programme of the parties of the extreme right, who have been obliged to abandon their other favourite themes (anti-

Communism and racism). For several years, these parties have increased their audience in a good half of the member states of the European Union. Nowhere do they play first fiddle but, here and there, they have become indispensable to the coalitions in power. If the latter want to remain in power, they need to satisfy the demands of the extreme right when it comes to immigration and cohabitation – otherwise they risk losing electors' votes.

This general xenophobia is strengthened by what has to be called Islamophobia, even if this term is sometimes used improperly. The two forms of rejection overlap only partially: Islamophobia concerns only one kind of immigrant, but it does not stop at a country's frontiers; nevertheless, most immigrants in Europe today are indeed of Muslim origin. Now, attacking immigrants is not politically correct, whereas criticizing Islam is perceived as an act of courage; so the latter can be found in place of the former.

There are many reasons, some of them very longstanding, why Europeans reject Islam. Islam long appeared to be a rival to Christianity. Today, it embodies a form of religiosity from which Europeans have taken a long time to free themselves: the secular-minded thus reject it even more violently than do Christians. Muslim countries were colonized by European powers over several centuries; ex-colonists were forced to return home when decolonization occurred, filled with a feeling of both superiority and bitterness. Members of the formerly colonized populations are now coming to settle in the homes of their former colonizers, though not as colonists: how can this not lead to hostility towards them? Add to this the resentment felt by those former colonized and new immigrants or their, by now European, descendants – a resentment that impels them to set off bombs in London and Madrid, Berlin and Paris: the danger they represent is not just imaginary. Finally, geographical (and geological) chance has meant that several of these Muslim countries hold the planet's main energy reserves. As the cost of petrol, or the bill for keeping one's house heated, increases, being dependent on people one used to rule is painful.

All of these reasons, and a few others too, no doubt, mean that the criminal, or shocking, acts committed by certain Muslims are explained by their identity as belonging to a certain religion and even as being originally nationals of certain countries. On the basis of this generalization, it becomes easy, by lumping things together in succession, to introduce into the public debate a discourse of stigmatization that is not suffered by any other group. Media personalities declare, pretty much on all sides, that Islam glories in hatred and violence, that it is also the stupidest religion in the world, that the children of immigrants speak broken French, and that one should be proud of being islamophobic. In the Netherlands, a flamboyant populist, Pim Fortuyn, published *Against the Islamization of Our Culture*; shortly after his assassination (by a true-born Dutchman), the party he had founded won 17 per cent of the seats in parliament. Filip Dewinter, the leader of the Flemish Interest party in Belgium, declared, 'Islam is the enemy number one, not only of Europe but of the whole free world.' Experts on Islam, who suddenly popped up all over the place, were all too glad to explain to the media that Islam is intrinsically wicked and needs to be fought. The effect of this hostile atmosphere? Those who claim a Muslim identity feel rejected by the society in which they live, and take refuge a little more in their real or imagined traditions.

Neither international relations nor relations between groups of the population inside a single country can be made harmonious by waving a magic wand. The causes of friction or hostility are often real, and do not result from mere misunderstandings. However, I do not think that we can reach any worthwhile results by waging war abroad and fomenting intolerance at home. But we should not pretend that the world is a rose garden, or stop actively combating terrorist threats. Resort to armed force cannot be eliminated from the relations between nations or groups of nations, but it requires a much more subtle analysis of each individual situation. On the other hand, democracy does not definitively suppress inner conflicts, but gives us the means to manage them in a peaceful way.

The military interventions of these last few years have not brought the hoped-for results. The same could probably be said of the war on Iran that Western leaders envisaged in their speeches starting in 2007. The choice of a different course of action would in no way mitigate any negative verdict on a theocratic regime, on its policing of morals and its attacks on press freedom, on the conditions of detention in the prisons of Iran or the provocative declarations made by its president. Nevertheless, rather than tagging along after the neo-conservatives of Washington, the European Union should in this regard set an example, hoping that the United States will fall in behind it.

Renouncing intolerance does not mean that *everything* needs to be tolerated. In order to be credible, an appeal to tolerance has to start out from an intransigent consensus about what, in a society, is considered as intolerable. It is usually the laws of a country that define this basis, together with certain moral and political values that are

10

not formulated, but are accepted by everyone. However, we need to distinguish this set of juridical injunctions (also known in France as the 'republican pact', specifying the rights and duties of every citizen) from the multiple and ever-changing cultural characteristics of individuals, of which religion is part. The interpretation of political and social conflicts in terms of religion or culture (or even race) is both false and harmful: it aggravates conflicts instead of calming them. Law must triumph over custom when there is a clash between them – but in most cases, there is not.

In today's and tomorrow's world, encounters between people and communities belonging to different cultures are destined to become more and more frequent; the participants alone can prevent them turning into conflicts. With the means of destruction currently at our disposal, any conflagration could endanger the survival of the human race. That is why it is necessary to do everything to avoid it. Such is the *raison d'être* of this book.

It is not enough just to utter pious wishes or to sing of the virtues of dialogue; it is necessary to face up to, and analyse, the facts. With this in view, I have chosen to tack back and forth between present and past, politics and anthropology, everyday life and philosophy. Here, then, are the main questions tackled in the following pages:

1. *Barbarism and civilization*. The first two chapters are devoted to setting up the instruments that will enable us to describe the facts unfolding before our eyes. To begin with, these are major categories with the help of which the different societies of the world are evaluated and judged to be barbarous or civilized.
2. *Collective identities*. Several major categories of these can be distinguished: belonging to a particular culture, civic solidarity, adherence to moral or political values. Culture comes to us from others, and each of us has several cultures; it is always a mixed phenomenon, forever being transformed. Different identities can enter into conflicts that then need to be managed. Might not a Ministry for National Identity be useful?
3. *The war of the worlds*. This analysis of the relations between societies starts with some comments on a well-known work by Samuel Huntington. Political and social conflicts must not be camouflaged as wars or religion or a clash of civilizations. The 'war on terror' is not altogether a war, and it is not really being waged on terrorism. Torture, which it legitimizes, is a gangrene on democracy.

11

4. *Steering between reefs.* Several particular cases of conflicts within European societies are here discussed: the murder of Theo Van Gogh in Amsterdam, the Danish cartoons of the Prophet, the Pope's Regensburg speech. In addition, I ponder current developments in Islam and the debate in Muslim countries.

5. *European identity.* This is not defined by a content, but by the status it grants to the differences between countries, societies or cultures. The foreign policy of the European Union does not live up to the expectations of its population. Finally, I suggest a few ideas on the frontiers of the Union.

Conclusion: Beyond Manicheism. In conclusion, a few thoughts on the dialogue between cultures and the direction that the policies of Western countries might take.

In discussing these sensitive questions, on which everyone already has an opinion, I have sought to avoid making approximate statements, lumping things together, resorting to Manichean distinctions and designating scapegoats, as well as adopting the self-important posturings of a righter of wrongs. The matter is too important for anyone to indulge in complacent self-congratulation.

— 1 —

Barbarism and Civilization

There has never been any value of civilization that was not a notion of femininity, of gentleness, of compassion, of non-violence, of respect for weakness...The first relation between a child and civilization is the child's relation with its mother.

Romain Gary, *La nuit sera calme*

If we are to talk of the relations between peoples or societies, we first need to tackle a difficult question: can we use the same criteria to judge acts that arise within different cultures? One often has the impression here that it is impossible to escape from one excess without immediately falling into another. Those who believe in absolute, and thus trans-cultural values, risk taking as universal values those to which they are accustomed, and falling prey to naive ethnocentrism and blind dogmatism, convinced that they have eternal possession of truth and justice. They risk becoming really dangerous on the day when they decide that the whole world needs to benefit from the advantages proper to their society and that, so as to better enlighten the inhabitants of other countries, they have the right to invade them. This is the line of argument taken by the ideologues of colonization in previous times, and it is also the line frequently followed by the current apostles of democratic inter-ference. The universalism of values thus threatens the idea that human populations are all equal, and hence the universality of the species.

However, those for whom all judgements are relative – relative to a culture, a place, a historical period – are in turn threatened, albeit by the opposite danger. If every judgement of value is subject to circumstances, will we not end up accommodating *everything*, just

13

so long as it happens in other countries? That would mean accepting that human sacrifice is not necessarily to be condemned, since certain societies practise it; the same applies to torture, and to slavery. It would mean deciding that one people is ripe for liberty, another not, and eventually leaving each of them to its fate, and ourselves too – since our values are not necessarily better than others'. As this relativism systematizes itself, it gradually ends up in nihilism. And if each person, equal in principle to every other, chooses his values arbitrarily, the unity of the species is again denied, albeit in another way, since people no longer have any common spiritual world.

Dogmatism and nihilism are the Scylla and Charybdis of transcultural judgement, and sometimes seem inevitable. And yet, every day, we are required to comment on deeds and customs that arise in different cultures, and we would like to transcend this alternative. We would simultaneously like to acknowledge the infinite diversity of human societies and have some unique and reliable scale of values that will enable us to find our way around them. But how?

To advance some distance in that direction, I propose to start with an old word filled with meaning, and to use it as a thread through the labyrinth. This word is *barbarian*.

Being a barbarian

I do not intend to relate here the story of this word 'barbarian' and the ideas that it covers, a story that has already been studied by various specialists.[1] Rather, I would like to reread certain pages of the past with a different aim in mind: starting with various older uses of the word, I will construct a meaning that can be of use to us nowadays. Between the past and the present there will be neither a complete break nor a strict identity, but rather the quest for a certain coherence.

As everyone knows, the word itself comes to us from Ancient Greece where it was part of common usage, especially after the Persian War. It was contrasted with another word, and together they made it possible for the population of the whole world to be divided into two unequal parts: the *Greeks* (or 'us'), and the *barbarians* (the 'others', the foreigners). In order to recognize whether a person belonged to one or other group, you resorted to the Greek language: the barbarians were all those who did not understand it or speak it, or spoke it badly.

14

We might well decide that there is nothing to object to in such a usage, even if Plato in *The Statesman* mocked those who behave as if all non-Greeks formed a coherent population, when in fact all those peoples had no resemblance to each other and, worse, did not even understand each other. But, after all, distinguishing between those who understand and those who do not understand our language is not a way of passing judgement, but of providing a piece of useful information. It is just that, for reasons to which we will need to return, the distinction was from the outset given a secondary meaning, and a judgement of value, with the contrast barbarians/Greeks being accompanied by a contrast – let us say, as a first approximation – between 'savage' and 'civilized' peoples.

The savagery of the barbarian was not defined with precision, and from one document to another the meanings of the word do not always overlap. It is, however, possible to isolate a set of characteristics that are convergent and suggestive:

1   Barbarians are those who transgress the most fundamental laws of common life, being unable to find the right distance to observe between themselves and their relatives: matricide, parricide, infanticide on the one side, and incest on the other, are definite signs of barbarism. In Euripides, a character speaks of Orestes who has murdered his own mother and says: 'Not even a barbarian would have dared to do that!'[2] In the first decades of the first century AD, the Greek geographer Strabo wrote a book in which he stated that the inhabitants of Ireland practised ritual cannibalism, and were thus barbarians. 'They are man-eaters as well as herb-eaters, and [...] count it an honourable thing, when their fathers die, to devour them.' They did this so as to absorb the father's power, thereby making no distinction between spiritual proximity and material absorption.

2   Barbarians are those who postulate a complete break between themselves and other men. Strabo, again, depicts the Gauls as barbarians since, he says, they have a particular custom: 'when they depart from the battle they hang the heads of their enemies from the necks of their horses, and, when they have brought them home, nail the spectacle to the entrances of their homes [...] We are told of still other kinds of human sacrifices.' By extension, those who systematically resort to violence and war in order to settle the differences between them are perceived as being close to barbarism. Here, the opposite of barbarism consists in practising hospitality, even towards strangers, or indeed

in cultivating friendship: you give to other people what you would like to receive yourself.

3 Another sign of barbarism: when performing the most intimate acts, certain people ignore the fact that they may be visible to others. In Ireland, according to Strabo, 'men openly [...] have intercourse, not only with other women, but also with their mothers and sisters',[3] as if it were animals and not men who were gazing at them. To couple in public, Herodotus had already said, is to behave like 'cattle'.[4] Modesty is a specifically human trait; it means that I am aware of the gaze of others.

4 Barbarians are those who live in isolated groups instead of gathering in common habitats or, even better, forming societies ruled by laws adopted in common. Barbarians are people of chaos and randomness; they are unacquainted with social order. In another way, countries are close to barbarism when all who live within them are victims of the tyranny of a despot; and countries are not barbaric when citizens are treated on an equal footing and can participate in the conduct of the business of the community, as in Greek democracy. In the view of the Greeks, the Persians are barbarians in a twofold sense: because they do not speak Greek and because they live in a country subject to a tyrannical regime. 'O tyranny, beloved of barbarian men!' as an ancient fragment puts it.[5] Helen, in the tragedy by Euripides that bears her name, utters these striking words: 'in barbarian lands all except one man are slaves'.[6]

These characteristics of barbarians, and some others too (we shall be returning to these), can be subsumed into one main category: barbarians are those who do not acknowledge that others are human beings like themselves, but consider them as similar to animals and thus consume them, or judge them as being incapable of reasoning and thus of negotiating (they prefer to fight), and unworthy of living freely (they remain in subjection to a tyrant); they frequent only their blood relations and are unacquainted with the life of the community as ruled by common laws (they are savages and live scattered apart). Parricide and incest, in turn, are categories that do not exist for animals; the men who commit these acts start to resemble beasts.

Barbarians are those who deny the full humanity of others. This does not mean that they are really ignorant or forgetful of their human nature, but that they behave *as if* the others were not human, or entirely human. This meaning of the word is not defined in this precise way in classical Greece, but it is suggested by usage. It is not universal in the sense of being already accepted at all times and in all places; but it may *become* universal: as it does not espouse the point of view of any particular population, this definition could be adopted by all.

If the Gauls cut off their enemies' heads and tied them to their horses' necks, this was not because they viewed these men as monkeys or wolves; it was because they wanted to proclaim loud and clear their victory over their rivals – a victory that was all the more precious because these rivals were, precisely, human beings like themselves. Nonetheless, by so doing, they refused to treat them as beings that resembled themselves, denying that they belonged to the same humanity as themselves: defeating these enemies was not enough for them, nor even their death – the humiliation of these former rivals, now mere booty, had to be displayed to the gaze of all, at the gates of the town; this is what made the Gauls barbarian. One passage in Herodotus makes this particularly clear. A Spartan military chief, Pausanias, has won a battle over the Persians. A Greek witness gives him this piece of advice: following a previous battle, the Persians had cut off the head of the king of Sparta and nailed it to a post; to avenge himself, Pausanias ought to do the same. But the latter vehemently refuses: 'that would be an act more proper for foreigners [*barbarois*] than for Greeks, and one that we view as blameworthy even among foreigners'.[7] Such reprisals carried out on the corpses of vanquished enemies would amount to doing to others something you would not wish to have inflicted on yourself, and you would then resemble barbarians. By refusing to imitate his enemies, to show them that he can beat them at their own game (violence), Pausanias emerges from a relation of rivalry and behaves like a civilized person.

The Greeks had merged together two oppositions, one formed from terms with an absolute moral value (barbarian/civilized), the other from neutral, relative and reversible terms (being able/unable to speak the language of the country). Their thinkers soon pointed out and criticized this conflation. In the third century BC, Eratosthenes, the author of a treatise on geography and ethnography that has since been lost (but is frequently quoted by Strabo), argues in these terms: 'Now, towards the end of his treatise – after withholding praise from those who divide the whole multitude of mankind into two groups, namely, Greeks and barbarians, and also from those who advised Alexander to treat the Greeks as friends but the Barbarians as enemies – Eratosthenes goes on to say that it would be better to make such divisions according to good qualities and bad qualities; for not only are many of the Greeks bad, but many of the

Barbarians are refined – Indians and Arians [i.e. Persians], for example, and, further, Romans and Carthaginians, who carry on their governments so admirably.' Not only do Greeks and non-Greeks resemble each other, but moral virtues are not divided up in virtue of the language one speaks. The opposition between vice and virtue needs to be maintained, but cannot be confused with the distinction between 'us' and 'them'. Strabo, who quotes these lines, does not agree with Eratosthenes on everything, but he himself sometimes sticks to the relativist conception of barbarity: barbarians are those who do not speak Greek well, 'as is also the case with us speaking their languages'.[8] So he knows that, to the 'barbarians' whose language we do not understand, we appear as barbarians.

We may well wonder, however, whether the coexistence among the Greeks of the two senses, absolute and relative, of the same word was a matter of confusion. It might be possible, on the contrary, to see a continuity between the first meaning of 'barbarian' (not acknowledging the humanity of others) and the second (not speaking the language of the country in which you happen to be). A being who cannot speak appears to be incompletely human. The use of the same word, *logos*, to designate 'word' and 'reason' simultaneously makes it easier to emphasize the value placed on being able to speak a language. The ignorance of my language that is characteristic of the foreigner prevents him from perceiving me as completely human; thus he is a barbarian. Linguistic impotence becomes a sign of inhumanity, and it is in this sense that the relative and absolute meanings come together. When the Greeks call foreigners 'barbarians', they admittedly omit to say that this 'barbarity' is provisional and easy to cure: you merely need to learn the language of others, those among whom you happen to find yourself, or, even more simply, to return home to your own people. The ignorance proper to the foreigner is a very temporary form of barbarity.

A first set of conclusions can be drawn from this quick reminder of the past. The concept of barbarity is legitimate and we must be able to draw on it to designate, at all times and in all places, the acts and attitudes of those who, to a greater or lesser degree, reject the humanity of others, or judge them to be radically different from themselves, or inflict shocking treatment on them. Treating others as inhuman, as monsters, as savages is one of the forms of this barbarity. A different form of it is institutional discrimination towards others because they do not belong to my linguistic community, or my social group, or my psychological type. Not all uses of the word 'barbarian' correspond to our definition; it is sometimes used to stigmatize those who attack us or those whom we do not like, and it sometimes helps disguise might as right, or camouflages our will to power as humanitarian intervention and a struggle for justice, since we are punishing 'the barbarians'. However, in spite of these abuses, the concept itself deserves to be preserved.

This choice does not coincide with what we have inherited from the Christian tradition. Within the framework of the latter, there has rather been a tendency to consider the notion of 'barbarian' as irrelevant, since it did not easily fit into Christianity's universal message. St Paul declares, in the First Epistle to the Corinthians, 'There are, it may be, so many kinds of voices in the world, and none of them is without signification. Therefore if I know not the meaning of the voice, I shall be unto him that speaketh a barbarian, and he that speaketh shall be a barbarian unto me.'[9] Barbarity has here become a mere question of point of view. For the true Christian, all that counts is unity in the faith, since all separations between human beings are held to be negligible. Thus, in AD 395, St Jerome summarized several remarks by the Apostle Paul: 'And since even in the flesh, if we are born again in Christ, we are no longer Greek and Barbarian, bond and free, male and female, but are all in Him.'[10] From this point of view, the category 'barbarian' has lost its *raison d'être*. However, in the world in which Christians dwelt, the category could not entirely be done away with: it was no longer used to designate all those who spoke the local language badly, or did not speak it at all, but those distant foreigners who appeared as a threat and were distinguished by their ferocity and inhumanity – the Germanic tribes who swept down from the North to pillage the Roman Empire, for example, or the Huns who emerged from the Mongol steppes.

The tension between the two possible meanings of 'barbarian', between the relative (a foreigner we cannot understand) and the absolute (a cruel person), was to become significant again from the sixteenth century onwards, at the time of the great voyages undertaken by the Europeans, who sought to classify populations of whose existence they had hitherto been unaware. Were these populations barbarians in the absolute sense, and not just the relative sense? Some Europeans were tempted to think so, especially since – considering them as inferior beings – they could then subject them to slavery, or put them to death without feeling too much remorse. On the other hand, it comes as no surprise that Bartolomé de las Casas, a fervent Christian who proclaimed himself the defender of the Indians, opposed any claim that they were inferior, and thus rejected any firm equation between 'barbarians' and 'Indians'. Las Casas knew the two meanings of the term, but neither of them seemed applicable to the native populations of America. For one thing, the Spanish surpassed them in inhumanity; and for another, the Spanish were even more ignorant of foreign languages than the Indians. After quoting the words of Strabo and St Paul, he concluded:

> We will call a man barbarian, in comparison with another, because he is strange in his ways of speaking and pronounces the other's language badly. [...] But from this point of view, there is no man or race which is not barbaric with relation to another man or another race. [...] Thus, just as we consider the people of the Indians to be barbarians, they judge us the same way, since they do not understand us.[11]

The book in which Las Casas wrote these words was to remain unpublished for centuries, but his ideas spread right across Europe. Several decades later, in France, Montaigne was still interpreting barbarity in similar terms: it is merely an optical illusion, due to our failure to understand others. So he criticizes his compatriots the French who, when they travel abroad, always prefer to stay with other French people, and confuse virtue with habit, like those mocked by Eratosthenes: 'If they come across a fellow-countryman in Hungary, they celebrate the event: there they are, hobnobbing and sticking together and condemning every custom in sight as barbarous. And why not barbarous since they are not French!' Hence his famous remarks on the encounter with the cannibals of America: 'I find (from what has been told me) that there is nothing savage or barbarous about those peoples in that nation, to judge from what has been reported to me, but that every man calls barbarous anything he is not accustomed to.'[12] This formula has lodged in people's minds, and is often enthusiastically quoted when ethnocentrism is being lambasted. How can anyone fail to accept that treating the other as a barbarian simply because we do not speak the same language is an inconsistent and untenable attitude? However, in these same texts, Montaigne, like Las Casas, cannot but resort to the term 'barbarity' in its absolute sense of cruelty – this time to stigmatize the wicked Europeans. Barbarity does not exist – but if it did exist, we would be more barbaric than the Indians! Christian universalism is here combined with a positive evaluation of noble savages.

From now on, I will be sticking to just the absolute meaning of 'barbarian' (barbarians are those who do not recognize the full humanity of others); I will move away from the Christian point of view and suggest that barbarity exists in itself, and not merely in the gaze of the naive observer; that it, too, forms a category of the first importance.

Barbarity results from a characteristic of the human being that it would be illusory to hope could ever definitively be eliminated. So, in my discussion, it will not correspond to any specific period in the history of humanity, ancient or modern, or to any particular group of the peoples who cover the face of the earth. It is within us, as well as being in others; no people, no individual, is immune to the possibility of carrying out barbaric acts. Prehistoric man, killing his fellow from the cave next door, Cain slaying Abel, the contemporary tyrant torturing his adversaries – all share in the same barbaric instinct, that of a sense of murderous rivalry that makes us refuse to grant others the right of access to the same joys and the same goods that we ourselves hope to enjoy.

We cannot say that barbarity is inhuman, unless we postulate, with Romain Gary: 'This inhuman side is part of the human. Until we recognize that inhumanity is something human, we will be stuck with a pious lie.'[13] By behaving in an odious way, human beings do not stop being human. More: their best qualities and their worst failings, what we call their 'humanity' and their 'inhumanity', stem from the same origin. Rousseau had already seen this clearly: 'Good and evil flow from the same spring', he wrote, and this spring is nothing other than our irreducible need to live with others, our ability to identify with them, our feeling of a common humanity. Contemporary primatologists confirm this intuition. 'Compassion and cruelty depend on the faculty an individual has to imagine the effect of his attitude on someone else.'[14] This faculty motivates us to help those who feel the need for help, even if they are strangers, and to recognize the equal dignity of others even if they are different from us. But it is also this faculty that guides us when we subject others to torture or when we engage in genocide: the others are like us, they have the same vulnerable points as us, they aspire to the same good things, so they must be eliminated from the face of the earth. I will be returning to this subject when I discuss torture.

Being civilized

If we have one term with an absolute content, 'barbarian', the same will be true of its opposite. A civilized person is one who is able, at all times and in all places, to recognize the humanity of others fully. So two stages have to be crossed before anyone can become civilized:

21

in the first stage, you discover that others live in a way different from you; in the second, you agree to see them as bearers of the same humanity as yourself. The moral demand comes with an intellectual dimension: getting those with whom you live to understand a foreign identity, whether individual or collective, is an act of civilization, since in this way you are enlarging the circle of humanity. Thus scholars, philosophers and artists all contribute to driving back barbarity. So the idea of civilization largely overlaps with what Kant calls 'common sense' or 'enlarged thought',[15] in other words the ability to pass judgements that take account of representations proper to the other people who dwell on the earth, at least partly escaping egocentric or ethnocentric bias. Kant sees in this ability to put oneself in the place of any other person a means for the human being to fulfil his or her vocation. In actual fact, no individual, let alone any people, can be entirely 'civilized', in this sense of the word: they can merely be more or less civilized; and the same goes for 'barbarian'. Civilization is a horizon which we can approach, while barbarity is a background from which we seek to move away; neither condition can be entirely identified with particular beings. It consists of acts and attitudes that are barbarian or civilized, not individuals or peoples.

The forms which the advance towards civilization takes are many and various. One concerns the very extension given to the entity that we are here designating as 'us'. In a short text dating from the year of his death, 'The Eras of Social Culture', Goethe presents a scale of values. Right at the bottom, closest to barbarity, is the human group in which you know only the human beings who are akin to you. This description is not far removed from that produced nowadays by palaeontologists and prehistorians: originally, human groups all lived in isolated territories, the presence of strangers was not allowed, and xenophobia was *de rigueur* – any stranger was a potential enemy. A step towards civilization is accomplished when this group meets other groups and establishes prolonged contact with them; and another when, together, they form higher entities – a people, a country, a state. Finally, the highest level is reached when they arrive at universality; when they discover that they share common ideals with the other members of the species and are ready, for example, to 'place all foreign literatures on an equal footing with the national literature'.[16]

Being closed in on oneself is the complete opposite of being open to others. Thinking that yours is the only properly human group, refusing to acknowledge anything outside your own existence, offering nothing to others, and deliberately remaining shut away within your original milieu is a sign of barbarism; recognizing the plurality

22

of groups, of human societies and cultures, and putting yourself on an equal footing with others is part of civilization. This progressive extension is not to be confused with xenophilia, or a systematic preference for strangers; nor with some vague cult of 'difference' as such – it simply indicates the greater or lesser ability to recognize our common humanity.

Another way of advancing from barbarity to civilization consists in a certain self-detachment, making it possible for you to see yourself from outside, as if through another's eyes, and thus exercising a critical judgement not only towards others but also towards yourself. In social exchanges, if you give up always putting your own viewpoint first, you draw closer to others. Here, too, it is not a question of preferring self-denigration to being proud of what you are: this would be to forget that neither barbarity nor civilization comprises any enduring essence of human beings, but merely their states and actions, certain of which are sources of pride and others of remorse. In return, we gain the ability, whenever necessary, of turning our scrutiny on ourselves, on our community, on the people to which we belong, and we will always be prepared for the discovery that 'we' are capable of acts of barbarity.

Yet another way of progressing towards civilization consists in behaving so that the laws of the country you live in treat all citizens equally, without distinction of race, religion or sex; the countries that maintain these differences, whether in the form of legal privileges or of apartheid, are on the contrary closer to barbarity. The practice of slavery is akin. The liberal state is more civilized than the tyrannical one, since it ensures that all can enjoy the same freedom; democracy is more civilized than the *ancien régime*, but also more so than any ethnic state, since the latter maintains a regime of privileges. For the same reason, but in another domain, magic is more the realm of the barbarian than of science: the one implies an irreducible difference between someone who knows and someone who does not, while the other proceeds by observation and reasoning which are not secret and which anyone can carry out in turn. Dialogue, which ensures that all interlocutors have an equivalent position, is a more civilized form of communication than the harangue, in which you utter certainties while everyone else just listens; or than the words of the oracle, the prophet or the seer. Accepting a proposal on somebody's word, or on an act of faith, implies that addresser and addressee of the message are unequal; accepting it by an act of reason places both on the same level, and the first practice is thus more barbaric than the second.

23

Within any community, the person who knows its codes and traditions is more civilized, since this knowledge allows him or her to understand the gestures and attitudes of the other members of the group, and thus to bring them closer to his or her own humanity. The idea of civilization implies knowledge of the past. Another person, limited in the capacity for understanding and self-expression, ignorant of the common codes, will be inevitably condemned to moving only within his or her small group and excluding others from it. The barbarian refuses to recognize him- or herself in a past distinct from the present. Politeness, which is an apprenticeship of life with others, is in turn a first step towards civilization; it is no accident that the world 'polite' used to mean 'civilized' as well as 'courteous'.

Torture, humiliation and suffering inflicted on others are marks of barbarity. The same is true of murder, and even more of collective murder or genocide, whatever may be the criterion by which you define the group that you desire to eliminate: 'race' (or visible physical characteristics), ethnic group, religion, social class or political convictions. Genocides were not a twentieth-century invention, but it cannot be denied that they lasted throughout the century – witness the massacres of the Armenians in Turkey, the 'kulaks' and the 'bourgeois' in Soviet Russia, the Jews and Gypsies in Nazi Germany, the inhabitants of the towns and cities in Cambodia, and the Tutsis in Rwanda. Waging war is more barbaric than settling conflicts by negotiation, as Strabo had already pointed out. But it is also an act of barbarity when the Yazidi (living in the north of Iraq) stone a young woman because she has fallen in love with a young Sunni man from outside the community. The decision to set up a tribunal at Nuremberg at the end of the Second World War – a judgement in conformity to law rather than a settling of accounts – is, on the other hand, a sign of civilization, whatever the imperfections and even the internal contradictions of this tribunal; and the same applies to the setting up of a Commission of Truth and Reconciliation in South Africa (or elsewhere), which means that all the defendants of the former regime are not merely categorized as monsters, criminals or sadists.

I used, above, the expression 'barbaric instinct' to designate the human capacity for scorning the humanity of others, but the fact of the matter is that I do not believe such an instinct has any autonomous existence. It is well known that, in the writings of his final period, Freud tried to present the life of the individual as an arena in which two instincts confront one another: one is on the side of civilization, the other of barbarism. 'And now, I think, the meaning of the evolution of civilization is no longer obscure to us. It must present the struggle between Eros and Death, between the instinct of life and the instinct of destruction, as it works itself out in the human species', he writes in *Civilization and Its Discontents*. The inclination to aggression is 'an original, self-subsisting instinctual disposition in man', and constitutes 'the greatest impediment to civilization'. According to Freud, we need to remain all the more vigilant towards this barbaric instinct in that we spontaneously tend to conceal it from ourselves. 'Those who prefer fairy tales turn a deaf ear when they hear people talking of man's innate tendency to "wickedness", to aggression, destruction and thus cruelty.'[17]

I do not altogether follow Freud's interpretation, and can here merely reiterate my own conviction: these acts find their origin in the same 'life instinct' as our acts of love; the difference does not lie in the initial motive, or in the goal pursued, but in the means chosen to accomplish it. My lack can be filled by the love given me by another, or by his or her complete submission. Barbarity and civilization resemble less two forces struggling for supremacy than two poles of one axis, two moral categories that enable us to evaluate particular human acts. On the other hand, we can accept the idea of Romain Gary quoted at the head of this chapter: the source of civilization, which takes into consideration the other's humanity, comes from the fact that human beings are obliged, for a long period, either to take care of their offspring in order to ensure they survive, or else to depend on this care. Unlike what happens in other animal species, here the period of protection and care lasts for ten years or so, and requires the collaboration not only of the mother but of the father too. This prolonged attention paid to a weaker creature surely fostered the flourishing of feelings of benevolence necessary to the advent of civilization.

I have illustrated these categories with examples drawn from different countries, and different periods. Does this mean that barbarity is always and everywhere the same? Certainly not. Once the meaning of words is fixed, a historical and typological analysis can be undertaken; the present book has as its theme the forms assumed by barbarity and civilization in the present era, when contacts between different cultures are becoming ever more frequent and rapid.

From civilization to cultures

Civilization is the opposite of barbarism. However, the meaning of the first word changes considerably if we put it into the plural.

Civilizations no longer correspond to an atemporal moral and intellectual category, but to historical formations that appear and disappear, characterized by the presence of several traits linked both to material life and to the life of the mind. It is in this sense that we speak of Chinese or Indian, Persian or Byzantine civilization.

Unlike what we have observed concerning the two senses of the word 'barbarian', relative and absolute, between which there was a certain continuity and which formed a hierarchy, the two senses of 'civilization', illustrated by the singular and the plural, are independent of each other. To avoid any ambiguity, I am thus choosing to use the word 'civilization' here only in the singular, and to designate the sense of its plural by one of its quasi-synonyms, which in any case bears the same double meaning: this is the word 'cultures', in the plural. These two terms, 'civilization' and 'culture', have been used differently in different European languages and by different authors. Here, 'civilization' will always be one, and opposed to barbarity; culture will always keep the sense it has in the plural.

However, for over two centuries, 'culture' has assumed a broader meaning than as a synonym of 'civilization'. Ethnologists have largely been responsible for this change. They realized that the societies studied by them, often lacking writing, and monuments, and works of art of the kind we habitually associate with culture, nonetheless possessed practices and artefacts that played an analogous role within them; they called these, in turn, 'cultures'. This 'ethnological' meaning has now gained ascendancy; furthermore, ethnology is also called 'cultural anthropology'. If the word is taken in this broad sense (as descriptive and no longer evaluative), every human group has a culture: this is the name given to the set of characteristics of its social life, to collective modes of living and thinking, to the forms and styles of organization of time and space, which include language, religion, family structures, ways of building houses, tools, ways of eating and dressing. In addition, the members of the group – and we should bear in mind that there may be just a few dozen of them, or several hundred thousand – interiorize these characteristics in the form of mental representations. So culture exists on two closely related levels, that of social practices and that of the image left by the latter in the minds of the members of the community.

It is not their content that determines their 'cultural' content, but their diffusion: culture is necessarily collective. It thus presupposes communication, of which it is one of the results. As a representation, culture also provides us with an interpretation of the world, a miniature model, a map, so to speak, which enables us to find our way around in it; possessing a culture means having at one's disposal a pre-organization of lived experience. Culture rests simultaneously on a common memory (we learn the same language, the same history, the same traditions) and on common rules of life (we speak in such a way as to make ourselves understood, we take into account the codes in force in our society); it is, at the same time, turned towards the past and towards the present.

Such is the shared opinion of the ethnologists of the twentieth century. Culture, writes Bronisław Malinowski, is 'a vast apparatus [...] by which man is able to cope with the concrete, specific problems that face him'. According to Claude Lévi-Strauss, culture includes 'all the attitudes or aptitudes learned by human beings as members of society'. 'There is no human nature independent of culture,' adds Clifford Geertz. 'Without human beings, there is no culture, obviously; but likewise, and more significantly, without culture, there are no human beings.'[18] It is in the very nature of the human being to have a culture.

Why should this be so? We can explain it by the physical characteristics of the human race. Compared with other animals, humans have greater freedom from their biological determining factors: in different places, they choose different food, organize their habitats or their daily timetables differently, look after their offspring in the most varied ways, and express their emotions differently. We would be plunged into chaos and commotion if the communities into which we are born and in which we grow had not made certain choices, and thus restricted the vast field of possibilities. Culture takes over where genetics leaves off. 'In short,' Geertz continues, 'we are incomplete or unfinished animals which become complete and finished by means of culture. [...] Between what our bodies tell us and what we need to know in order to function normally, there is a vacuum which we need to fill ourselves, and which we fill with information (or disinformation) from our culture.'[19] Without the instructions given to us by culture, we could not be sure of having communicated even our most elementary emotions, whether of joy or fear. The case of language is perhaps the most striking: the human child is not born within a natural and universal language, but within a particular linguistic community, without the aid of which he could not pick up any language at all, and thus all of the innumerable advantages that ensure from this would be debarred him; in a word, he could not become human.

Every human being needs a set of norms and rules, traditions and customs, transmitted from the older generation to the younger;

27

without these norms, the individual would never achieve the fullness of his humanity, but would be reduced to the condition of the 'wild child', condemned to *anomie*, in other words to the absence of all law and all order – an absence that can create severe disturbances. This is the way certain children live today, no longer in the forest, but in the streets of big cities, barely speaking, fighting off aggression, selling themselves to the highest bidder, stupefying themselves with drugs. The destruction of culture is called 'deculturation': the condition of a human being who has lost his original culture without acquiring another, and who risks being led, in spite of himself, to a state where he cannot communicate – to barbarism.

It is thus easy to understand (if not to condone) the fact that various populations consider themselves as the only ones to be fully human, and view foreigners as outside the pale of humanity: this is because the culture of foreigners, being incomprehensible, is judged non-existent, and without culture man is not human.

An Enlightenment heritage

It is no accident if these two concepts of 'civilization' and 'cultures', whatever the words used to designate them, entered European thought at the same time, the second half of the eighteenth century, in the wake of the Enlightenment. In French, the word 'civilization' first appeared, it seems, in 1757 in *L'Ami des hommes ou Traité de la population* [*The Friend of Men, or Treatise on Population*] by the Marquis de Mirabeau, who had also planned (but without carrying it out) a complementary work with the title *L'Ami des femmes ou Traité de la civilisation* [*The Friend of Women, or Treatise on Civilisation*]. Here, the word has the sense of a process that makes human beings 'polite' in the old sense, i.e., both courteous ('polished') and benefiting from the progress of knowledge. In the following years, several authors were to contrast 'barbarism' with 'civilization' and conceive the history of humanity as a one-way process, leading from the former to the latter. In 1770, D'Holbach described the process that led men from the savage state to civilized society; in 1776, Diderot contrasted the primitive state of barbarism with the possibility of civilizing a nation. The same applies to other European countries. In England, in 1767, Ferguson described the progress of humanity as a passage from brutality (what he called 'rudeness') to civilization. In 1772, Boswell defended the use of 'civilization' as a perfect antonym to 'barbarism'. In Germany, at the end of the century,

28

Klopstock makes *Kultur* (rather than *Zivilisation*) the synonym of 'de-barbarization' (*Entbarbarung*).[20] At the start of the nineteenth century, these terms and these meanings entered common usage.

At the same time, there was a growing interest in 'cultures'. This was grafted on to an old tradition, which in France went back to Montaigne, with his insistence on the power of 'custom'. Pascal said of custom that it was a second nature; he thus prefigured the formulae of later anthropologists. The travels of Europeans East, South and West became increasingly frequent in the seventeenth and eighteenth centuries, and their protagonists would bring back detailed, sometimes admiring descriptions of the customs and manners observed in the countries they visited, even though these customs were far removed from collective European practices. At the same period, there was a new interest in history, and thus for ancient social forms, no longer perceived as arising from a now inaccessible golden age, or as a mere, imperfect preparation for the present; henceforth, it was deemed that every period had its own ideal and its own coherence. In Italy, at the start of the eighteenth century, Giambattista Vico acknowledged that all the societies which had succeeded one another in the history of humanity had a comparable dignity.

The thinkers of that period gave themselves the conceptual means to understand unity and plurality simultaneously. Leibniz brought in the idea of a multiplicity of possible worlds, independent among themselves but all structured with the same rigour and contributing to the same order. It was Montesquieu, in France, who gave shape to the first attempt to describe all human societies at once, in their diversity and their unity; he sought to view them as different paths to the same goal. In his great work *On the Spirit of the Laws* (1748), he introduced two series of categories. The first are absolute and timeless: they correspond to the rules that constitute natural law and to the central contrast between legitimate states and tyrannies; they are thus evaluative categories. The others are historical and local, what Montesquieu calls 'the spirit of nations'; they include the physical conditions of every country and the norms and customs that regulate its social life. There is no value judgement here; as Montesquieu writes, 'I do not write to censure that which is established in any country whatsoever. Each nation will find here the reasons for its maxims.'[21] The balance that he sought here was sought equally by his disciples, such as Jean-Nicolas Démeunier, the author of an extensive compilation entitled, in homage to the master, *L'esprit des usages et des coutumes des différents peuples* (*The Spirit of the Uses and Customs of Different Peoples*) and published in 1776, in which he states, on the one hand, that he wishes to 'follow the advances of civilization' but, on the other hand, that he will endeavour to describe the manners of all the peoples of the world without privileging European culture or the culture of classical antiquity. From this point on, it would even be possible to speak of a civilization – or a culture – of savages.

For a long time, Enlightenment thought served as a source of inspiration for a reformist, liberal current, which fought against conservatism in the name of universality and equal respect for all. As we know, things have changed these days, and the conservative defenders of a higher Western culture have arrogated this idea to themselves, believing themselves to be engaged in a struggle against 'relativism' that – they say – emerged from the romantic reaction at the start of the nineteenth century. They cannot do so, obviously, unless they amputate the real tradition of the Enlightenment, which was able to combine the universality of values with the plurality of cultures. We need to get away from clichés: this idea was to be confused neither with dogmatism (my culture must impose itself on everyone) nor with nihilism (all cultures are pretty much the same); placing Enlightenment at the service of a denigration of others which gives one the right to subject or destroy them represents a wholesale hijacking of the whole Enlightenment project.

Let us spend a moment or two on the case of the German philosopher and historian, Johann Gottfried Herder, who is sometimes presented as the founder of the contemporary relativist current. In reality, Herder adopted the same positions as Montesquieu, though he decided that the latter's categories were too schematic; he would try to make them more detailed and closer to the facts. In works such as *Another Philosophy of History* (1774), or *Ideas for a Philosophy of the History of Mankind* (1784), he set out from a critique of what he felt to be an excessive penchant for abstraction on the part of the French Encyclopedists or Voltaire, which entailed a certain contempt for previous eras and distant peoples when they did not resemble one's own milieu. Now, each society has its own requirements, and the desires of individuals are shaped by 'the country, the period and the place'.[22] Herder explains this diversity by drawing a comparison with the ages of an individual life: you do not like the same things when you are ten, forty, or seventy years old. The child liked school, but once he has turned into a young man, he is happy to escape it! In a society everything holds together; you cannot isolate any element and judge it separately: what is a failing in one group of people becomes an advantage among another. In order to appreciate it, you first need to examine it in its own context.

Aware though he was of the plurality of cultures, Herder did not abandon the idea of the unity of humanity. The latter is founded on both the biological origin common to all men (the unity of the species) and the common goal that they pursue. Herder believes that they have the same ideals of happiness, human love and the flourishing of the mind, the same notions of the true and the good. 'On what is pure intelligence and equitable morality, Socrates and Confucius, Zoroaster, Plato and Cicero all agree: in spite of the many differences between them, they all acted on one point, on which the peace of our whole species rests.'[23] All of Herder's writings are imbued with the effort to bring together the plurality of cultures and the unity of civilization, or, in his own words, to understand the unity of nations in their diversity, to unite the disparate scenes without muddling them, to show the same forces at work producing diverse forms, the same principle acting through societies irreducible to one another. Far from being an enemy of Enlightenment thought, Herder thus presents, in the words of the Czech philosopher Jan Patoka, a warmer version of it. As for that thought in itself, which is sometimes limited just to its universal and abstract side, it represents, on the contrary, a first brave attempt to conceptualize ethics and history, civilization and cultures, together in one framework.

Judging cultures

It seems highly likely that, if the term 'culture' designates the set of forms of collective life, its contents are far from being homogenous. One way of distinguishing between its diverse elements would be ask oneself whether they call for a value judgement or not. I have chosen to give the word 'civilization' the sense of a moral judgement, while 'cultures' are morally neutral; but this does not mean they are equivalent. We need, rather, to accept the fact that all of their ingredients do not possess the same status.

In the case of several customs, we can state merely that they are what they are. For example, it is important to know whether, in a culture, it is the paternal uncle or the maternal uncle who plays a privileged role within the family; but there is no reason for having to decide whether one of the systems is, in itself, better than the other. Similarly, unlike what the colonizers who moved into Africa in the nineteenth century thought, eating with your fingers rather than with

31

a fork is a characteristic trait of a culture but does not allow you to deduce that those who do so are barbarians. Alimentary habits are an important element in everyone's culture, and one of the most resistant there can be: even if you have sampled the most exquisitely cooked dishes in the world, you always keep a particular fondness for the tastes you have been used to since you were a child. It would be foolish to try and draw up a unique scale of values in this domain. That Leopold Bloom eats sautéd kidneys for breakfast, while the typical Frenchman Jean Dupont dips his slice of bread and butter in a bowl-sized cup of white coffee, and Kim, a Korean student living in Paris, feels reassured when he pulls a few leaves of fermented cabbage out of a pot that he has brought from home, does not enable us to declare any one culture superior to any other. Nor does the fact that you eat halal meat, or kosher food, or neither of them. Of course, for sociologists studying a society, there is nothing arbitrary about such a choice. It depends on the foodstuffs you find in the country of origin, on the techniques of transformation to which you subject them, on the traditional commercial contacts with other regions or countries, on beliefs, and so on. Nonetheless, it cannot be declared better, in any absolute sense, than any other; here, everything is relative. A chef may cook a traditional dish better than his competitor, but this is a personal success, not a cultural characteristic.

However, this is far from being the case with all the elements of a culture. In every society, big or small, ancient or modern, certain members are better acquainted with its codes and traditions than others; for this reason, they are listened to and appreciated. This knowledge can be transmitted orally – within families, or from older to younger people, or from specialists to apprentices – or, as in our societies, within schools, or it may finally be mediated by books and computers. Anyone who masters this knowledge is a well-informed person, whatever his or her speciality may be: an ancient language that died out 2,000 years ago, or the slang spoken by a gang of youths. In certain cases, the specialist contributes, as we have seen, to the advance of civilization, by making communication possible with a growing number of members of society, and indeed of humanity. Occasionally, this enables the specialist to win games such as *Trivial Pursuit* or the TV quiz *Who Wants To Be a Millionaire?* More generally, the specialist has the virtue of keeping a great deal of information in his or her head. What is measured and valued here is the sheer amount of information held ready for use. We can also, of course, take account of the quality of this information, and appreciate the knowledge that may have, in some way, an impact on the fate of humanity as being worth more than the futile knowledge that is rewarded in quiz shows. Ray Bradbury's *Fahrenheit 451* showed how precious the memory of certain books could be, constituting as they did a universal patrimony.

Another way of evaluating knowledge consists in judging, not its quantity or quality, but the use we make of it. A long tradition in European culture, which began in classical antiquity and is still alive today, having passed via Montaigne and Rousseau, privileges the knowledge that is put to work in a creative way rather than just being passively accumulated; it prefers judgement rather than memory, a good mind rather than a head full of facts, wisdom to information. The good worker is the one who is able to transform his or her knowledge into know-how and, if the case should arise, can adapt it to circumstances; the good scholar is the one who is ready to question what he or she learned at school, and to boldly think what nobody has ever thought before. But this preference for autonomy can never be emancipated from its repetitive side: it is of the very nature of education to start out from a tradition. In any case, it is far from certain that anyone can gain wisdom without any knowledge, and when Montaigne says that we should prefer good minds to ones stuffed with information, he does not require them to be empty: he is indicating a hierarchy, the subordination of memory to understanding, not the exclusive presence of the latter. Knowledge is indispensable, but it remains a means: 'the more our souls are filled, the more they expand'.[24] From this point of view, all cultures do not resemble each other: some of them forbid anyone tampering with the traditions, in the literal sense of sacred texts, while others encourage questioning and innovation; now, the latter have undeniable advantages for those who practise them, especially in the field of technology.

How can we describe the relation between 'civilization' and 'cultures'? We need first to insist on the autonomy of the two concepts, which belong to two different orders, the first passing an absolute judgement of value, while the second is limited to identifying a segment of the world forming part of history. They are not, of course, incompatible: every stable human group necessarily possesses a culture; also, certain groups are more civilized than others. Having a culture is a necessary condition for the process of civilization: without a minimal command of a cultural code, the individual is condemned to isolation and silence, and thus to separation from the rest of humanity. However, it is far from being a sufficient condition; certain cultures (the Aztecs, for instance, with their human sacrifices) seem to us to exemplify barbarism rather than civilization. Mastering a culture and advancing towards a more civilized state are two different things – but they do not harm each other, either.

We cannot advance on the road to civilization without having previously acknowledged the plurality of cultures. If we refuse to take into consideration visions of the world that are different from ours, we will find ourselves cut off from human universality, and end up nearer the pole of barbarism. On the other hand, we advance in civilization if we agree to see a humanity similar to our own in the representatives of other cultures. The two senses of the word 'civilization' or 'culture', depending on whether it is used in the singular or the plural, here approach each other; so the *trans-cultural* value judgement is legitimate. A culture that encourages its members to become aware of their own traditions, but also to be able to distance themselves from those traditions, is superior (being more 'civilized') to that which contents itself with pandering to the pride of its members by assuring them that they are the best in the world and that the other human groups are not worthy of interest. We reach this critical distance by examining our traditions critically, or comparing and contrasting them with those of another culture. Taking others' point of view into consideration does not mean that you opt for altruism to the detriment of egoism, or for xenophilia instead of xenophobia: it is in our own interest to enrich our understanding of the world in this way.

Technology and works of art

When they discuss 'civilizations' or 'cultures', the classical authors often quote another type of facts, which deserve to be examined separately. In his description of Gaul, Strabo states that its inhabitants are evolving – they are leaving their caves and no longer sleep on the ground, and are starting to wash: having been nomadic hunters and warriors, they are now becoming, under the beneficent influence of the Romans, sedentary people who practise agriculture (this description is, of course, a caricature: the Gauls were sedentary and starting to cultivate the land before the Romans came along). He judges that this is a progress towards a greater degree of civilization. The Britons, on the other hand, seem to him to be more barbarian than their neighbours since, 'although well supplied with milk, [they] make no cheese'.[25] Herder, in his *Ideas*, considers the domestication of wild animals, the cultivation of the land, the development of trade, science and the arts to be all stages in the acquisition of culture.

34

It is certain that such practices are not just different: they demonstrate a greater or lesser degree of development. The Neolithic revolution, 10,000 years before our era, during which men managed to domesticate animals and to replace hunting and gathering by agriculture, was a superior and irreversible phase in the history of humanity. When the European crusaders of the Middle Ages encountered the Arabic populations of the Middle East, they were amazed to discover that the latter were able to heal a wounded leg without having to amputate it: they realized, without any shadow of a doubt, that the Arabic medicine of the period was superior to European medicine. A society that can write has several advantages over one that has only an oral memory.

We can give the name 'technology' to a great number of the means used in these activities – and this enables us to compare and classify such technological means. An iron axe definitely cuts better than a stone axe. A society that knows about the wheel can solve heavy-goods transport problems more easily than one which does not; the same applies to one which has motor cars when compared to one that only uses horse power. This gradation is not linear, and the evolution of technology sometimes goes off at a tangent or even backwards. And sometimes we discover the unforeseen consequences, the perverse effects of allegedly superior technology. The pollution caused by motor engines may outweigh their advantages, and the violence of a certain medicine used in hospitals may make us nostalgic for more traditional, less technological and more 'human' approaches to sickness. Even the invention of agriculture, which supplanted previous modes of production, is not as beneficial as we are accustomed to believe: thanks to agriculture, the population may grow, but its consequences also include famines, wars, and restrictions in the freedom of women. Jean-Jacques Rousseau caught this ambiguity in a lapidary formula: 'It was iron and corn, which first civilized men, and destroyed humanity'.[26] We appreciate the benefits of technology, but every day we become more aware of its harmful effects and of the damage it inflicts on our environment and our way of life. The fact remains that, in most cases, different forms of technology can be compared, and the kinds of efficiency that they make possible can be rigorously evaluated.

Technology comprises a subset of its own within the characteristics of a society. Can these technological traits be called an index of civilization? If we give this word the sense of 'an acknowledgement of the humanity of others', the answer has to be negative. The reason is clear: civilization concerns the relations between one set of human beings and another, whereas technological forms have to do with the relations between human beings and the surrounding material world. So, as well as the judgements of moral value that arrange human acts on an axis stretching from barbarism to civilization, we need to accept other, no less legitimate judgements, of a pragmatic and existential rather than ethical order. They concern the greater or lesser degree of efficiency of the instruments at one's disposal, or the possibility of living for longer, or feeding more people: in short, people's well-being, rather than their virtue. Technology is not to be confused with culture, either, since culture concerns the rules of common life, not the manipulation of objects. The proof lies in the fact that technology is in essence universal: the same planes, telephones or watches are found on every continent; culture is different for every human group (otherwise, these groups would not exist).

The practice of the arts, associated by Herder with technology, calls yet another kind of judgement into being. Literary, pictorial, musical and other works arouse spontaneous opinions on the part of each of their consumers, and these reactions are not as arbitrary as they at first appear. As has been known since at least the age of Kant, aesthetic judgements are not 'objective', and thus are not mechanistically deducible from the material properties of the works; but that does not mean that they are 'subjective', i.e., left to the individual's free choice. Taste is 'inter-subjective', in other words it lends itself to an argued debate that may lead to a consensus. Certain works are admired outside the frontiers of the countries and periods in which they were created, since they are judged to be more beautiful and true than others; this ability to transcend their context of origin is perceived as an index of quality. What we have here is a truth of a particular kind, established on the basis of a common opinion rather than by any direct confrontation with segments of the world, but it is no less certain: we can easily agree these days that the statues of Michelangelo, like the paintings of Rembrandt, teach us something essential about human beings. All the same, these judgements remain relative – to our culture, our identity – and nothing guarantees that these works will always be admired.

This aesthetic judgement is sometimes passed within one genre ('Elvis Presley is the best rock singer of all time!', 'Tolstoy and Dostoyevsky are the greatest Russian novelists of the nineteenth century'), but also between genres within the same culture: it is possible to make a convincing claim that *War and Peace* is a richer work of art than the tale of Baba Yaga, or that a Mozart concerto is musically more interesting than a Georges Brassens song, even if this does not stop

anyone preferring the tale or the song. This does not entail that there
is a radical discontinuity between the two: Mozart knew the popular
music of his time well and used it as a point of departure, just as
Tolstoy could sometimes do for the stories and tales in circulation
around him. 'High culture' is not the contrary of 'popular culture'
– it is not separated from it by an impassable wall; the one is often
a purer, more complex, sublimated version of the other. And the
products of the two can sometimes achieve the same intensity: Goethe
acknowledged that there was as much beauty in Serbian popular
songs as in the works of the most celebrated poets. A traditional
carpet can be more beautiful than an abstract painting.

Finally, trans-cultural aesthetic judgements are in their turn legitimate: there is nothing untoward in asserting that the German instrumental music of the nineteenth century is superior to Bulgarian music
of the same period, or that *Hadji Murat* (Tolstoy again) is more
profound than all the contemporary stories from Chechnya. Everyone
knows that Shakespeare's plays were condemned in eighteenth-
century France for being too coarse: French culture at that time
demanded a separation between the elevated and the vulgar style,
whereas the English dramatist mixed them together; today we can
see the greatness of the works, and the pettiness of the reactions
which they aroused at the time. It is not arbitrary to say that, between
the fifteenth and twentieth centuries, European painting went through
a period of exceptional brilliance which surpasses all that had preceded it as well as all that has since been produced. Such judgements
are not to be explained by whether one belongs or not to a certain
class, or by snobbery or fashion: they are based on the characteristics
of the works themselves, as related to the expectations of the members
of the society that receives them.

Let me take an example from my immediate experience. In the
region of France where we spend the summer, we went, on two consecutive days, to listen to musical performances. On the Saturday, in
a church, there was a woman playing the violin – works by baroque
composers, including Bach's Second Partita. On the Sunday, sitting
in the shade of the lime trees, we listened to traditional music, *bour-
rées* from the Berry and Burgundy – the prototypes of which date
perhaps from the same period as the works of Bach (who was well
acquainted with contemporary gigues and other sarabandes). The
pieces performed on the two occasions belonged to their respective
cultures, German and French. It can also be said that they are all
beautiful, each in its genre, that some are made to accompany dances
while others are not, that they deserve the attention and respect of

their listeners: our experience, although different, was in each case gratifying. But it would be rather cursory to leave it at that. On another level, that of musical excellence, of spiritual depth and richness, there was one of the peaks of the European tradition on the one hand, and a perfectly simple, minor kind of music on the other. Not to recognize the huge difference in level between the two sorts of music would be to demonstrate a peculiar deafness.

It must also be admitted that these judgements will always have an inevitable degree of approximation and that any attempt to establish a single and definitive order of merit is doomed. When we are asked whether Chekhov's plays are better than Molière's, we feel like replying that both sets are good and that they are, above all, different. We prefer to say of a work that it is 'great' rather than that it is 'greater' or 'the greatest'.

Works of art and technology are related to the culture of a society in that, by passing judgement on the former, we are inevitably evaluating the latter too. It might be thought that there is a certain injustice at work here, insofar as every technical invention, every work of art, is the product of an individual, not of an entire collective body. Responsibility lies with the individual to overcome the weight of the old ways of thinking and seeing, so as to discover unprecedented solutions; it is the individual's task to examine the human condition with fresh eyes, to push forward with the work of the spirit, with what Wilhelm von Humboldt called *Bildung*, the individual's spiritual education. However, the surrounding culture can be more or less favourable to the arising of these major works of art. It becomes so, in particular, by putting a positive value on creation, innovation and audacity, rather than on strict respect for tradition, by cherishing excellence rather than conformity to order, and thus by creating a space in which the free criticism of others and of oneself can circulate. It becomes so, also, by reserving an appropriate place for its creators and thinkers, rather than treating them with contempt, or condescension, or indeed by shutting them away in a ghetto, however gilded it might be. In Stalin's Russia, enlightened readers expected writers to be the conscience, the spokesmen and spokeswomen, of a people deprived of freedom: a challenging but stimulating demand.

So what makes us appreciate certain works of art more than others is not how far removed they are from barbarism, or their more civilized character. If we prefer these works, it is because we judge them to be rich and profound, because they open up and refine our minds, because they allow us better to understand the world and ourselves, because, thanks to their harmony and beauty, they provide us with a unique and intense pleasure. Aesthetic judgements do not run counter to ethical judgements, but neither do they follow them. It can also be seen that the quality of works of art does not stem from whether they belong strictly to a culture and a tradition; nor does it arise from their degree of emancipation from the spirit of a nation: the detailed knowledge of one particular culture is often the path that leads to the universal, as is demonstrated by the masterpieces of the most various traditions that have acquired a worldwide audience. Two examples from a thousand possible cases will illustrate this. Mu Qi was a Buddhist monk who lived in the thirteenth century, in South China; he had never left it, and knew nothing outside the local tradition. However, his ink drawings, his persimmons, wagtails and wild geese these days attract the gazes of people from every land. Tadeusz Kantor, the Polish dramaturge, so immersed himself in his native Wielopole and his childhood memories that he was able to address spectators from the whole world. Once a certain depth of exploration is reached, art – like thought – becomes universal.

A dream of Enlightenment

The spread of knowledge, from the growth of literacy and the adoption of modern technology to familiarity with great works of art and the most recent discoveries of the sciences, should make mankind better: this was one of the great dreams of Enlightenment. It was the role of what was called 'civilization'. 'The more civilization extends across the world,' as the oft-quoted words of Condorcet from 1787 put it, 'the more we shall see wars and conquests disappear, as well as slavery and poverty.'[27] Now this latter objective, which for my part I call 'civilization', does not depend directly on the spread of technology and works of art, as those Enlightenment thinkers had hoped: this is the lesson that we cannot fail to draw from the centuries that separate us from Condorcet's words. These latter elements of cultures are circulating more and more quickly over the surface of the planet and a greater and greater percentage of the world population is becoming aware of them; however, wars and conquests have not stopped, poverty has not lessened and even slavery has been banished only in the rule books, not in actual practice.

The twentieth century was particularly instructive in this respect: the greatest acts of barbarity were not carried out by particularly uneducated groups. The commandants of the *Einsatzgruppen*, the mobile killing units that exterminated the Jews behind the Russian front, had all had a higher education. In his spare time, Eichmann played the beautiful German chamber music of the nineteenth century. Mao knew his classics, though this did not stop him being the instigator of the greatest massacres of the century. Causality can even sometimes operate the other way round: the artistic and intellectual flourishing of Athens in the fifth century BC was probably dependent on the presence of slaves in Greek society, and the court of the Medici in Florence, in the fifteenth century, which encouraged the blossoming of the Renaissance in the arts, was not reputed for its liberal and democratic tendencies. It may be that we have to choose between these different aspects of societies; in that case, as Benjamin Constant said of ancient Greece, 'we prefer to have fewer poets, and no slaves at all'.[28]

People have often pointed out with relish that this is part of a paradox revealed by the twentieth century: barbarity, they exclaim, sprang from the very heart of European civilization. But there is not really anything all that paradoxical here, once it is admitted that civilization cannot be reduced to the production and enjoyment of works of art, and that the relationship between them is indeed far from direct. Mankind's existential, ethical and aesthetic achievements do not depend mechanically on one another, and yet they are all perfectly real. We need to think them in their plurality and not deduce them from each other; nor transform the one into a means for attaining the other; nor indeed consider them as opposites that we need to choose between in an 'either/or' way dictated by an exclusivist logic. Such simplifications would come down to giving into the facile modes of thought associated with the mass media and demagogy. The human being needs a certain material comfort, but also a spiritual life and an openness to the rest of humanity that will enable her to turn her back on barbarity. Perhaps certain periods and societies channel human energy rather towards the creation of accomplished works of art, while others tend towards technological innovation, and others focus on erecting political structures. Yet it is pointless to urge us to prefer – as did Russian radicals in the nineteenth century – a pair of boots to Shakespeare; it is also pointless to lament – as did Sartre – the fact that the hunger of a child is not appeased by any work of art. We perish in the absence of earthly *and* spiritual food.

A first warning – and a powerful one – against the illusions entertained by certain supporters of the Enlightenment is found in their most lucid representative in France, Jean-Jacques Rousseau. In his first work, the *Discourse on the Sciences and the Arts*, he was already breaking away from the *philosophes* and encyclopedists who were

40

his friends, abandoning their belief that the spread of works of art and technological advances would make mankind better. Far from contributing to the progress of moral life and an increased benevolence towards others, he declared, the growth in the sciences and arts is detrimental to moral progress. The vocation of human beings is to live (well) with others, and for that there is no need to accumulate a great pile of knowledge; nor to be what is called 'a cultivated person'. 'We can be men without being knowledgeable,' Rousseau concluded in his *Emile*.[29] A few years later, it was precisely in this dissociation between knowledge and wisdom, between the accumulation of knowledge and respect for men, that Kant was to locate Rousseau's innovation.

> I feel the full thirst for experience, the full desire to extend my knowledge, and indeed the satisfaction at all progress accomplished. There was a time when I thought that all this could constitute the honour of humanity, and I despised the common people, who are ignorant of everything. It was Rousseau who disabused me. This illusory superiority vanished, and I have learned to honour men.[30]

The absence of any parallel in the evolution of civilization on the one hand, and cultures, technology and works of art on the other, does not mean, as we have already seen, that there is no contact between these different things (Rousseau's thinking on this matter is more complex than is sometimes claimed). Let us return to the case of the sciences. The status reserved to them in society is one of the characteristics of its culture. Now, through the appeal they make to reason, they affirm the unity of the human race. Through the spread of their results, they share in universal communication and thus help the process of civilization to advance. Works of art, in their turn, can bring together people of different periods and different continents, and in this sense are the opposite of barbarity, even if they do not manage to prevent it.

It is this multiplicity of activities in which members of any society are engaged that explains the difficulty we have in knowing whether human history is progressing, whether the judgements that we pass on different periods are absolute, or relative, or merely arbitrary. If we define civilization as a better understanding of others in their full humanity, we can say that, on the biological scale, the progress is undeniable. Originally, the earth was peopled by tribes who were unaware of each other's existence and shared the conviction that every stranger was an enemy whom it was better to see dead than alive, or enslaved rather than free. These days, human beings in the

41

four corners of the earth can communicate with each other thanks to advanced technologies, they can hear the voices and see the faces of those who live in the antipodes, they use products and objects that have come from elsewhere and they can travel to each other's homes without having to fear for their lives.

But this biological scale, however reassuring it might be when seen from above, does not tell us much about the unfolding of human history, in which we see barbarity and civilization experiencing peaks and troughs, ebbs and flows, without our being able to find any reason for feeling reassured as to the future. As far as we know, the individuals who lived in ancient Greece could be no less hospitable, noble and friendly than contemporary Europeans. These days, states wage war on each other with no less ferocity than Greeks and Persians at the time of Herodotus; what has changed, more than anything, is their capacity for mass destruction. In the best of cases, we might point out that the way in which individuals are treated by their states, as in liberal democracies, is constantly progressing, since they are obtaining ever more equal rights. But it must immediately be added that, in other respects, our contemporary societies are less human than are some others, including those that have preceded us, as exemplified by our way of treating old people, or our indifference towards the drift of certain groups of young people.

Science and technology, for their part, do progress in their respective domains, and this progress is cumulative: every scientist appropriates the results of his predecessors, and seeks to go further; today's physics student knows more than the geniuses of the past. Works of art lend themselves in turn to judgements that remain relative (with regard to their genre, country or period), but the framework within which they have an impact can vary considerably, from a small circle of friends to the whole West over a period of twenty-five centuries. Here, the successes of one person do not benefit those who come after, and art as such does not progress. On the other hand, within any system of values, we have the right to declare one moment of its history to be superior to others. Finally, several other characteristics in the culture of a people do not lend themselves to collective value judgements, even if the individual member of society may cherish them above all else – or loathe them.

As a result, a particular action that falls within several categories at a time will be judged in contradictory fashions. Thus the explosion of the atom bomb over Hiroshima was simultaneously an index of scientific-technical progress and the proof of a regression in civilization since, whatever the justifications invoked, it resulted from the cold-blooded decision to slay several hundreds of thousands of people who belonged to the civilian population of the 'enemy'.

Civilization and colonization

It is the same plurality of dimensions of experience that explains the contradictory judgements made of a phenomenon such as colonization as it was practised by the European powers in the nineteenth and twentieth centuries. A famous quotation from Napoleon clearly illustrates the possibility of considering the same event from different points of view. On the eve of his disembarkation in Egypt, on 30 June 1798, he harangued his troops with these words: 'Soldiers, you are about to undertake a conquest whose effects on civilization and commerce are incalculable'.[31] It is plausible to imagine that, by 'civilization', Bonaparte meant the spread of technology and works of art and science, and in this respect his prediction was correct: commerce and the circulation of knowledge were indeed reinforced by this expedition. On the other hand, the very existence of a 'conquest' was the index of a retreat of civilization to barbarity, since the French general was here postulating that the submission of a foreign population was in itself legitimate.

The same contradiction occurred later on. The French prided themselves on bringing civilization to the Africans and the Indochinese, and thereby justified their conquests; by that they meant, in the best case, the building of roads, the opening of schools, and the introduction of medicine; in other words the introduction of a technically more advanced set of skills. The colonized natives complained, not about the technological advances that were imported, but about the personal humiliations that they underwent, since they were treated as beings of a lower category. What one group of people calls 'civilization' conceals, for another group, an incarnation of barbarity. The colonizers believed, or pretended to believe, that the republican principles which they claimed to uphold were illustrated by the social order which they imposed; the colonized had the impression that these principles served as a mask for an attitude of conquest and exploitation, and that these same principles of freedom and equality were more in agreement with their own struggles against colonialism and for independence.

We find an amusing illustration of the different meanings that scholars and colonialists placed in certain words in the report on a meeting organized in May 1929 in Paris. The newly created Centre International de Synthèse devoted one of its first meetings to the theme 'Civilization: The Word and the Idea'. Great professors were invited, including the historian Lucien Febvre and the anthropologist Marcel Mauss: they explained at length the double meaning of the word 'civilization', depending on whether it was used in the singular or the plural. The debate was also attended by several French politicians interested in the question. One of these was Paul Doumer (1857–1932), President of the Centre's board of directors, who had been Governor General of Indochina, but also a minister and president of the Senate, and later became French President in 1931.

After listening to several scholarly papers, Doumer put his foot right in it.

M. Doumer: Nobody has yet given a plain definition of civilization. We claim that we are bringing civilization to the peoples that we colonize. What do we mean by that?

M. Berr [director of the Centre de synthèse]: Every people has its civilization; so there are many different civilizations. The problem lies in knowing whether, in spite of this diversity, we can still speak of 'civilization', and in what sense.

M. Doumer: The general public gives this term quite a concrete meaning. Civilization is the order, established by the police, that guarantees security for individuals and for property, and that protects the freedom to work and the freedom of commercial transactions.

Marcel Mauss tried to introduce a few nuances into this peremptory assertion, but Doumer carried imperturbably on:

European civilization is spreading and gaining more and more territory, thanks to its material power, if not indeed thanks to its moral side. It is also acknowledged that there are savage and barbarian peoples, among whom abominable cruelties are committed – horrors. Civilization has rights against barbarity.[32]

The debate was not as anachronistic as it might at first seem, since in 2005 the French Parliament voted in a law that obliged French schools to recognize 'the positive role of the French presence overseas', in other words the benefits of colonization (the law was blocked by President Chirac). But the fact that, in the past, the terms 'civilization' and 'barbarity' have been abused is no reason to give up using them now.

Some misunderstandings

We can decide to use the words 'civilization', 'barbarity', 'culture', 'works of art' and 'technology' in a sense different from that adopted here; but, one way or another, we need to distinguish between the concepts and the realities to which they refer. If we fail to do this, we risk getting bogged down in misunderstandings caused either by the authors themselves or by their readers who allow themselves to slip from one meaning to another. Some examples drawn from authors of the past or the present, either respected or disputed, may illustrate this necessity of not reducing to a unique dimension the complex field that is circumscribed by these words.

One of the most frequently mentioned quotations on this topic comes from the German critic and philosopher Walter Benjamin, who wrote 'There is no document of civilization which is not at the same time a document of barbarism.'[33] These words come from a text written in 1940 but published posthumously in 1950 under the title 'Theses on the Philosophy of History'. In these pages, Benjamin contrasts two ways of writing history: that based on historical materialism (the 'hist-mat' of the Marxists) and that which he calls 'empathy', in which the historian identifies himself with a character, or a group of characters from the past, by adopting their values. Now these characters are, generally speaking, the victors. The goods of a culture or civilization, one type of booty that falls to the victors, present themselves, to be sure, as the work of great artists, but, in order to be realized, they also demand the bringing together of certain social conditions, for instance, slave labour. And it is here that barbarism intervenes. 'For without exception the cultural treasures he [the historical materialist] surveys have an origin which he cannot contemplate without horror. They owe their existence not only to the efforts of the great minds and talents who have created them, but also to the anonymous toil of their contemporaries.' Then comes the quotation above, and Benjamin concludes: 'And just as such a document is not free of barbarism, barbarism taints also the manner in which it was transmitted from one owner to another.' If, these days, we go to the museum in which these goods are preserved – we are given to understand – we are participating in the cult of this barbarity.

It is easy to see why Benjamin's words stick in the memory: the paradoxical coincidence of contraries cannot fail to make us think. But it is also easy to see that the word 'civilization' is being used in a highly idiosyncratic sense. It is not the sense we are adopting here – that of recognizing the humanity of others. This is not in itself a problem, except that this is the only sense that is opposed to 'barbarism'. The meaning given to the word by Benjamin is not that of 'cultures' either – 'culture' as a set of lifestyles. The goods he has in mind are obviously works of art alone. But 'works of art' are not opposed to 'barbarism': works of art may be barbarous and misanthropic – this is perfectly obvious. But bringing these two terms together is not in itself paradoxical.

Can we nonetheless claim that all the works of art of the past are, at the same time, documents of barbarism? The assertion can be accurately applied to monuments such as the pyramids of Egypt or the temples of Angkor or the Gothic cathedrals of France, and perhaps to any architectural wonder of the world, which will have required the collaboration of a visionary genius and a political leader who set a whole host of labourers to work. But, faced with the generalization of this observation, two objections immediately come to mind. The first is that it is difficult to see what is the equivalent of these masses of slaves in the case of many other works of art: what back-breaking task was imposed on anyone so that the works of Sappho, or Shakespeare, or Van Gogh could see the light of day? The second is that the conditions of origin do not completely determine the meaning of a work of art, whatever the adepts of historical materialism may think. A work created at the court of a king may serve as an inspiration to those who will overturn this same king; the works of writers who belong to the colonizing powers have managed to help the colonized peoples to liberate themselves.

The same move – reducing civilization and culture to works of art alone – is found in several other European writers too. Most of the time, the reasons for this are not the same as in Benjamin. Rather, in its history, 'Europe' has not always been an example of superior civilization and, from the point of view of cultures, other traditions can be placed on an equal footing. If, on the other hand, we restrict ourselves to works of art, how can we not be filled with a sense of pride when we see ourselves belonging to the same tradition as some of the greatest geniuses of mankind? This theme is abundantly present in a book written by the Italian journalist Oriana Fallaci published shortly before her death, her anti-Muslim tract *The Rage and the Pride*.

'It irritates me even to talk about two cultures', she writes. They cannot be put on 'the same plane'. In order to prove the incommensurable superiority of one of the two cultures over the other, Fallaci draws up two series of proper names. On the European side we find Homer, Socrates and Phidias, Leonardo da Vinci and Raphael, Beethoven and Verdi, Galileo and Newton, Darwin and Einstein. On the Muslim side, 'looking and looking', she can find only 'Muham-mad with his Koran and Averroes with his scholarly accomplish-ments', and the poet Omar Khayyam. And, she insists, 'I like Dante Alighieri more than Omar Khayyam', and more than the *Thousand and One Nights*.[34] Doubtless certain readers, even if they in turn are rather irritated by Fallaci's peremptory tone or by the racism that surfaces in her remarks, will agree to prefer the sum total of the works in the first series to those in the second, and will tell themselves that Fallaci's merit is that she has said aloud what everyone secretly thinks without daring to say so, for fear of attracting the indignation of the 'politically correct' (even though what we have here is a false impres-sion: books by Fallaci and other islamophobic writers regularly show up on best-seller lists).

Of course, we might utter a few reservations as to the fine detail. We might say, for example, that the *Thousand and One Nights* should be compared to other collections of folk tales – not to Plato or Dante but, for instance, to the tales of the Brothers Grimm; and, from this point of view, the comparison is not in the least shocking (but who would wish to choose the one to the detriment of the other?). It could be added that Averroes is not the only Muslim phi-losopher and that in any case he is not a mere commentator. It is also curious that the name of Omar Khayyam is the only one that Fallaci remembers, when Dante himself was acquainted with the Arabic poets who had preceded him, and Goethe admired Hafez so much that he drew inspiration from him for his *West–Eastern Divan*. But if we restricted ourselves to suchlike remarks on method and history, we would miss the main thing, which is the way civilization and cultures are being reduced to works of art alone. I have already insisted on the absence of any direct relation between the latter and civilization; here we need to refer back to the relationship between works of art and cultures.

To state that Muslim culture (supposing that it is a single homo-geneous entity) has not produced a Michelangelo or that Zulu culture has not given birth to a Tolstoy (as Saul Bellow once remarked) is not false, but it does not teach us very much: we all know that what we call the novel in the strict sense is a genre that came into being in the European tradition, contemporary with the rise of individualism, as were the sculpture and painting of the Renaissance. Reciprocally, Zulu culture as well as Persian culture include genres and forms of expression of which Europeans are completely ignorant. If the com-parison between Tolstoy's *Hadji Murat* and the Chechen stories of the same period has any sense, this is because on both sides we have

47

stories dealing with the same events: the two cultures have a minimum of shared characteristics.

Beyond this self-evident fact, we can observe that what characterizes the Western tradition is not merely the existence of great scientists, but also the possibility of establishing an impermeable separation between research itself and its positive or negative consequences. The secret of atomic fission was discovered within Western culture, but the decision to drop the atomic bomb on several hundreds of thousands of Japanese was also made possible there, probably thanks to the same mechanism of fragmentation and dissociation between the end and the means, between ethics and knowledge. As Jared Diamond puts it in reference to the Neolithic revolution: 'In addition, when we count up the specialists whom society became able to support after the advent of agriculture, we should recall not only Michelangelo and Shakespeare but also standing armies of professional killers.'[35] This is why the judgement that this or that culture, taken as a whole, is superior to another, is ultimately meaningless, whereas we can condemn acts for their barbarity, whatever culture they emerge from, and we can claim that a Bach chaconne is superior to a *bourrée* from Burgundy.

Another facile misunderstanding comes from the confusion between the two meanings of 'civilization' and 'culture', depending on whether they are used in the singular or the plural; and we can well wonder whether this confusion is always involuntary. A famous quotation from Ernest Renan, taken from his lecture 'What is a Nation?' (1881) says: 'Before French culture, German culture, and Italian culture, there is human culture.'[36] Renan is here arguing against what he presents as the German conception of the relations between community and individual, in which the latter is completely determined by the group from which he or she comes; Renan adheres to the Enlightenment principle expressed by Montesquieu, who said that he was a man necessarily, and French merely by the chance fact that he had been born in this place rather than in another.

However, a problem arises from the repetition of the word 'culture' in Renan's quotation, which is the reason for which it is memorable. When joined with the word 'human', the word 'culture' does not have the same meaning as when it follows the word 'French'. Human culture is a synonym of the intellectual and moral capacities of human beings, while French culture is a set of characteristics that have become consolidated in the course of history. Only if we distinguish between these two meanings can we justify the word 'before' in Renan's sentence: the human brain possesses certain general dispositions for speech even before the child learns to speak this or that language. If, however, we are discussing the order in which the local and the universal succeed one another, it is clear that learning about human rights comes 'after' the acquisition of national language and culture. No child learns to speak and reason in a universal, merely human language, and it is only once the child has reached adulthood that it discovers the universal laws of logic. The same applies to ethics: the separation between the couple us/them and the couple good/evil is a belated acquisition, coming only after childhood. The play on the two senses of 'culture' allows Renan to construct a pretty phrase but it muddles the meaning of his assertion.

We find a similar slippage in the meaning of words in another author who is currently trying to put us on our guard against the dangers of Muslim fundamentalism. In *Les Religions meurtrières*, Élie Barnavi gives his conclusion the title 'Against the "Dialogue between Civilizations"', arguing as follows: 'There is civilization and there is barbarity, and between the two there is no possible dialogue.'[37] This time, it is the word 'civilization' which bears the weight of the paradox. If we say (as I am doing in the present work) that 'civilization' is opposed to 'barbarity', it is impossible to speak in the same breath of 'civilizations' in the plural – whether to preach dialogue or, as Barnavi does, war. It is between cultures, in the plural, that dialogue, exchange and interaction are possible. More precisely: every culture is already also comprised of the encounter between cultures, but certain of these contacts have simply been established under constraint, have been imposed by the sword, while others have appeared peaceably. Is it absurd to encourage the latter at the expense of the former? No culture can be reduced to barbarism; favouring mutual understanding between cultures is indeed one of the best means of driving this barbarism back. It is difficult to imagine that Barnavi has not noticed the double meaning that he is here loading on to the word 'civilization'.

A third type of misunderstanding seems to come from the fact that certain authors present the relation between 'civilization' and 'cultures' as an antinomy: if we cherish the former, we need to renounce the latter, or vice versa. In a famous text entitled *Race and History* (1952), Claude Lévi-Strauss emphasizes the equal legitimacy of all cultures. He affirms that each of them is organized around the solution of a particular problem. Western culture has, for several centuries, devoted itself to the invention of ever more powerful mechanical means. The Esquimos and Bedouins have, better than other peoples, managed to adapt to hostile geographical conditions. The Far East has found the best way of mastering the relations between body and mind. The Australian aborigines have developed the most complex family relations; and so on.

The impact of this text played a great part, in France, in the process of recognition that non-Western cultures have their own dignity. But Lévi-Strauss takes a step farther: he impugns the relevance of the opposition between 'civilization' and 'barbarism', and thus the very idea of civilization. This does not mean that he ignores the existence of barbarism, and he defines it in the same way that we have here: as the attitude that consists in rejecting others outside the pale of humanity. But he thinks he can observe in this context what he calls 'a rather significant paradox', which lies in the very act of designating this or that person as barbarian: 'By refusing to see as human those members of humanity who appear as the most "savage" or "barbaric", one only borrows from them one of their characteristic attitudes. The barbarian is first of all the man who believes in barbarism.'[38] Whereupon, Lévi-Strauss refuses to pass any judgement on cultures and their elements: all societies are equally good (or bad), and value judgements are necessarily relative, while trans-cultural judgements are impossible.

Actually, the real paradox here lies in Lévi-Strauss's own argument. If we define barbarism, as he does, by the way in which certain members of mankind cast some other members out of mankind, then nobody becomes a barbarian merely by denouncing acts of barbarism: it is enough merely to recognize that barbarism is not inhuman, and not to exclude barbarians from humanity. There is a paradox only if one has previously postulated the fundamental goodness of mankind; now, if we qualify someone as human, I can also (or especially) be thinking of his ability to torture. The barbarian is *not* the person who thinks that barbarism exists; it is the person who thinks that a population or a human being do not belong fully to mankind and that they merit treatment that he would resolutely refuse to apply to himself. The absolute meaning of 'civilization' barely disappears merely because everyone sees the mote in his neighbour's eye and ignores the beam in his own: acts of barbarism remain such in every clime. A realization of this nature does not prevent one from recognizing the plurality of cultures, as Lévi-Strauss recommends: in order to call *myself* barbarian I need first of all to admit that barbarism exists.

In other authors we find the opposite line of argument, claiming this time that maintaining the civilization–barbarism axis must entail a refusal to recognize the legitimate plurality of cultures. One example of this position can be seen in Alain Finkielkraut's *The Undoing of Thought*, which indeed presents itself, in part, as a questioning of Lévi-Strauss's ideas on cultures. After tracing a somewhat summary history of European Enlightenment thinking, Finkielkraut expresses his fear that the recognition of multiple cultures will destroy the very idea of civilization. 'Speaking of culture only in the plural means refusing to the men of different periods or of distant civilizations the possibility of communicating around thinkable meanings or values that can be lifted out of the context in which they arose.'[39] In short, the plurality of cultures destroys the universality of judgements.

Such a conclusion, however, is far from inevitable. Civilization is not the opposite of culture; nor is morality the opposite of custom; nor the life of the mind the opposite of everyday life (the popularity of this idea is not enough for it to be correct). In reality, the one draws its nourishment from the other. The existence of multiple cultures has not stopped them making contact with one another, influencing each other mutually; one culture can sometimes systematically glorify another. A decisive step towards civilization is made on the day when it is admitted that, although they are human beings as we are, the others do not have the same culture as we do, do not organize their societies in the same way, and possess different customs from ours. To have a culture does not mean being its prisoner; on the basis of every culture, it is possible to aspire to the values of civilization.

In short, there is no necessary reason for following these authors in their rejection of one of the terms of the relation, even when we can benefit from their attachment to the other. Let us reiterate the point: the plurality of cultures (an indisputable fact) does not in any way prevent mankind from being a unity (another indisputable fact); nor does it hamper our ability to judge that the distinction between acts of barbarism and civilized behaviour is real. No culture is barbarian in itself, no people is definitively civilized; all can become either barbarian or civilized. This is what defines the human race.

— 2 —

Collective Identities

Culture always puts what nourishes human beings before what nourishes culture.

Roman Gary, *Ode à l'homme qui fut la France*

These days, in Western countries, collective identity no longer enjoys a good press. It is viewed with suspicion: the suspicion that it is a sort of conspiracy against individual freedom. When it comes to finding a specifically human trait, people prefer to lay the emphasis on the capacity that each person has of opposing all definition-from-outside, all physical or cultural heredity. Other, very varied reasons are added for disputing the relevance of this notion. The example is given of all those who lose their collective identities unwillingly, those whom economic need or political constraint have thrown into a life of wandering far away from their homes, in a world in which the movements of populations are merely becoming faster and more frequent. At the other extremity of the social spectrum, people point to the existence of a globalized elite composed of prosperous businessmen, media stars and showbiz personalities, but also famous scientists and writers, who spend a great deal of time in airports, speak several languages fluently, and say that they feel at home everywhere.

This abandoning of collective identity is obviously not shared by everyone, neither in Western countries nor, in particular, in the rest of the world. In order to understand the reasons for this disjunction, we need to take a closer look at these collective identities. For there are several types of them. Without splitting hairs, I will suggest that we distinguish, at least, between cultural belonging, civic identity and adherence to a political and moral ideal. This will enable us to envisage the conflicts that sometimes arise between them all; the recently created French Ministry of National Identity will enable us to pinpoint the effects of this confusion.

The plurality of cultures

The human being, as we have seen, is born not only within nature but also, always and necessarily, within a culture. The first characteristic of one's initial cultural identity is that it is imposed during childhood rather than being chosen. On coming into the world, the human child is plunged into the culture of its group, which precedes it. The most salient, but also probably the most determining fact, is that we are necessarily born within *one* language, the language spoken by our parents or the people who look after us. But language is not a neutral instrument, it is impregnated with thoughts, actions and judgements that are handed down to us; it divides reality up in a particular way, and imperceptibly transmits to us a vision of the world. The child cannot avoid absorbing it, and this way of conceiving the world is transmitted from generation to generation.

The extent of the traits inherited in childhood can vary greatly. Language is common to millions or indeed tens or hundreds of millions of people: but we also receive other, more restrained heritages from the human grouping in which we grow up: ways of moving, or organizing time and space, as well as relating to other people – in short, lifestyles. During childhood, we also adopt tastes for food that remain with us throughout our lives; we interiorize certain landscapes, we memorize counting rhymes, songs and tunes that will constitute our mental universe. This local sense of belonging is the 'hottest', the most affective of all, and all of us draw a precious part of our identity from it.

A little later, the circle widens, for children go off to school, where they learn the basic history of the country in which they live: a few great events from the past, the names of characters who have left their mark, the most common symbols. They familiarize themselves with the literary works that are taught there, together with the names of the scientists and artists who are part of the collective memory. The common language and a set of shared references constitute what has been called the 'essential culture',[1] in other words a command of the common codes that enable us to understand the world and address other people – a basic culture on to which are grafted the types of knowledge proper to the different domains of the mind, art or science, religion or philosophy. These codes are all given in advance, and not freely chosen by each individual.

Another trait of the cultural affiliation of every individual is immediately obvious: we possess not one but several cultural identities, which may either overlap or else present themselves as intersecting sets. For example, a French person always comes from a particular region – the Berry, for instance – but from another angle this person also shares several characteristics with all Europeans, and thus participates in Berrichon, French, and European culture. On the other hand, within one single geographical entity, there are many different cultural stratifications: there is the culture of teenagers and the culture of retired people, the culture of doctors and the culture of street sweepers, the culture of women and that of men, of rich and of poor. A particular individual may recognize herself as belonging simultaneously to Mediterranean, Christian and European culture.

Now – and this point is essential – these different cultural identities do not coincide with one another, and do not form clearly separated territories, in which these different ingredients are superimposed without remainder. Every individual is multicultural; cultures are not monolithic islands but criss-crossed alluvial plains. Individual identity stems from the encounter of multiple collective identities within one and the same person; each of our various affiliations contributes to the formation of the unique creature that we are. Human beings are not all similar, or entirely different; they are all plural within themselves, and share their constitutive traits with very varied groups, combining them in an individual way. The cohabitation of different types of belonging within each one of us does not in general cause any problems – and this ought, in turn, to arouse admiration: like a juggler, we keep all the balls of our identity in the air at once, with the greatest of ease!

Individual identity results from the interweaving of several collective identities; it is not alone in this respect. What is the origin of the culture of a human group? The reply – paradoxically – is that it comes from previous cultures. A new culture arises from the encounter between several smaller cultures, or from the decomposition of a bigger culture, or from interaction with a neighbouring culture. There is never a human life prior to the advent of culture. And for a good reason: 'cultural' characteristics are already present among other animals, notably the primates.

There are no pure cultures and no mixed cultures; all cultures are mixed ('hybrid', 'cross-bred'). Contacts between human groups go back to the origins of the species, and they always leave traces on the way in which the members of each group communicate with each other. As far back as we can go in the history of a country like France, we always find an encounter between several populations, and thus between several cultures: Gauls, Franks, Romans and many others.

A particularly eloquent example of what may occur when cultures meet can be observed in America, in the sixteenth century, during the years following the conquest of Mexico by the soldiers of Spain. The conflict between the two political forces had a devastating effect: nothing of the legal and administrative structures that had been in force in the time of Moctezuma (or, further south, of Atahualpa) remained. The two cultures, Spanish and Aztec, were totally ignorant of one another before 1519; they differed in language, religion, collective memory and customs. The encounter did not leave them intact, but none of them disappeared entirely. An active role was very quickly played by individuals who, coming from one of the cultures, managed to know the other culture from inside and assumed the role of mediators. This is true of the Spanish who fell into the hands of the Indians and ended up adopting numerous traits of their lifestyle; it also applies to the Indians who, once they had been vanquished, learned Spanish, transcribing their native language with the aid of the Latin alphabet and producing writings that participated in both cultures at once.

One of the most complex examples of this cultural cross-breeding is provided by the work of the Spanish Dominican Diego Durán. His initial aim was to extirpate the pagan superstitions of the Indians. In order to do this, he felt obliged to study them in detail; and, as he did so, he allowed himself to be influenced by them. He also wrote a history of the Conquest, in which he shifted from the point of the view of the Spanish to that of the Aztecs, and vice versa, so that eventually his reader inevitably comes to this conclusion: he is dealing with a new, *Mexican* point of view. Everywhere in the country, the Christian ritual was 'contaminated' by pre-Columbian traditions, and in this way a new culture – that of Mexico – was born.[2]

Another characteristic of cultures, no less easy to identify, is the fact that they are in perpetual transformation. All cultures change, even if it is certain that the so-called 'traditional' ones do so less willingly and less quickly than those that are called 'modern'. There are several different reasons for these changes. Since each culture includes others within itself, or intersects with them, its different ingredients form an unstable equilibrium. For example, granting women the right to vote in France, in 1944, enabled them to participate actively in the country's public life: as a result, French cultural identity was transformed. Likewise, when – twenty-three years later – women were granted the right to use contraception, this entailed a new mutation in French culture. If cultural identity never changed, France would not have become Christian, to begin with, and then secular subsequently. As well as these internal tensions, there are also external contacts, with nearby or distant cultures, which in turn lead to new changes in direction. Before it influenced other cultures in the world, European culture had already absorbed Egyptian, Mesopotamian, Persian, Indian, Islamic and Chinese influences.

We also need to taken into account the pressures brought to bear by the evolution of other series that are constitutive of the social order: the economic, the political, even the physical. These changes happen all the more easily in that cultures – a common memory, common rules of life – are formed by agglutination and addition, and do not possess the rigour of a system. In this sense, they resemble the lexicon of a language rather than its syntax: one can always add a new word, while another word can easily fall into disuse. But the most eloquent image is still that of the mythical ship of the Argonauts, the *Argo*: each plank, each rope, each nail had to be replaced, since the voyage took so long; the ship that returned to port, years later, was materially completely different from the one which set off, and yet it was still the same ship *Argo*. Unity of function is more important than difference of substance, and the identical name counts more than the disappearance of all the original elements. However, the shifting identity of cultures should not lead us to abandon the very notion of culture, as certain anthropologists have done, finding it difficult as they do to think of an entity whose contents are constantly evolving. Cultures are in a process of constant transformation – but without any common culture for the group, the human being perishes. We can acknowledge the necessity of talking about cultures without falling into the misperceptions of 'culturalism', or the deduction of all of an individual's characteristics from his or her cultural belonging, in the way that racism proceeded in the past.

If we keep these two characteristics of culture in mind, its plurality and its variability, we see how disconcerting are the metaphors most commonly used to evoke it. We say of a human being, for instance, that he is 'uprooted' and we pity him for it; but it is not legitimate to equate human beings with plants, since a human is never the product of just one culture, and in any case the animal world is distinguished from the vegetable world precisely by its mobility. Cultures have no essence or 'soul', in spite of the fine works that have been written about these things. Or else people talk of the 'survival' of a culture (this time humanizing the representations instead of dehumanizing man); by this they mean its conservation in identical form. Now a culture that has stopped changing is by definition a dead culture. The expression 'dead language' is much more judicious: Latin died on the day it could no longer change. Nothing is more normal, more common than the disappearance of a previous state of culture and its replacement by a new state.

However, for reasons that are easy to acknowledge, the members of the group find this obvious fact difficult to understand. The difference between individual and collective identities is illuminating here. Even if, one day, we dream of discovering within us a 'deep' and 'authentic' self, as if it awaited us patiently lurking somewhere in the depths of our being, we are conscious of the changes, wished for or not, that our being undergoes: they are perceived as normal. Everyone remembers the decisive events from his past, and we can also take decisions that send our identities off in a new direction, when we change jobs, or partners, or countries. A person is nothing other than the result of innumerable interactions that mark out the stages of a life.

Collective identity works in a completely different way: it is already fully formed by the time the individual discovers it, and it becomes the invisible foundation on which her identity is built. Even if, seen from outside, every culture is mixed and changing, for the members of the community that it characterizes, it is a stable and distinct entity, the foundation of their collective identity. For this reason, all change that affects culture is experienced as an attack on my integrity. One need merely compare the facility with which I agree, if I am capable of it, to speak a new language while on a visit to a foreign country (an individual event) and the disagreeable feeling I have when, in the street where I have always lived, only incomprehensible words and accents can now be heard (a collective event). What we have found in the original culture is no longer shocking, since this has helped actually to shape the person. On the other hand, what changes by force of circumstances over which the individual has no power is perceived as a kind of degradation, for it makes our very sense of being feel fragile. The contemporary period, during which collective identities are called on to transform themselves more and more quickly, is thus also the period in which groups are adopting an increasingly defensive attitude, and fiercely demanding their original identities.

Culture as construction

The same two characteristics of cultures help us to understand why the way the members of a community represent their culture to themselves has nothing automatic about it, but is, at every moment, the product of a construction. The social practices of a group are multiple and changing; now, in order to construct a representation, we must proceed to choices and combinations, operations which do not passively reflect the nature of things, but organize them in a certain manner. In consequence, individuals are immersed, not in purely physical contacts with the world, but within a set of collective representations that, at a given moment, occupy a dominant place in the hierarchy of a culture. These representations constitute an oral knowledge that is transmitted from generation to generation, or else are set down in writing; it is these which give meaning to the different events that constitute a person's life. In this sense, culture is the image that society makes of itself. It is with this representation that individuals seek to identify themselves – or from which they aspire to free themselves; it does not unfold mechanically from the facts themselves. Let us take one example: all the inhabitants of France did not suddenly become Christian overnight. One day, however, the image of French culture as being Christian became dominant; and the same goes for the day when, centuries later, France was declared to be secular. Representations are not mere reflections of facts or statistical approximations: they result from choices and combinations that might have been different.

The internal hierarchy of the different ingredients of a culture is fixed or modified in accordance with conflicts between the groups which carry these ingredients within a society, or between the whole society and its external partners. Thus religion becomes the determining characteristic when the invaders from a neighbouring country have another religion, as for the Irish with regard to the English in Ireland, or the Bosnians and the Croats as against the Serbs. But it is language that becomes this crucial factor in the case of the Basques in Spain, since they are as Catholic as the Spanish who surround them. The case of Quebec is equally revealing here. So long as the other in relation to which Quebecois identity was constituted was the English-speaking population of Canada, the dominant trait of this identity was the French language. The policies that arose from this fact, in this country of immigration, favoured the arrival of groups from the former French colonies, in North Africa and sub-Saharan Africa. As a consequence, the balance between new arrivals and native inhabitants was modified, and the latter became aware of another element in their identity, and also of the need to emphasize it – namely, religion. Catholic or atheist Quebecois do not recognize themselves in the devout Muslims who have become their fellow citizens, and so they construct their identities in a different way.

Of course, representations are determined by practices; but they in turn also act on behaviour. They do so as norms that are adopted explicitly by society, but also as an image of the world – incomplete, inevitably, and thus unfaithful, but shared by the majority of the population. All perception, as is well known, is already a construction: not because the objective world does not exist, but because it is necessary to choose from among its countless properties, in virtue of pre-established schemas, in order to identify objects and events that present themselves 'to our eyes'. Perception always mixes together 'realities' and 'fictions'. These schemas in turn are former selective constructions: the past image affects the present perception.

Equally well known, in the psychology of the individual, is the mechanism of the 'self-fulfilling prophecy'. If a child is frequently told that it is naughty, it will assume this negative image and deliberately exaggerate it even more: it will become even 'naughtier' than it is accused of being. Deciding that it owes nothing to the society by which it feels rejected, it will reject it in turn and rejoice in its destruction. The same phenomenon can be observed in the behaviour of groups within a wider community. The immigrant population of a particular ethnic origin, for instance, will be at one and the same time identified as being distinct from the majority (its members look different, speak another language, have their own customs) and as undervalued (because they have not properly mastered the codes in force in global society and are less able to succeed than the others). In short, it is the same continuity as that between the two meanings of the word 'barbarian' among the Greeks: these individuals do not speak our language, so they are not civilized. In their turn, they interiorize this image of negative strangeness, and on it they mould a pattern of behaviour which, perceived as aggressive, provokes repression on the part of the 'forces of law and order', and arouses a hostile attitude on the part of the rest of the population. This repression is then felt by the group discriminated against as a provocation, leading it to riot. Thus a vicious circle kicks in: the image created by the neighbours of a group affects the group's self-image, and this in turn guides the behaviour of its members and finally, once again, the image of its neighbours.

At the basis of each culture we find the collective memory of the group bearing that culture. Now a memory is in itself necessarily a construction, in other words a selection from the facts of the past and their arrangement in a hierarchy that does not belong to them as their own, but comes to them from the present members of the group. This collective memory, like all human memory, carries out a radical selection from among the countless events of the past, and this is why forgetting is no less constitutive of identity than is the safeguarding of memories. The selection of facts and their arrangement in a hierarchy are not carried out by specialists (historians themselves habitually stop the guardians of memory from repeating the same clichés), but rather by influential groups within society who are trying to defend their interests. The aim of these groups is less the exact knowledge of the past and more the recognition by others of their place in the collective memory and thus in the social life of the country.

An eloquent example of the constant reconstruction to which collective memory (and thus also the culture of the country) is subjected can be found in the recent aspirations of various groups, in France as in other Western countries, to assume the role of principal victim in the past. Whereas being a victim of violence is a pitiful fate, it has become desirable, in a contemporary liberal democracy, to obtain the status of a former victim of acts of collective violence, a status that is supposedly transmitted from generation to generation.

In this respect, it is significant that a transformation in contemporary memory has occurred: these days, it is the former victims rather than the former heroes who are granted the maximum of attention and most often canvassed for their opinions; the wrongs suffered weigh more heavily than the exploits accomplished. In the aftermath of the Second World War, people spoke with the greatest respect of political deportees, former resistance fighters: they had acted, and thus they deserved the recognition of their own country. Even the existence of 'racial' deportees – the Jews – was often ignored: they had done nothing, so there was no need to talk about them. Thirty years later on, the situation had been reversed and the former resistance members had started to feel neglected, since attention had now shifted to the victims of anti-Semitic persecution, the object of the supreme crime, the crime against humanity. Those victims had not acted, and so the evil committed against them was even greater. This consecration of the narrative of the victims over that of the heroes, with the former now placed at the summit of a symbolic hierarchy, is indirect evidence of a reinforcing among us of the idea of justice: who would have any idea of demanding to occupy the victim's place if he did not have any hope of seeing his suffering acknowledged and obtaining reparation?

For several decades, the victim par excellence was thus identified with the Jewish deportees, the victims of Nazism. However, for several years, this unenviable privilege has aroused the desire of a similar recognition on the part of new groups that have, in the past, been subjected to injustice and ill-treatment, which has created the phenomenon of a competition between different memories. These demands are often made by the children, the grandchildren or the more distant descendants of other former victims: the colonized peoples of the nineteenth and twentieth centuries, the populations reduced to slavery in the seventeenth and eighteenth centuries. These sometimes assume the form of a call for repentance, or at least for the public acknowledgement of the fault committed, on the part of the state authorities, the president or the parliament. In France, as we have seen, these criticisms lead to a corresponding demand from other groups in the population for a public recognition of the positive role of French colonization, or even the erection of monuments to the former members of the OAS.

These struggles to rewrite collective memory illustrate the processes of construction and reconstruction to which the past is permanently subject, and which have palpable results: for some time now, in France, Napoleon has started to leave his place as a national hero, since people are lending a more attentive ear to the voices of his victims (as expressed through the voices of their descendants or defenders). From the point of view of civilization, or indeed of history, we must proscribe the Manichean reading of the past, in which whole societies and cultures are reduced to playing the roles of barbarian or victim. On the other hand, we need to emphasize the importance of the moment when the individual becomes aware of the identity of his own group and becomes capable of observing it as if from the place of another; he even becomes capable of critically scrutinizing his own past to discover the ancient traces of humanity as well as of barbarism. We cannot really know our own traditions and culture unless we can take a certain distance from them, which is in no way to be confused with systematic self-denigration and public lambasting – or, of course, with the bland self-assurance of having always been right. Exclamations of pride and tears of penitence, rather, should be replaced by an investigation into the causes and the meaning of past events.

The functions of culture

What use is culture? Depending on the point of view we adopt, we can give different answers to this question. It plays the role, as I have said, of an image, a key to understanding the world, without which everyone would have the impression they were immersed in a terrifying chaos. It acts as a link between the different members of the community that shares it and allows them to communicate with one another. A human being without culture is not completely human. But culture also has functions of a different kind. It provides the material and the forms that each individual needs to construct his or her own personality. The human being is not satisfied with mere biological life, and needs to feel that he exists, which can happen only when he is included within a specifically human society: the latter constitutes the environment which he cannot live without, since it is not within himself that he can find the proofs of his existence. Self-awareness springs from recognition by others; the inter-human realm precedes and founds the human.[3]

This inclusion into a larger whole takes several forms, some of them individual – the child seeks its mother's gaze, the lover seeks her beloved's – while others are social, and mediated by the fact of belonging to a group: I feel confirmed in my existence if I can say to myself that I am a schoolboy, or a peasant, or a Frenchman, if I can recognize myself in any kind of group whose existence is undeniable. The South African archbishop Desmond Tutu, a former president of the Truth and Reconciliation Commission, also emphasizes the traditional African interpretation of identity: 'It also means my humanity is caught up, is inextricably bound up, in theirs. We belong in a bundle of life. We say, "a person is a person through other people". It is not "I think, therefore I am". It says rather: "I am human because I belong." I participate, I share.' (W. H. Auden, as a typical Westerner, revised the Cartesian adage in a more individualist way: 'I'm loved, therefore I am.')[4]

Social recognition can come in the form of distinction, or simply from belonging to a collective identity, that of the group whose culture one shares. If the gaze of others does not gratify my sense of individual excellence, I can seek the confirmation of my being in the community (preferably as a valued member) of which I am part. This is what is called the need for belonging – a feeling that is not at all an anachronism, but a constitutive trait of the human person. This is why the wish that is sometimes formulated, to free ourselves from the weight of all collective identity, will never be realized. It is true that traditional identities are often growing weaker these days: up to a certain point, this affects the identity of a country's inhabitants, obliged as they are to move further and more often and to have greater contact with foreigners; to a greater extent, that of the members of territorial or social groups within a country, condemned to mobility and flexibility if they wish to have successful careers. However, more often than not, the reaction to these constraints takes the form of a constitution or rediscovery of other collective identities, either imaginary or provisional, which is a good illustration of the vital need we have of them. This belonging does not necessarily serve our immediate interest; on the other hand, it brings us a deep satisfaction by appeasing our anxieties.

A human being is always born into a culture, but this does not mean that she is destined to remain its prisoner. There is no need to choose between 'belonging to a culture' and 'acting as a free individual': the one does not prevent the other. On the contrary, mastery of one's culture encourages one to be individually creative – but 'mastery' does not mean, as fundamentalists of every creed would have it, 'following obediently'. Conservatives who reject the idea of man as an empty page, or as a shapeless dough to be moulded, are right, for we always have an initial culture at our disposal; but this does not mean that reformists or revolutionaries are wrong to affirm that change is possible. Cultures do exist, but they are not immutable or impermeable to each other. We need to move beyond the sterile opposition between two conceptions: on the one side, that of the disembodied, abstract individual existing outside culture; on the other, that of the individual shut away for life in his original cultural community. Among other animal species, ours is characterized by the increased role of cultural mechanisms and, at the same time, by our greater capacity to adapt to new conditions, and thus tear ourselves away from our original environments.

This can already be observed in human babies. Right from the start of the first year in its life, a child is driven by contradictory instincts. On the one hand, he wishes to feel *comfortable*, in other words to find himself in a familiar physical and human environment: his bedroom, his toys, his mother, his father all reassure him. But on the other hand, he wishes to be *surprised*, in other words he tries to discover and appropriate new postures for his own body, to enlarge his own space by exploring his surroundings, and to familiarize himself with new people. A child who sought only security would be mentally and physically handicapped; a child who was after novelty alone would be unstable and tormented. So we find this need for equilibrium in the adult, even if it is less easy to observe: individuals seek belonging, of course, and a confirmation of the identity which they possess already; but at the same time they are driven by curiosity, the capacity for surprise and admiration, the desire to annex new domains and thus to transform their original culture. These two ingredients of the human psyche are both equally necessary to each individual, and it is impossible to choose between them, any more than we can resolve the antinomy between determinism and freedom, or unity and diversity.

At the time of decolonization, a conflict arose regarding the two choices. Was it enough to replace British nationalism by Kenyan nationalism, or that of the French by that of the Algerians? The dominant culture of the colonist would seem to have been supplanted by another hegemonic culture, of local origin, but the individual may well have remained subject to a collective – perhaps even more so. Or might it be possible to dream of a more radical liberation, not only that of one group from another group, but also that of the individual from his own group?

To seek to tie the individual down to his or her own group of origin is illegitimate, since this comes down to denying this precious characteristic of the human race, the possibility of tearing oneself away from the given by preferring to it something which one has chosen for oneself. The Nazis wrote the word *Jude* on the identity card of every Jewish person, forbidding him to forget his origin for a single moment. In the USSR, the political police marked you down in your records as bearing the stigmata of your 'bourgeois' origin, from which you could never emancipate yourself. Voltaire wrote, 'Every man is born with the natural right to choose a country for himself,'[5] which is an idealistic point of view – countries also have something to say about welcoming people in; but it is true that preventing an individual from changing culture, or punishing a change of religion as apostasy, brings us back towards barbarity. We will never be able to free ourselves of certain traits that are determined by genetics: unless I undergo a rather problematic operation, I am condemned to keeping my sex, my physical appearance and the individual shape of my body. But here, precisely, culture cannot be confused with nature.

Certain external conditions prove favourable to this kind of critical distance. If the group that bears a culture is persecuted or discriminated against, any distance from one's traditions may be experienced as a betrayal, and thus rejected. The Nazi persecutions led many hitherto 'assimilated' Jews to discover or rediscover Jewish traditions. These days, the discriminations sometimes suffered by people from the Maghreb in European countries lead some of them to lay claim, with pride, to their identity of origin and arouse a desire to return to their traditions. If I am insulted or viewed with suspicion because of my Algerian or Moroccan origin, I feel attacked in part of my identity, and to wish to detach myself from it at that moment would involve joining my attackers and enfeebling my sense of being. It is much easier to commit oneself to the way of 'violent detachment' if my culture, and the community which bears it, are not being undermined at that precise moment.

On the other hand, detachment is easier when I also receive personal gratifications that reinforce my sense of being – whether they be linked to my work, to my wealth, to my physical appearance or to my power. The country's elite, in the business world or that of politics or the arts, easily adopts a cosmopolitan point of view. When, however, a person lacks education, work, or any possibility of future success, group belonging is still an effective fall-back: I belong, therefore I am. In order to tear oneself away from an identity, one must already possess it.

Nor need this surprise us: not all people live their need for identity and collective belonging in the same way, for, as Benjamin Constant noted long ago, 'the object that escapes your grasp is necessarily quite different from the one which is pursuing you'.[6] If one day I had been forbidden to speak Bulgarian, my native language, I would have experienced this restriction as an intolerable act of aggression on my identity. I have chosen, freely and step by step, to make French my everyday language: the new identity took over from the previous one without any violent shocks. However much the individual is crisscrossed by forces that he cannot control, unconscious instincts or social determinations, his choice and his desire can give a new meaning to the event; the exile that he desires will not be lived in the same way as the expulsion inflicted by an occupier.

We are well aware that identities can become murderous. A necessary condition for the eruption of violence is, as Amartya Sen has shown, the reduction of multiple identity to single identity. Before I kill my neighbour because he is a Tutsi, I need to forget all his other kinds of belonging: to a profession, an age, an environment, a country – or to humanity. Violence carried out in the name of identity is no less violent because the groups that practise it consider themselves, rightly or wrongly, to be the victims of other groups, threatened in their very existence, or in that of their nearest and dearest. Many women and children, it has been said, have been massacred in the name of the defence of 'our' women and 'our' children. But there is nothing wrong with identity as such and, as Amin Maalouf says,[7] we are not driven back on the choice between wholesale fundamentalist identity and the disintegration of identity.

It is impossible to live outside all culture; it is a disaster to lose one's culture of origin without acquiring another. Living within one's culture without having to feel embarrassed about it is legitimate, as is leaving one's initial culture and adopting a new one: both situations enable us to feel that we exist, and to maintain our dignity. However, acquiring – by one means or another – the ability to recognize ourselves in people different from ourselves, and treating them as if they were like us, is to take one step further. The idea of such a hierarchy was not foreign to the Christian doctrine. Thus, in the Sermon on the Mount, Jesus declared that our neighbour, in the evangelical sense of the word, is precisely the one who is most distant in cultural terms. 'For if ye love them which love you, what reward have ye? do not even the publicans the same? And if ye salute your brethren only, what do ye more than others? do not even the publicans so?'[8] The aspiration to an identity and the acquisition of a culture provide the necessary condition for the construction of a fully human personality; but only opening up to otherness, with universality (and thus civilization) as its horizon, will provide us with the sufficient condition.

States and nations

In his dialogue *The Laws*, written in 52 BC, Cicero, the Roman politician and philosopher, formulated a distinction that had a great impact on European thinking on the subject. Here are his words:

> Surely I think that [...] all natives of Italian towns have two fatherlands, one by nature and the other by citizenship. Cato, for example, though born in Tusculum, received citizenship in Rome, and so, as he was a Tusculan by birth and a Roman by citizenship, had one fatherland which was the place of his birth, and another by law [...] so we consider both the place where we were born our fatherland, and also the city into which we have been adopted. But that fatherland must stand first in our affection in which the name of republic signifies the common citizenship of us all. For her it is our duty to die, to her to give ourselves entirely, to place on her altar, and, as it were, to dedicate to her service, all that we possess. But the fatherland which was our parent is not much less dear to us than the one which adopted us.[9]

The first of these two 'fatherlands' is of the same kind as our 'culture'. I belong to it without having had to choose it, it is the land of my ancestors, of the impressions that cradled my child-hood, and in it – as Cicero adds – I find something mysterious that makes it a particularly precious place. 'Do they not say that, in order to see Ithaca again, the wise Ulysses turned down immor-tality?' The second 'native land', on the other hand, is our state, the country of which we are citizens. Some three centuries after Cicero, in the year 212, a famous decree of the Emperor Caracalla declared that all the inhabitants of the empire, from North Africa to England, were citizens on an equal footing, even though they were the bearers of very different cultures. The state is not a 'culture' like others; it is an administrative and political entity with well-established frontiers, and it obviously includes individuals who are the bearers of several different cultures, since in it we find men and women, young people and old, of every profession and every condition, from various regions, indeed countries, and speak-ing different languages, practising several religions and respecting different customs.

The modern idea of the nation, born in the eighteenth century, has two sides: in it, power is attributed to the whole set of citizens rather than to a monarch with divine right; and the state is deemed to coin-cide with a human group which has the same language and the same traditions (including religion) – what is sometimes called an ethnic group. This conjunction produces the nation-state. In reality, the second condition is never entirely satisfied. Human populations have become mixed and displaced on many different occasions and the establishment of as many states as there are ethnic groups is materi-ally impossible; furthermore, the very identity of an ethnic group is often problematic. There is no ethnically pure nation. The figures are there to prove it: there are, today in the world, some 6,000 languages (language being the easiest element to identify in a culture) but fewer than 200 states.

It can also be claimed that such a coincidence between state and single culture is undesirable, both because, in the contemporary world, a microscopic state is not really viable and because the pres-ence of heterogeneous elements ensures that a society remains dynamic. A modern democracy is to be distinguished from an *eth-nocracy*, i.e., a state in which belonging to a particular ethnic group ensures you of privileges over the other inhabitants of a country; in a democracy, all citizens, whatever their origin, language, religion or customs, enjoy the same rights.

67

In spite of the difficulty, indeed the impossibility, of establishing a true nation-state, a mono-ethnic state, there has been no lack of attempts to do so in the course of the last few centuries. The nationalist movements that have been involved in attempts have served the cause of freedom, toppling a tyrannical regime or an oppressive foreign yoke. However, nothing guarantees that nationalists will establish a just society once they are in power: national oppression may be replaced by religious or political oppression, carried out by a class or a clan, that is worse than the previous one. And it is in the name of their explicitly affirmed principle – preference for one's own people to the detriment of others – that the new injustice may be perpetrated. It is altogether possible – and even frequent – that, having thrown off the foreign yoke, the new majority that holds power will oppress its own ethnic or cultural minorities. Its policies then consist in imposing on them a brutal choice between assimilation and expulsion. If they remain in place, they risk suffering various discriminations and persecutions, and having legal inequalities and apartheid imposed on them.

The end of the Second World War saw massive displacements of population, illustrating the principle of distinction between state and ethnic group. Thus millions of Poles had to leave land given to the Ukraine (and thus the Soviet Union) so that the latter territory could be inhabited by Ukrainians; millions of Germans were expelled from Poland, Czechoslovakia and lands that had been German. Later, the Palestinians were obliged to leave what had become the state of Israel. Even more recently, the same principle of ethnic purification led to civil wars in Yugoslavia. The Serb Communist power, sensing that it was weakening in the wake of a general disaffection with its ideals, decided to play the nationalist card, replacing its failing ideology by a tried and tested passion, a preference for 'us' over 'them'. In their turn, and in the name of the same national principle, the former minorities of Yugoslavia demanded their political independence. In the military conflict that resulted, the army and the Serbian auxiliaries, who were better armed, succeeded in committing more massacres than their opponents.

The last episode in this civil war, the conflict in Kosovo, was the scene of an additional agent. To begin with, the situation seemed familiar: the Serbian power was persecuting a minority from a different culture, to which the response was the constitution of an Albanian-speaking independence movement; both parties aspired to govern homogenous entities, to ensure that the fields of political action and cultural identity would coincide. This time the surprise came from the third party, the Americans and Europeans, who (as opposed to what had happened in Bosnia) not only accepted but also powerfully reinforced this change in the country's destiny, by intervening in the conflict on the military level. Indeed, the form of intervention chosen – the bombing of one of the groups in the name of the other – could lead only to an easily foreseeable result: an acceleration of ethnic purification. In response to the bombings, the Serbs multiplied the exactions against the Albanian Kosovars, perceived as being the allies of their enemy and the cause of their misfortune; in the wake of the NATO military victory, the Albanian minority embarked in turn on a persecution of the Serbs, who had become its own minority, under the complicit eyes of the international community.

Ethnic purification, condemned in official law courts, was the principle of action that was tacitly accepted by all, with a result that one hesitates to endorse. From this point of view, the experiment that was first tried in Kosovo served as a model for episodes of Western interference in the following years. Thus the war in Iraq seems to aim at the constitution of homogeneous groups that do not mix (a material wall now separates them in certain towns) and are inevitably rivals with one another: Sunni Arabs on one side, Shiite Arabs on another, Sunni Kurds on yet another.

The non-coincidence between states and cultures, not to mention that between different forms of cultural belonging, is the rule, not the exception. When a minority is oppressed or discriminated against, two theoretical solutions are possible: re-establishing one's rights within the pre-existing state or creating a new state in which the former minority will be in the majority. This second path is sometimes the obvious choice: the Algerian 'minority' within the French Empire had to gain independence. In numerous other circumstances, it is the first path that is preferable; though it is true that it does not have the same simplicity as the other measure – dropping bombs on the enemy.

The fragile state

These days the national state faces several challenges. The first, to tell the truth, is quite old, since it results from the new status to which the individual has aspired ever since the Enlightenment. Referring to Cicero's text on the two homelands, Benjamin Constant, at the beginning of the nineteenth century, had already realized the change that had occurred: the contemporary individual no longer wished, he said, to 'give all' for the state, and times had changed:

> it is because the fatherland embodied [at the time of Cicero] all that was dearest to a man. To lose one's country was to lose one's wife, children, friends, all affections, and nearly all communication and social enjoyment. The age of that sort of patriotism is over; what we love now in our country, as in our liberty, is the property of whatever we possess, our security, the possibility of rest, activity, glory, a thousand sorts of happiness.[10]

Except during international football matches, one's 'political' homeland, in Cicero's sense (the state), is not the object of any affection in Europe, where one's feelings usually go towards a more restricted group made up of elements that are close to one: family, friends, places, habits. This is easy to understand: the state, even if we suppose that it is protective, is cold and distant – a coldness and distance that seem destined to increase every year, whereas the community from which I come and which I miss if I emigrate is closer and warmer. The recognition of my own people enables me to exist in a more intense manner than the abstract awareness of being one citizen among others.

A second reason for seeing the national state retreat comes from the reinforcement of the communities that constitute it, communities of ethnic origin, or sexual inclinations, or other cultural choices; a movement that in France is called (pejoratively) 'communitarianism'. The question is sometimes asked: should we be moving towards a multicultural society? But the terms of the debate are the wrong ones to choose. In fact, as we have seen, every society and every state are multicultural (or crossbred), not merely because populations have been intermixing for time immemorial, but also because the constitutive groups in society – men, women, old, young, etc., – possess distinct cultural identities. The difference does not lie between pluricultural and monocultural societies, but between those which (in the images they form of their own identity) accept their inner plurality by emphasizing its value and those which, on the contrary, choose to ignore or denigrate it. In this respect, the contempt in which the realities designated by terms such as 'crossbreed' or 'hybrid' have long been held reveals a desire for 'purity', not its real presence. It is perfectly pointless to be against multiculturalism: in this sense of the word, there is nothing else – and lucidity and realism are preferable to the maintenance of illusions.

However, the word has taken another sense, especially in the United States – one that is no longer descriptive, but prescriptive: it valorizes the separation of communities and, at the same time, the submission of the individual to the group's traditions. I am an Afro-American, I prefer to remain among my own kind, and this sense of belonging is responsible for the main lines that my behaviour will follow. Such a sense attributed to the word 'multiculturalism' is, it has to be said, fairly paradoxical, since it enjoins each individual to remain, in a word, monocultural, and Amartya Sen is right to speak in this regard of a 'plural monoculturalism'.[11] In the name of *that* monoculturalism, in other countries, a young girl will be forbidden to go with a boy from another religion, on the pretext that she is thereby offending the group's honour.

Such a decision does indeed need to be disputed. Condemning the individual to remain trapped within the culture of his ancestors presupposes that culture is an immutable code, which, as we have seen, is empirically false: not all change is good, perhaps, but all living culture changes. There is no drama for the individual in the loss of a culture, on condition that he acquires another; it is having a language that constitutes our humanity, not having *this* language; it is being open to spiritual experiences, not practising *this* religion. Communitarianism leads to the opposite result of the one it had proposed, defending the dignity of the group's members: each individual is now enclosed within his little cultural community, instead of profiting from exchanges with people different from himself, as national integration allows him to do. To know a tradition well, yet again, does not mean that you have to obey it docilely.

Finally, the nation-state is also currently weakened, especially in Europe, by the strengthening of trans-national networks. These are, to begin with, institutions of the European Union, which can force national governments to modify their politics. In addition, there are the effects of economic globalization, which mean that a government no longer has control over a major part of the lives of its citizens – the part that is subject to trans-national economic agents. This weakening is indisputable, and yet it is far from signifying that old-style states are perishing. The European Union does not eliminate the state structures of member countries, it coordinates them; there will never be a European nation or people. It is clear that, in the eyes of the population, the major political stakes remain tied to the national state – witness the way that the big beasts in each political party engage in the struggle for power within the country. And if the latter can no longer entirely control economic power, it is not thereby deprived of all means of intervention – far from it.

The national state has thus lost several of its attributes, but this does not mean it has become superfluous. It is within the nation that the great social solidarities find a place. It is the taxes paid by all citizens that make medical care available to those who cannot afford it. It is the work of the active citizens that enables retired senior citizens to pick up their pensions. It is their contributions, too, which help to supply a fund for the unemployed. It is thanks to national solidarity that all children in the country benefit from a free education. Now health, work and education all form an essential part of everyone's existence. The fact remains that a person's attachment to the country of which she is citizen is civic rather than sentimental. When I emigrate, I may change country and thus solidarities; on the other hand, I will never be able to have a childhood other than my own. Our spontaneous reactions to the two are not the same: we love (or hate) our language, the place we grew up in, the food we ate at home; but we do not 'love' our social security system, our pension fund or the Ministry of Education – we simply ask them to be reliable.

Likewise, an individual can never demand his rights except insofar as the state guarantees them and, in case of need, intervenes to defend them. We may feel that our souls are profoundly cosmopolitan, but we are never citizens of the world. In a moving page from *The World of Yesterday*, Stefan Zweig tells of the revelations he experienced: he, the Viennese Jew from a good family, able to speak several languages fluently, popular and celebrated in all the countries where books were read, was in the habit of thinking of himself as a European, as a cosmopolitan, as a man without ties – up until the day when the Nazi anti-Semitic persecutions really did make him stateless. And this was a traumatic experience. For many people in the modern world, civic identity is like air: you feel the need for it only when it becomes threatened; but on that day, it reassumes all its rights.

It would be good to have this lucidity *before* finding yourself in the situation where you have to flee, flee further and further away. Far from being just a threat, as an individualist and anarchist vision of the world would have it, states are also a source of support, not only in the form of the welfare state, i.e., redistributing its revenue in such a way as to ensure that everyone has a certain level of comfort, as well as education, health and accommodation, but also because of the way it protects us against aggression that may come from individuals as well as from groups.

A state without common culture?

One question remains: can we remain content with a state that is essentially reduced to its administrative solidarities and to national solidarities, to the exercise of political rights and partisan struggles for power? If they are to agree to show solidarity to one another, and thus to deprive themselves of part of their income in order to benefit those who have less, the inhabitants of a country must also feel a sense of nearness to each other, in other words possess a certain cultural identity in common. We have just seen that this identity will not be the only one, that it will also involve cultures of lesser extent, regional cultures or the cultures of one's country of origin, or of the social group to which you feel strongly that you belong; and of even greater extent, since I can also feel essentially European, Western, or indeed Christian. This does not prevent a national culture from also existing. What is the content of this, at a time when there are ever more international exchanges, increasingly rapid population turn-overs and, at the same time, a need to recognize the dignity of other cultures?

This question might be set in a concrete environment: schools. In a country like France, all state schools follow a common syllabus and education is obligatory up to the age of sixteen. So, at the end of that period, everyone will have been put in contact with a set of information that constitutes educational culture. These days, nobody really knows how to address a population as varied as that which goes to inner-city schools. Things were doubtless simpler in the days of colonial France, when young Senegalese, Vietnamese and so on learned, just like the French boys and girls in metropolitan France, the history of 'their' ancestors the Gauls! The social hierarchy concealed cultural plurality. But these days? It is sometimes recommended that schools should again be made places where 'children learn to recognize themselves in a common past'.[12] But what are we to do if this common past does not exist, since in the class there are children of ten, or fifteen, or twenty nationalities of origin, who do not wish to remain ignorant of their initial cultural belonging?

The problem is real: children from immigrant backgrounds find it difficult to project themselves into the traditional French heroes, whereas this kind of pride-filled identification, this demand for positive figures, is useful for the constitution of a healthy self-image, which is itself indispensable for all harmonious social life. Anyone who lives in a state of self-hatred or self-contempt – which may be particularly powerful when they are unconscious – can only reject the society that surrounds him, too, for it is a society with which he cannot identify. What are we to do if we wish simultaneously to take into account the cultural diversity of origin, proper to the children in a class, and work towards a culture shared by all future citizens?

In order to break out of this impasse, it has sometimes been suggested that the study of national history be enriched by certain episodes drawn from the history of the peoples from which the children who have now settled in France originally sprang, in particular, the episodes that illustrate the influences to which French or European culture were subjected. The example of Arab scholars of the Middle Ages, such as Avicenna or Averroes, easily comes to mind. However, one may hesitate to go down that path. It would be difficult to find, in the history of every people whose current descendants live in France, appropriate heroic figures; difficult and, to tell the truth, pernicious: it is not because their ancestors contributed to the flourishing of European culture (or to that of their countries of origin) that we should now respect the children of immigrants from Mali or Morocco, Romania or Turkey; it is because they are human beings just as much as the others. Respect for human dignity is not something you have to deserve: it is a given.

However, another type of intervention can be imagined, the principle of which would be less the multiplication of positive cultural references than an encouragement to critical reflection on the very notion of cultural identity, on the plurality of our affiliations (which overlap only minimally), on the problematic, and not always positive, character of each national history. Thus, in classes in civic education, given in France from primary school onwards, it can be shown, with the aid of examples and stories, that while citizenship remains singular, the cultural identities of each person are multiple and changing; certain elements in national culture are governed by the principle of unity (language above all, mastery of which ensures that everyone can have access to the same social space), whereas other elements, such as religions, are governed by the principle of secularism and tolerance.

In France, when children are between eleven and fifteen years old, they follow a course on the entire history of France; now history cannot be taught without values being at the same time transmitted. But mentioning acts that illustrate the notions of good and evil does not mean that we should favour a Manichean view. Without going as far as embarking on a systematic critique, the course can become an opportunity for showing (as is sometimes already the case) that this country, France, has not always played a role that should arouse

74

admiration or compassion – that of the valiant hero bringing the benefits of Christianity and civilization to distant peoples, or that of the innocent victim subjected to the vile aggression of its ill-intentioned neighbours. Light can be thrown on several episodes from history if we remember the way they were perceived by the 'enemies' of bygone days. We need to move, as the German sociologist Ulrich Beck puts it, 'beyond arrogance and self-betrayal' to 'a culture of shared ambivalence'.[13] The episodes of the Crusades and the great geographical discoveries followed by the intensification of the slave trade, the Napoleonic Wars, colonization in the nineteenth century and decolonization in the twentieth, would enable pupils to dissociate their judgements of good and evil from their sense of collective identity.

Finally, in French secondary schools it is possible to imagine a study of literature that puts them in contact with great works from various world cultures, and not just from the French tradition. This would show that the flourishing of the spirit can assume the most varied forms. All of these modest measures taken together, together with others of the same kind, would make it possible to become aware of the way everyone has a plural identity, and everyone belongs to the same humanity.

Moral and political values

When we debate the national identity, one of the texts most frequently mentioned is Ernest Renan's lecture already mentioned, 'Qu'est-ce qu'une nation?' ('What is a Nation?'), which stemmed from his reflections on the Franco-Prussian War and was published in 1882. Its aim was, in particular, to demand that Alsace and Lorraine should belong to France, because of the desire clearly expressed by the populations of those regions, and despite their greater cultural proximity to the rest of Germany. This was summed up in his celebrated formula: 'The existence of a nation is [...] a daily plebiscite.' The expression of the desire represented by this plebiscite means that people accept a set of values: 'A nation is a spiritual principle,' Renan adds. What is often forgotten, however, is that in the same text Renan mentions a second criterion that is necessary if we are to decide whether someone belongs to a nation – a criterion which this time rests fairly and squarely on the existence of a common cultural basis. 'The nation, like the individual, is the end result of a long past of efforts, sacrifices and acts of devotion. Ancestor-worship is the most legitimate of all forms of worship; our ancestors made us what we are. [...] You love a home that you have built and can hand on.'[14]

It is of little importance to us here to know how Renan manages to reconcile these two criteria when their results do not go in the same direction; it is the very distinction between them that is of value. So, on the one side, we have that which comes from the past and which we cannot choose, which we love, too, without having to think about it: we recognize here the characteristics of what we call 'culture'. On the other side, no longer a common past, but a common future, a political project, acceptance of a set of principles and norms to which we agree to submit. So it is not just a question of administratively belonging to a state, by virtue of the fact that I am the citizen of this rather than that state, but instead of a choice of ideals – which enable me, should the case arise, to criticize the reality of my country. A third type of collective identity appears here, after belonging to a culture and a state: we recognize ourselves in certain moral and political values.

Thus, these days, in the countries of the European Union, everyone supports the ideas of a democratic regime, universal suffrage, equal rights for individuals, the state of law, the separation of the political and the theological, the protection of minorities, the freedom to seek the truth and the freedom to aspire to happiness. The idea of civilization, in the sense that enables us to contrast it with 'barbarism', is part of these values. We cherish them because we think they are good, not because they are our exclusive property. Furthermore, this is not the case: all these values possess a universal vocation and are actually claimed, in variable combinations, throughout the world.

These values as a whole are precious to us; protecting them might even justify our risking our lives for them, as Cicero was prepared to do for his own land. An attachment to certain values forms the basis of an identity that is different from those previously envisaged. Nobody can tear from out of us the heritage we received in childhood; we can change our loyalty as citizens without necessarily suffering as a result. On their side, the moral and political principles to which we are attached are both fragile and irreplaceable. It is in the name of these principles, which can be shared by all peoples but which are proper to just a few, and independent of our particular culture as well as of the state whose citizens we are, that – to take a few current examples – we are ready, today, to defend intransigently the freedom of women to organize their personal lives the way they see fit; or secularism, understood as the separation of the theological and the political, which confines the exercise of faith in the personal sphere alone, the corollary of which is the freedom to criticize religions; or else the banning of physical violence, whether it be domestic or practised illegally in the name of *raison d'état*, such as torture.

These principles happen to be integrated into the Constitution or the laws and institutions of several countries, but they do not belong to them essentially. The dissociation between this set of values and the national framework is all the more obvious these days in Europe since the majority of the population of the European Union demonstrate that they are attached to them, whereas the states themselves preserve their borders and their sovereignty. We can go even further: many of these ideals today feature in the Universal Declaration of Human Rights and inspire the legislative systems of other cultural or national traditions; conversely, we must remember that the European heritage contains many elements other than the defence of human rights.

In his influential work *The Clash of Civilizations*, Samuel Huntington illustrates the confusion between political project and what he views as the heart of Western civilization.[15] The following are, according to him, the constitutive features of the latter: the heritage of classical Greek and Roman culture; the Catholic and Protestant variants of Christianity; many different languages, but mainly Romance and Germanic; the separation of the spiritual and temporal powers; the state of law; the plurality of social groups; political representation, as in parliament; the individual considered as a value. Even if we disregard the extent to which each of these characteristics is actually correct, we can immediately see that this description freely mingles cultural characteristics, over which an individual has no power (classical heritage, religion, language), with political choices such as secularism or pluralism – forgetting, in the meanwhile, that opposite choices have also appeared in the course of Western history. To this we can add an anthropological characteristic such as individualism, which has yet another status. Such an amalgam is perplexing: wishing to share with others a moral and political ideal is legitimate, but presenting it as indissolubly linked to particular cultural characteristics is much less so.

Let us sum up: even if the individual is in no way their prisoner, even if she can always escape from them and does not fail to do so, collective identities exist and we can ignore them only at our own expense. Every individual participates in numerous identities, of variable extent. I have here distinguished between three major types: cultural identities, themselves already multiple; civic identity, or belonging to a country; finally, identity as adherence to a common project, to a set of values whose vocation is often universal, even if only certain countries have introduced them into their legislation.

The dissociation between these different identities in contemporary European countries creates a new situation, whose consequences we are only now starting to glimpse. In the recent past, it was possible to believe, even if this had never been entirely true, that our different affiliations, and thus our loyalties, all coincided with one another. The nation-state's ambition was to fuse cultural entity with administrative entity; at the same time, the nation was deemed to provide the basis of all values. The nation is the origin of everything, said the Abbé Sieyès on the eve of the French Revolution; it is the law itself. But these days, for a citizen of the European Union, these three dimensions have become separate. An inhabitant of Barcelona can claim to share simultaneously in Catalan culture, in the Spanish nation, and in European values. This separation in itself raises no problems: the human being, as we have seen, can easily cope with multiple affiliations, which are in any case inevitable. But the question then arises: to which of these three entities does her main loyalty go? Or to put it in more dramatic terms: for which of them would she be prepared to die?

Who, these days, desires to 'die for his native land'? All the surveys carried out in Europe show that this feeling is less and less widespread. In any case, modern states no longer ask their population for this kind of commitment: the conscripted army, which implied a gathering together of all the males of a people, has these days been replaced by an army of professionals. Being a soldier has become a profession, with all the advantages and disadvantages that entails. Certain tasks, indeed, are even frequently entrusted (as is the case with the United States in Iraq) to mercenaries, i.e., to private armed groups, in a way similar to what happened before the nation-state, when men would join the army tempted by the lure of booty, or were constrained by force, or were obeying the call of God – but not in order to defend their nation.

This does not mean that the contemporary individual would never agree to sacrifice his existence or his personal satisfactions: such an overturning of the previous order would have meant a radical mutation in our species; but the object of his attachment is no longer the same. To sacrifice oneself for one's nearest and dearest is an attitude that everyone can understand, even if not everyone is ready to assume it. Wishing to risk one's life for the state or for democracy is rarer, but does exist. It is probable that loyalty to others, which used

78

to be directed solely to the nation, will not disappear, but will be divided out in the future between different collective entities, on the basis of personal preferences and new threats. What used to be the fate of certain minorities within the nation-state – for example Jews by culture, French men and women by loyalty, cosmopolitans by conviction – will thus become the general rule.

A Ministry of Identity

If we do not wish to debar ourselves from understanding the world in which we live, it is indispensable to keep in mind the distinctions that we have just been emphasizing, whatever name we give them. Nobody will be surprised, in this context, at the unease that spread through France when, in May 2007, a Ministry of National Identity was set up. The idea for it had been launched in the course of the presidential campaign of the previous months by the candidate Nicolas Sarkozy. It was not easy to know what exactly was meant by the expression 'national identity', or why it needed to be entrusted to a ministry. The candidate said: 'France is all the people who love it, who are ready to defend its ideas, its values ... Being French means speaking and writing French.' But these words could not be taken literally: we know, alas, that nearly a quarter of the French population finds it difficult to master reading and writing, whereas many foreigners who live in other countries express themselves in French without difficulty. As far as values are concerned – the candidate quoted secularism, or equality between men and women – these belong, not to French identity, but to the Republican pact to which the citizens and residents of the country are subject. It is not because it is contrary to French identity that the oppression of women is to be condemned; it is because it transgresses the laws or constitutional principles in force.

But the candidate's aim was obviously far removed from these terminological quibbles: with this formula, he was attempting to capture part of the popular vote. In her book on the electoral campaign, Yasmina Reza reports these off-the-cuff comments he made: 'If we didn't have National Identity, we'd be trailing Ségolène ... If I've got 30%, it's because Le Pen's voters are behind me.'[16]

Since the candidate was elected, the ministry has indeed been created; it bears the name of the Ministry of Immigration, Integration, National Identity and Co-development. The element in its name that causes problems is, of course, 'national identity'. In a reply to the criticisms that had been levelled at him, the first holder of the post, minister Brice Hortefeux, tried to specify the meaning of the formula as he understood it.[17] However, if we read the words, we do not feel much more enlightened. 'Knowing who you are also means understanding where you are going,' he notes at the beginning of his discussion. That is a highly disputable postulate, according to which the past and the present determine the future, as if we could never tear ourselves away from what we are and head off in a different direction. In any case, one has the impression that identity is first and foremost cultural in nature, since the minister goes on to say that in the past it had been inculcated by state-run television, while today it finds itself undermined by the globalization of information brought about by the Internet. However, the minister continues: 'Being a French person is now experienced as a choice rather than as a condition. France creates a sense of acceptance rather than subjection.' Now what we accept are values: so what we have here is another type of identity, in which we choose our moral and political principles rather than attaching ourselves in any emotional sense to a piece of land. Finally, the minister adds that every French person will have the 'duty of serving' his or her country: we are thus moving into the register of the citizen, to whom the fact of belonging to the state attributes rights, but on whom this belonging also imposes obligations.

If I am here striving to distinguish between these different ingredients in 'national identity', it is not out of any pedantic pleasure, but rather because, when we wish to modify them, we need to resort to different kinds of intervention. There is no such thing as a single, homogeneous French culture, but a set of diverse and even contradictory traditions, in a state of permanent transformation, the hierarchy between which varies and will continue to do so. The French Ministry of Education is already, via the syllabus of what pupils study during the period of obligatory schooling, entrusted with the task of producing an image (itself changing) of what all children need to know about the culture of their country. However, this schematic image obviously does not exhaust everything that can be brought under the label of 'French culture'. In the second place, there are no French values, but moral and political values, potentially universal and in any case officially adopted by all countries in the European Union. On the other hand, there *does* exist a French civic identity, which depends on the laws in force in France and which is dependent on parliamentary and government responsibility. A newcomer to the country can be required to respect its laws of the social contract that binds together all its citizens, but not to love it:

public duties and private feelings, and values and traditions, are not all on the same level. Only totalitarian states make the love of one's native land obligatory.

The phrase 'national identity' mixes these different levels together and leads one to transpose onto one level what is true on another. Thus, by a decree defining his competences (31 May 2007), the new minister is entrusted with defining 'a politics of memory', and the minister's text gives us a glimpse of its main tendencies: no longer to privilege those who died 'because of' France (more simply, the victims of slavery and colonization) to the detriment of those who died 'for' France (the French soldiers). This submission of memory to the need to glorify what is judged meritorious at a given moment, and thus the submission of the search for truth to what is deemed to be the good, does however contradict the principle of secularism, an integral part of the values to which the French claim to adhere, since it entrusts the political power with the task of defining what citizens must think and believe (this was already the problem with the Loi Gayssot, which punished Holocaust deniers, and with other laws in memory). Granting exclusive control over the politics of memory recalls the practices with which the defunct Communist governments of Eastern Europe were familiar. Should the values to which one is obliged to adhere be decided uniquely in virtue of patriotism? Should the French soldier who was led to torture and massacre Algerian villagers and who lost his life in so doing be celebrated as much as the resistance fighter who defended his country against the invaders and democracy against Nazism? Should we forget the inhabitants of Algeria – who indeed at that time fell within the jurisdiction of the French state – simply because they had not been born in mainland France?

Other initiatives taken within the context of the new ministry are no less problematic. This is true of the decision to expel, every year, 25,000 foreigners 'without ID papers', a decision which involves placing oneself in a quantitative rather than qualitative perspective, setting up an arbitrary figure that needs to be reached, whatever the individual cases involved. Problematic, too, is the law that subjects the family group to DNA tests, which amounts to allowing the children of foreigners to live in France only if the latter are their biological progenitors. Is it not disturbing to see physical identity taking over from civil identity, as if we were animals? Does not the long process during which the newborn child attains the autonomy of the adult, conducted under the responsibility of the parents (whether or not they are biological parents), deserve to be taken into consideration? Each time, the foreigners are associated with criminals, since it is the latter who are locked up and expelled, or else identified by their DNA. So what we have here is a real lesson in xenophobia – or, if you prefer, of barbarity.

If certain persons living in France these days refuse the state of law, oppress their women or systematically resort to physical violence, they are to be condemned not because such types of behaviour are foreign to French identity (they are not), but because they transgress the laws in force, which in turn are inspired by a core of moral and political values. It is for every individual to look after his or her own affective choices; neither the government nor parliament have any reason to meddle with them. It is in this respect that our democracy is liberal: the state does not entirely control civil society, and within certain limits each individual remains free. National identity too is independent of the laws, and is made and unmade on a daily basis by the action of millions of individuals living in France.

In addition to these disadvantages endemic in the expression 'national identity' is the problem that it is joined to three other terms that all have to do with foreigners: immigration, integration (when they live among us) and co-development (when they stay in their own countries). It is difficult not to sense, here, that foreigners are perceived as a threat to French identity. Now while it is normal for every state to draw up a policy to control its frontiers, the granting of visas, and international projects, it is also groundless to present foreigners as a problem as such and as a threat to national identity. Do we need to recall, yet again, that all modern nations are the result of encounters between populations of different origins, in France as elsewhere? Or that the newcomers are, generally speaking, more enterprising than the natives and thus particularly valuable to the country? Finally, when it comes to the transformations of national identity, we can see that they stem less from the impact of foreigners than from competition between different groups belonging to the same society: yesterday's inferiors seize the top places, and turn out the former privileged class. Pointing these things out does not mean that we are desperately trying to see the world as a rose garden, or forgetting the difficulties presented by integration.

Culture and values

The specificity of civic identity is relatively easy to establish (you either are a citizen of a country or you are not), but the same does not apply to cultural traditions on the one hand and to spiritual values on the other. We have seen that several characteristics of different cultures were not susceptible to value judgements; however, this is not the case for all of them. Values themselves are born within particular cultures before being exported elsewhere. In this latter case, they may come into conflict with those prevalent in the new country. We can see this today, with the growing number of contacts between people who have emigrated from different countries, in particular the peasant societies of several Muslim countries and the culture of big European cities.

The point at which the collision is the most damaging concerns the status of women, who in certain cultures are considered as inferior beings unable ever to enjoy a freedom comparable to that of men, and deserving physical punishment if they disobey. This is a cultural heritage that is directly opposed to the fundamental principles of democratic countries (establishing equality before the law, individual freedom or outlawing violence – even if practice often lags behind theory). Several cases have recently featured in the news, linked in particular to what are called 'crimes of honour'. It is fathers or brothers who decide to punish their daughters or sisters by locking them up, treating them brutally, or even putting them to death. These 'crimes of honour' are often described as *faits divers* and pass unnoticed by the public; at other times they are identified as what they really are. In 2005, a young woman of Turkish origin, Hatun Sürücü, was killed in Berlin by her brothers because she had stopped wearing the veil, visiting her family regularly and frequenting the friends who had been imposed on her.[18] In 2006, a young girl from Brescia in Italy, brought up in a Pakistani family, Hina Saleem by name, was murdered by her father because she had decided to earn a living for herself, to live far away from her family and to dress in accordance with her own taste: a Western lifestyle that her father considered to be dishonourable. In 2007, Sadia Sheikh, a young woman of Pakistani origin, who lived in Charleroi, Belgium, was killed point-blank by her brother, for refusing a marriage arranged by her parents, and wanting to decide the course of her life for herself. All countries in Western Europe have witnessed similar cases; as for the more 'benign' types of physical violence, they are much more frequent.

It must be emphasized, to begin with, that these violent customs do not come from Islam but from previous traditions that were widespread within the area between the Mediterranean and India, and as far as South Africa, persisting among Christians or pagans as much as among Muslims. We should also bear in mind that brutalities inflicted on women are also found among the native population of countries such as France, Spain or Italy, or indeed on the American continent (in France, one woman dies every three days as the result of violence inflicted by her partner). Nor should we forget that the equality of women before the law is a recent achievement: until the end of the Second World War in France, women were regarded as, in certain respects, inferior beings, since they did not have the right to vote; only in 1965 did married women obtain the right to have a separate bank account – in other words, to enjoy financial autonomy. But once we have mentioned these gains, we still need to demand that such crimes, acts of violence and murders, be punished with all the rigour of the law, without the fact that they have been absolved in certain traditions being used to grant their perpetrators a plea of attenuating circumstances. The same applies to other customs, such as clitoridectomy, forced marriages, or purdah imposed on women. But the law courts still hesitate: in the summer of 2007, the Italian Court of Appeal quashed the sentence handed down to the parents of a young girl for kidnap and torture, on the pretext that they had thought they were acting for the good of their child. Similar cases have also occurred in other countries.

How can we distinguish between what is acceptable insofar as it forms part of a tradition, and what is not acceptable insofar as it contradicts the constitutive values of democracy? The answer is in principle not difficult, even if its application in particular cases can pose a problem: in a democracy, law is higher than custom. This precedence does not affect Western, or European, or even French culture, but the basis of the values to which the country is faithful. The values of a society find their expression in the Constitution, the laws or indeed the structure of the state; if custom transgresses them, it must be abandoned. The Universal Declaration of UNESCO, adopted in 2001 and confirmed by the UN in 2002, says in Article 4: 'None may invoke cultural diversity in order to attack the human rights guaranteed by international law, nor to limit their effectiveness.' We could add: 'nor to attack all the laws guaranteed by the laws of a democratic country'. If the law is not broken, this means that the custom in question can be tolerated: it can be criticized publicly, but it cannot be forbidden. For example, marriages in which the choice of partner is imposed by the family become a crime only if they are imposed by force; if they are accompanied by the consent of the bride, they may be regrettable, but they cannot be treated as being against the law.

Whereas, from this point of view, the cases of ill-treatment or murder can be easily classified, other situations require a more nuanced response. Can we demand of a Muslim nurse that she remove her veil when she meets patients? Should we withdraw a man's benefit because he refuses to shake hands with the woman who has authorized it? Should we agree that a husband can always remain present when his Muslim wife is being examined? Can we accept that certain beaches are reserved for Muslim women so they are not obliged to share them with women in swimming costumes? The reply here requires that we keep in mind the context of every act, of its frequency, of the reactions it arouses, and of its consequences. But it is likely that the existence of clear rules, set out in advance, will prevent many conflicts from arising. This is one of the lessons that can be drawn from the 'affair of the veil' in France: whereas, in abstract terms, it was possible to argue for the authorization of the veil as much as for its prohibition within state schools, the decision to legislate on the matter finally made it possible to eliminate the tension surrounding every individual case, in which the decisions taken by teachers and head teachers might sometimes appear arbitrary.

Nonetheless, in order to submit to the law, we need first to know it. 'Ignorance of the law is no excuse' – true, but in practice, there are many adults who *are* ignorant of the law, and who transgress it unknowingly, something that is especially easy if they are acting in agreement with an ancestral custom. In the contemporary world, it is for the state to ensure that the inhabitants of the country, whatever their origin, have some idea of the great principles on which the laws rest. Basic education should be free and obligatory for all, as it is for the native-born children. And this, in turn, requires a basic knowledge of the country's language. Pondering how best to respond to these demands, and what might be asked in exchange, could well be the task of a service of immigration and integration, which would then have freed itself from the unrealizable objective of controlling national identity.

— 3 —

The War of the Worlds

The Americans cannot tolerate the idea of a problem without a solution. They are less than any other people capable of coexisting pacifically with any insoluble problems around and within them. The 'human condition', in the sense of the irremediable, of failure, sends them scuttling off to psychiatrists or on a headlong rush for various replacements: power, money and world records. The greatest danger for the world would be an America reduced to powerlessness.

Romain Gary, *Au-delà de cette limite votre ticket n'est plus valable*

Every human being participates simultaneously in several cultures, and thus the possibility of their pacific coexistence cannot be questioned. But one can imagine that the situation may change once we move on to the collective level, in particular when culture coincides in extent with one or several states. This was already the case with the nation-states of Europe, and in the past people have frequently commented on the specific nature of German or English traditions, on Spanish or Italian manners, on French wit and Polish soul, and on the impossibility of reconciling them. Ever since these countries have formed part of a single political entity, the European Union, the same question has arisen at a higher level: people now ask whether the cultural differences between Europeans and Americans or, more globally, between Westerners and Chinese, or Indians, or Muslims, do not risk leading to masked or even overt conflicts. The title of a recent work has provided us with a formula that allows us to designate this type of conflict in a nutshell: *The Clash of Civilizations* by Samuel Huntington. His ideas have spread far and wide and have inspired certain political decisions; for this reason, they are a worthy starting point for consideration of the encounter between cultures.

Make love or war?

Huntington's book, published in 1996, presents us with a curious paradox. Based on an article published under the same title in 1993, which had already caused a considerable stir, it tries to take account of the many various criticisms formulated on the occasion of its publication and to 'cover' itself on all sides. It appears as a rather shapeless work of political science, stuffed with statistics and results of opinion polls, and resting essentially on other books of synthesis. Its different claims are not always easy to reconcile. Criticisms of the book (and already of the article) did not hesitate to highlight its weaknesses. So it might be imagined that it had remained without readers and without any impact on public opinion. But quite the opposite happened, with the result that its title – actually borrowed by Huntington from another influential academic, the Islamologist Bernard Lewis – went all round the world and today belongs to the vocabulary of countless more people than the book's actual readers.

How are we to explain such a success? By the fact that title, article and work offer an explanation of the complexity of the international world that is simple and accessible to all, as well as indicating the way undesirable consequences of the current situation can be prevented. Concretely, Huntington asserts that the well-being of Westerners (i.e., North Americans and West Europeans) is under threat, and he suggests a remedy for this problem. Two sentences at the beginning of the work sum up its main argument. The first is presented as a fact: 'the potentially most dangerous enmities occur across the fault lines between the world's major civilizations'. The second is a recommendation: 'The survival of the West depends on Americans reaffirming their Western identity and Westerners accepting their civilization as unique not universal and uniting to renew and preserve it against challenges from non-Western societies.'[1] Civilizations clash, we are in mortal danger and we need to defend ourselves. This is clear and easy to grasp: it is obvious where the seduction of such an argument comes from. But what is seductive is not necessarily just. Is the contemporary world as simple as Huntington suggests?

His analysis starts with the fall of the Berlin Wall. Up until then, things were clear: two superpowers, the United States and the Soviet Union, were opposed in every respect but did not embark on any direct war; the other countries took up a greater or lesser distance from these two giants. With the end of the Cold War, the situation inevitably changed. From now on, as Huntington diagnoses the situation, it is no longer ideological and political blocs that confront one another, but cultural areas, and groups of countries belonging to the same civilization. These groups, he says, are eight in number, and the civilizations are Chinese, Japanese, Hindu, Muslim, Orthodox, Western, Latin-American and, potentially, African. Their relations consist in rivalries that inevitably lead to a clash; the greatest danger for us Westerners thus comes from other civilizations. Concretely, this threat is embodied above all by two particular civilizations – those of China and Islam.

The most obviously fragile aspect of this claim is the status of the 'civilizations' themselves. Using the word in the plural, Huntington gives it the meaning of 'great cultures' in space and/or time. However, just by reading the enumeration of these eight candidates, it is clear that the author is slipping from one criterion to another: sometimes it is religion that decides; sometimes language; sometimes geography. As a result, these civilizations do not form a coherent system: certain of them correspond to a big country, while others bring together extremely heterogeneous populations. The common denominator of over a billion Muslims, for example – the fact they possess the same holy book – does not appear enough to ensure the unity of this 'civilization' which extends from Indonesia to Senegal. Islam itself has not been interpreted in the same way throughout its existence, neither in the different schools of exegesis nor within this or that territory.

The characteristics of every civilization, as we have just seen for 'Western civilization', have very different statuses: some are purely cultural, while others are attached to values; some are specific, while others can be shared by all. In addition, Huntington writes as if it were possible to identify, once and for all, the hard core, or essence, of every civilization – the thing which it must, as matter of sacred duty, never betray; the same number of civilizations has been maintained right from the start. However, even a rapid glance at world history reveals that this is far from the case: Western culture – supposing that such a generalization has any meaning – was profoundly transformed between year zero, year 1000, and year 2000. As is also well known, the representation that it chooses to give of itself is the result of bitter conflicts between influential groups and of compromises that change from one generation to another.

Not only are living cultures in a state of constant transformation, but every individual is the bearer of multiple cultures. Now, this pacific cohabitation and the interactions that it creates can be observed to an equal extent if we adopt the standpoint of different cultures. By rubbing shoulders with each other, these cultures have influenced

88

each other, have borrowed elements from each other and produced hybrid forms – which, after several centuries, appear as the most authentic characteristics of each of them. The Christianity that prospered in Europe was an import from the Middle East, just as Buddhism, born in India, was to leave its mark in particular on the countries of the Indochinese peninsula, China, and Japan. But in Huntington's eyes, these borrowings and mixtures do not really diminish the originality of every civilization. Perhaps under the influence of Oswald Spengler and his lament over the 'decline of the West', the author of *The Clash of Civilizations* imagines cultures as living beings: they are born and flourish, before becoming weak and feeble old men. Or, even more, they resemble human individuals as depicted by an extremely individualist psychology: self-sufficient characters bent on freeing themselves from all dependence and extending their domination.

A warlike model, perhaps unconsciously (and in any case prior to his empirical research) seems to have guided Huntington's description of the encounter between cultures: like young combatants, each convinced of his own superiority, they confront one another until the one triumphs and the other dies. If we are going to resort to anthropomorphic metaphors, we may well wonder whether a sexual model might not be more suitable to describe the encounter between cultures. Rather than two young males ready for everything in their desire to win, cultures behave like a man and a woman drawing near each other and 'mingling', thereby giving birth to progeny; the latter keeps certain characteristics of both of them. The encounter between cultures does not usually produce a clash, a conflict, a war, but – as we have seen – interaction, borrowing, and cross-fertilization.

Religious wars and political conflicts

We could leave aside the precise meaning of 'civilization' that Huntington had in mind – whatever the difficulties rising from its definition – to examine another part of his argument, namely, the idea that current global conflicts stem mainly from civilization or culture. This clearly implies that these conflicts originate in differences of religion. 'Religion,' writes Huntington, 'is the principal defining characteristic of civilizations'; it is 'possibly the most profound difference that can exist between people'. Thus it is religious wars that represent the biggest danger today, and the heartland of this threat can be clearly identified: Islam has 'bloody borders'.[2]

Several other authors have been treading on Huntington's heels in a rush to announce that Islam had entered on a state of war with the West. Oriana Fallaci, for instance, writes in her pamphlet: 'What's under way here is a reverse Crusade. We have here a reverse crusade [...] a war of religion [...] that [...] certainly envisions the conquest of our souls. The disappearance of our liberty and our civilization.'[3] Or Élie Barnavi: 'A Muslim terrorist International has declared a war to the death against the "atheist" West.' The author of *Religions meurtrières* tries to move away from Huntington, whom he describes as an 'arrogant WASP patrician',[4] but in fact there is only one step from civilizations that clash to religions that kill each other. This was also the thesis of the George W. Bush government: attacks on the US are not to be explained as resulting from demands on the part of their adversaries that could be taken into consideration and possibly satisfied – they are the pure product of a radical and hostile ideology.

This thesis arouses several objections. We should first remark that, if it is indeed a war of religion or ideology that is being waged, this constitutes something quite novel in the world history of warfare. Previously, wars always had essentially political, economic, territorial or demographic reasons behind them. Hitler unleashed the Second World War to ensure his domination over Europe and its resources, not to eradicate a hostile ideology; and the same goes for Japan, which attacked and occupied China. Things are even clearer when we turn to the First World War or, if we go back in time, to the Franco-Prussian War, or the Napoleonic Wars, or the Hundred Years' War. And even the Crusades, the emblematic example of a war of religion, were far from being exclusively motivated by the desire to liberate Jerusalem: this was perhaps what the soldiers enlisted thought, but the same was not necessarily true of those who sent them. Today, it is well known that those military expeditions occurred in the context of a reconquest of lands that had previously been lost to the Muslims (the Umayyads in Spain and North Africa, the Turks in Asia Minor) and that they were attracted to the magnet of the supposed fabulous wealth of the East.

Wars of religion, when they do take place, usually happen within a country, not between countries. Religion has been responsible – *inter alia* – for many acts of violence (among Christians themselves, for example: persecutions of heretics, witch hunts, attacks on Jews), but for few wars. In order to impose its will, it needs the support of the secular arm and its laws: but in wartime, the laws are suspended. It is perhaps Huntington's point of departure that leads him to neglect this obvious fact. His initial question, 'What has replaced the Cold War these days?', presupposes that the Cold War was one particular embodiment of a permanent state of affairs; but there is nothing less certain. The ideological conflict between totalitarian regimes and liberal democracies that lay behind the Cold War created a rather exceptional situation. And, let us not forget, this was a *cold* war: so long as other interests did not come into play, the weapons remained silent. The United States and the Soviet Union intervened in an imperial, and not a religious way, each in its reserved sphere of interest, Latin America or Eastern Europe; their military forces did not engage in direct combat with each other.

On the other hand, the idea of a global war between Islam and the irreligious West does fit the declarations of the *jihadist* leaders themselves – who use it to recruit new supporters. Could Huntington ever suspect that he would find a disciple of his theories in the person of the most popular of them? On 20 October 2001, the journalist of Al Jazeera asked his interviewee: 'What is your opinion about what is called the "clash of civilizations"? Osama Bin Laden replied: 'I say there is no doubt that it exists. The "clash of civilizations" is a very clear story, proved by the Quran and the traditions of the Prophet, and no true believer who proclaims his faith should doubt these truths.' In 2002, other Islamists published a brochure entitled *The Inevitability of the Clash of Civilisations*; ever since then, the idea of a 'clash' has been greeted with wild enthusiasm in their circles.

These declarations do not, however, prove that the religious explanations for conflict are correct. Indeed, the very fact that they serve the propaganda of those leaders makes them suspect. The theory of the clash of civilizations has been adopted by all those who have an interest in translating the complexity of the world into the terms of a confrontation between simple and homogeneous entities: West and East, 'free world' and Islam. It was in the interests of Bin Laden to depict the West as a single, coherent tradition, engaged in a mortal combat against Muslim countries: if this were true, everyone would be obliged to choose his party and all Muslims would line up behind him. It is in the interest of governments of countries such as Syria or Iran to turn the West into a scapegoat, a homogeneous civilization and political bloc, solely responsible for everything that is going wrong: this enables the frustration and the anger of the population to be contained by turning it from what might otherwise be its target – namely, a dictatorial or corrupt regime whose yoke it is forced to suffer. Such descriptions of the world may well be false at the moment when they are formulated, but they still incite men to act as if they were true. Such descriptions, indeed, aim at becoming self-fulfilling prophecies.

When we examine, not the language of propaganda, but the witness of the combatants themselves, religion does not occupy the first place. Their motivations are more often secular: they mention their sympathy for a population reduced to poverty, the victims of the whim of ruling classes that live in luxury and corruption – rulers able to maintain themselves in power thanks only to the support of the American government (as in Pakistan, Saudi Arabia and Egypt). They speak of the members of their families or their local communities who have suffered or died by the fault of these governments (and thus of their protectors); and they want to avenge them. The thirst for vengeance did not wait for Islam to appear in the world, and the appeal to the law of an eye for an eye and a tooth for a tooth is universal. Thus there comes into being, little by little, what Stephen Holmes, in his detailed analysis of the motivations that might have driven the suicide attackers of 11 September, sees as a particular narrative of blame,[5] a scenario of resentment that legitimizes the punishment of the American enemy. In September 2007, a potential terrorist was arrested in Germany; after lengthy sessions of interrogation, the German police chief drew this conclusion: his principle motivation was his 'hatred for American citizens'.[6] So we are not really forced to opt for religious reasons when trying to explain acts of aggression: by so doing, we risk forgetting political passions, in the broad sense of the word.

Here is the portrait of another *jihadist*, Shaker al-Abssi, as depicted by his brother (the man was killed recently by the Lebanese police). At the age of twelve, says the latter, the young Shaker had already 'that character common to the young Palestinians in the camps who had seen their parents humiliated and dispossessed: the anger and frustration that lead to activism'. Humiliation and the desire for vengeance become the founding experiences of such people; just like the slave freeing himself from his master, they seek to emancipate themselves in a combat between equals against those whom they consider to be responsible for their situation. Indeed, this combat gives them the only space in which they have the feeling that they find themselves on the same level as their enemies. And religion? 'The Palestinians have tried Marxism and Arab nationalism. It all failed. For Shaker, Islamism was the ultimate solution.'[7] Frustration and personal anger need a framework and a narrative of legitimation. Those offered by secular doctrines – Marxism, nationalism – have turned out to be ineffectual; what remains is traditional religion, now transformed into an ideology of war.

Here is another example, that of an Indonesian *jihadist*, Ali Ghufron, awaiting execution in prison. 'He says it's a war,' relates his brother-in-law. 'America killed our civilians in Chechnya [*sic*] and Afghanistan and so on, so we are taking revenge on them.'[8] Such stories are legion. 'Their religion', as Barnavi recounts of the European *jihadists*, 'is a pretext, a tool of power and a dream of belonging. [...] In fact, they are religious illiterates, interested only in direct action.'[9]

Just after the 11 September 2001 attacks, the Turkish writer Orhan Pamuk (who later won the Nobel Prize) observed, in Istanbul, the ordinary and peaceable inhabitants of the city displaying great joy at the collapse of the Twin Towers. What was the explanation? 'It is neither Islam nor even poverty itself that directly engenders support for terrorists whose ferocity and ingenuity are unprecedented in human history; it is, rather, the crushing humiliation that has infected the third-world countries.'[10]

Why, then, do we so often have the impression that we are dealing with religious or cultural wars? First of all, it is because this kind of language is available to all, and enables them to affirm their sense of belonging to a respectable community. When an angry mob demands the death of a female English schoolteacher alleged to have insulted the Prophet, as happened in Sudan in November 2007, the real objective was not the defence of Islam but of honour, which – it was felt – had been slighted for many long years by the Western powers. This 'spontaneous' use of religion was accompanied by its deliberate instrumentalization by those who are pursuing other objectives, but who prefer this disguise. Even the Crusades, as I have said, had several motives other than religious ones, but these motives were merely less easy to admit to; so they preferred to declare that Jerusalem needed to be liberated. Such a cause appears nobler; and, in addition, the appeal to cultural identity allows more powerful inner resources to be mobilized. This identity is forged in the course of childhood, as we have seen, and for that reason possesses an emotive charge far superior to that of decisions about one's interests, which are supported by utilitarian arguments alone. The religious motivation transforms the pursuit of interest into passion.

It is for the same reason that, in wartime, appeals are so often made to patriotic rhetoric. Thus Stalin, attacked by Hitler in 1941, immediately laid aside Communist phraseology, and now spoke simply of the 'Great Patriotic War', of the need for Soviet peoples to defend their lives, their land and their dignity. In this way, war chiefs could call on soldiers who were, if not fanaticized, at least ready to sacrifice themselves: a state of mind ensuring the combatant would be an effective fighter. And yet it is not identities in themselves that cause conflicts, but conflicts that make identities dangerous.

These days, tensions sometimes exist between certain Western countries and certain segments of the Muslim populations here and there. But it is far from evident that these tensions constitute wars of religion or a clash of civilizations, rather than more familiar forms of political and social conflicts. In the rare cases where everything does seem to indicate that the religious element really is playing a major role, one ought to identify a new actor – the political movements organized by believers – and to draw a clear line of separation between Islam (a religion) and Islamism (a party). Now this distinction is unacceptable to Huntington, since it would undermine his whole argument. So he postulates that the central problem for the West is not Islamic fundamentalism, but Islam.[11] Or, in Fallaci's more vivid language: 'Behind every Islamic terrorist there is inevitably an imam.'[12] This remark has been taken up by several commentators, with the effect of giving a pejorative meaning to the words 'Muslim' and 'Islam'. If we want to neutralize this, we are obliged, in the West, to add the qualification 'moderate', as if Islam in itself were intrinsically extremist. But repeating a cliché does not make it any the truer.

If multitudes of the downtrodden, in several countries of the third world, demonstrate their sympathy for Bin Laden, this is not because they judge him to be a good Muslim, but because they see in him the man who defies the power of the West. The presence of ideology or religion is not neglected, but it is not enough to produce a religious or ideological war. It is not cultures that wage war on one another, or religions, but political entities: states, organizations, parties. And, in one sense, this is a good thing: political conflicts can be resolved by discussions, but wars between civilizations isolated from one another (if they existed) would be impossible to stop. In Northern Ireland, it will perhaps never be possible to reconcile Catholicism and Protestantism, but all the inhabitants can be assured of an equal dignity and an equal justice; if these are achieved, blood will cease to flow.

Men like us?

We could, from the same standpoint, examine the riots that shook the suburbs of the cities of France in November 2005 (followed since then by others, as in November 2007). Some hasty analyses had immediately jumped to the conclusion that these represented an attack on France and its values, an anti-republican pogrom to be added to the long list of threats which terrorist Islam holds over the West. However, observers closer to the action saw nothing of the kind. The Attorney General of Paris announced in January 2006 that among the people arrested for acts of violence, 63 per cent were minors, 87 per cent were of French nationality, 50 per cent were unknown to the police and 50 per cent were school drop-outs. As for their motivation, there was 'no trace of any demands based on identity. And no stigma to show any political or religious impulse, or any manipulation by political or religious authorities'. Indeed, during these events, the only Islamic voices that could be heard were those of religious personalities asking the young people to return to their homes. Jean-Marie le Pen, always ready to stoke conflicts of a cultural or racial type, was forced to admit as much himself: he declared that he 'completely disagreed' with those who saw 'ethnic and religious reasons' behind these acts of violence, this time the result of a 'far from revolutionary game'. Once again, the 'clash of civilizations' was unknown to the people on the front line.

It is not enough to condemn violence. If we wish to prevent its return, we need to understand it: it never explodes without reason. The violence that broke out in 2005, or more recently, is no exception. Its origin is to be sought not so much in the conflict between two cultures as in the absence of that initial minimal culture which every human being needs to construct his identity. The participants in this violence suffer not from multiculturalism but from what ethnologists call deculturation. Inner-city children have often come from families where the father is absent, or is a humiliated figure without much prestige. Since the mother is at work all day long, or herself deprived of any social integration, they have no context in which they might interiorize the rules of common life. From the time they first enter school, they feel excluded. They often emerge from an immigrant background, but are separated by one or two generations from that origin, and they have no prior identity that they could put in the place of that which they find it difficult to construct *in situ*. They do not always have a good command of the language, and also find it difficult to work quietly at home, where conditions are cramped and the television is always on. Once they are of an age to work, they do not manage to find employment: they have no particular skills, and their physical appearance is not judged to be very reassuring. None of the other paths that lead to social recognition is accessible to them, and a certain number of them turn to violence and the destruction of the social framework in which they live.

The foreigners they choose to imitate are not the imams of Cairo but the rappers of Los Angeles. They find their inspiration from figures on television, and they often confuse fiction and reality, fed as they are by TV images. They do not dream of the Quran, but rather of cutting-edge mobile phones, designer trainers and video games. Wealth is displayed to them while they live in deprived inner cities that are crammed in between motorways and railway lines, without nice streets, shops or services; their council flats are falling apart. They might as well set fire to them! With regard to the riots that broke out in the black districts of the cities of the US in 1968, Romain Gary spoke of our 'society of provocation', a society that 'pushes people into consumption and possession by means of advertising [...] while leaving a significant fraction of the population excluded'. How can anyone be surprised, he concluded, 'if this young man ends up flinging himself, at the first opportunity, on the wide-open shelves behind the smashed shop windows?'[13] While he should obviously not be *excused*, it is an urgent and crucial matter to *understand* him: only the most spineless demagogy will confuse these two acts.

It is true that powerlessness added to envy contributes towards the social explosion, not just in the suburbs of big European or American cities, but also in the poor countries of the rest of the world. There is such a huge distance between the dream, nourished by images of wealth that are spread all round the planet, and the wretched reality, that physical violence alone seems able to reduce it. It is this feeling of frustration, experienced in particular by young men, and often disguised by them as a form of faithfulness to religious prescriptions (this is all they retain of religion): feeling dispossessed and powerless in the face of the outside world, they will try to dominate and lock away their wives, sisters or daughters. Male pride (which is exalted by traditional Mediterranean culture), when combined with the sense of humiliation, is the motive for their sudden interest in a fantasmatic Islam and, at other times, for their destructive rage.

Explaining behaviour by seeing it as the result of an individual belonging to a particular group, rather than of causes that are each time specific, is convenient: no need to bother exploring particular situations, for you already have an answer – one which it is easy for the public to understand and remember. Furthermore, such an explanation has the advantage of postulating the inferiority of those individuals: *we* are able to exercise our freedom and choose our acts, which thus fall within the remit of a political or psychological analysis, while *they* blindly obey the customs of their group and belong to the domain of ethnology or cultural studies. If the youths in the suburbs burn their neighbours' cars, or the buses that link them to the rest of the city, or the schools which their younger brothers and sisters attend, this is because they are obeying their cultural DNA: it is pointless to ask any further questions. The original culture then plays the role reserved for race in the nineteenth century.

This rigid determinism more particularly concerns those who come from predominantly Muslim countries. All other human beings act for a variety of reasons: political, social, economic, psychological, even physiological; only Muslims, it is alleged, are always and only impelled by their religious affiliation. As in Huntington's work, Orientalist stereotypes become a universal explanation for the most varied types of behaviour, deemed to characterize the billion men and women living in tens of countries in Africa, Europe and Asia. The freedom of the individual demanded on behalf of the population of the West, is denied them: in every respect they follow their immutable and mysterious essence as Muslims.

From this point of view, the perpetrators of violence in the rundown districts of European cities are seen as similar to international terrorists, who also are moved to act only by their cultural and religious identity, and thus by their collective affiliation. Our acts have reasons, but theirs only have causes. 'In order to remain within the circle of reason, [...] we must at all costs find arguments to attribute to the killers', writes Pascal Bruckner.[14] So, in fact, they seem not to have any arguments of their own, merely murderous impulses that drive them on unwittingly. Élie Barnavi adds: 'This terrorism is something we cannot understand, since it is radically foreign to us.' The formula should be turned round: it is because we postulate a priori that those people are radically foreign to us – who are free and rational, in other words fully human, while they are determined, irrational, and thus incompletely human – that we cannot understand them. For it is not a sufficient explanation to conclude: 'we do not know what they want, except to kill as many people as possible, that is all'.[15] Really?

Wars are motivated by the need to seize the wealth of our neighbours, to wield power, to protect ourselves from real or imagined threats: in short they have, as we have seen, political, social, economic or demographic causes. There is no need to refer to Islam or the clash of civilizations to explain why the Afghans or the Iraqis resist the Western military forces occupying their countries. Nor to speak of anti-Jewish sentiment or anti-Semitism to understand the reasons why the Palestinians are not overjoyed by the Israeli occupation of their lands. Nor to quote verses from the Quran to give a meaning to the reactions of the Lebanese who, in 2006, resisted the destruction of the infrastructures of their country.

The argument that states these people are irrational and unpredictable, so that we need to reduce them to powerlessness as a preventive measure, is also found in conservative American circles. Thus, in November 2007, a report of the American intelligence services deemed it necessary to state that the Iranian regime and its leaders are capable of reflecting rationally. However, we may wonder: is it Osama bin Laden who is irrational when he sends a suicide mission to the Twin Towers in New York and to the Pentagon in the hope that the violent reaction of the Americans will reveal to the rest of the world the 'imperialist' and 'bloody' nature of their regime? Or is it the President of the United States, who presents his policy of the military occupation of a Muslim country as a means of bringing its population round to supporting Western values? It is obviously the former who chose the most appropriate means for his end. Or are we to suppose that the real aim of the latter was completely different? But when we look at the catastrophic situation caused by the intervention in Iraq, we wonder whether such an aim existed or whether this was not also a case, not just of electoral and economic reasons, but also of a 'particular narrative of blame', of the 'irrational' desire to wipe out by a wound which you yourself inflict the consequences of a wound you have suffered.

Instrumental rationality, the sort which allows one to find the means adapted for the ends envisaged, is part of the essence of all human beings, Muslims as much as Christians or atheists, even if certain individuals are more cunning, and better calculators than others. From this point of view, Stalin, Hitler and Mao were perfectly rational individuals. On the other hand, they were not all wise, far from it: wisdom concerns the choice of ends, not of means. We can dispute the values in the name of which certain combats are conducted; we do not need to deny all reason and all liberty to the combatants, or to claim that we ourselves are without any unconscious drives.

In the preface to his book, Huntington formulates the question that we should ask in order to judge of the value of his work: 'The test is whether it provides a more meaningful and useful lens through which to view international developments than any alternative paradigm.'[16] The answer, in my view, would be 'no'.

The Manichean vision

We may conclude that when 'civilizations' meet, they do not produce clashes, and that 'clashes' concern political rather than cultural entities. There is a third aspect to Huntington's thesis, namely, the fact that clashes, conflicts and wars express the truth of international relations. The point of departure of his inquiry is, as we have seen, to seek what in the contemporary world has replaced the old Soviet Empire; the idea does not occur to him that this division of the world into friend/enemy is maybe not adequate and that it was the previous situation, that of the Cold War, which was really exceptional. Or rather, the idea *does* occur to him, only to be rejected in the name of a sort of anthropological postulate: 'enemies are essential'.[17]

This part of Huntington's argument enjoyed wide success in its turn, in particular after the attacks of 11 September 2001. Many commentators proclaimed that the third (or fourth) world war was already under way, pitting the West against Islam. The denunciation of this danger from outside, sometimes designated by the term 'islamo-fascism', is a traditional aspect of the discourse of the far right. However, it is these days found in broader political or intellectual circles, in which the craving to be purer than pure and the naivety of another sector of public opinion are berated for leading to an excessive passivity and tolerance, comparable to those which, between the two world wars, enabled the other fascism, that of European nationalisms, to rise: by rejecting war, they say, we are preparing for our own defeat. 'The democratic West is at war against a global ideology which intends to use terrorism at an unprecedented scale so as to put it to death.'[18] The supporters of more tolerant attitudes are stigmatized as 'multiculturalists' and seen as collaborators, if not traitors. This vision of the world has also spread among the leaders of the United States who have declared a 'war on terror'.

This is obviously not the first time that the world has been described as being divided into two quite distinct parts, friends and enemies. The term 'enemy' has a clear and simple meaning when it is applied to a war situation: it designates the country whose army is trying to conquer ours and which, consequently, is ready to destroy us; in response, we ourselves seek to neutralize and destroy the enemy. Murder then ceases to be a crime and becomes a duty. However, a much broader usage of the term was found in the totalitarian regimes of the twentieth century. In my Communist youth, we heard about enemies all day long, even when we were living at peace. The lack of economic success was invariably attributed to enemies outside, the principal among them being the Anglo-American imperialists, and enemies within, spies and saboteurs, a name designating all those who did not demonstrate enough enthusiasm for Marxist-Leninist ideology. So the totalitarian regime imposed a warlike language on situations of peace and did not accept any nuances: every different person was perceived as an adversary, and every adversary as an enemy – whom it was legitimate, and indeed praiseworthy, to exterminate like vermin.

Nor can it be said that the totalitarian vision was an absolute novelty. In one sense, it was merely systematizing and concretizing a very ancient tradition emblematically designated by formulae such as 'man is a wolf to man' (Plautus), 'he who is not for me is against me' (the Gospels), or 'the war of all against all' (Hobbes) – a tradition which in turn can be traced back to the origins of mankind. More relevant is the link between this vision and those Christian heresies of the first centuries of our era, the *Manichean* and *Gnostic* heresies, which divided the world into two parts hermetically sealed from each other: evil down here; good in the beyond. Projected on to earthly affairs, this moral opposition merges into that between us and them, and it lies behind the desire to destroy evil, and thus the enemy who incarnates it. Since, as creatures driven by exclusively good intentions, we are completely different from the enemy and since, furthermore, we risk becoming the innocent victims of his criminal intentions, how can we fail to desire his disappearance? When eliminating evil from the face of the world is within our reach, should we still hesitate? The dream of such a sublime end makes all the means leading to it permissible. Communist propaganda did not often use this moral vocabulary; however, it has reappeared with American presidents, and this allows them to speculate on the religious convictions of their citizens. So they take it on themselves to fight against 'the evil empire' or 'the axis of evil'.

The Manichean vision of the world does, however, have another and more complete contemporary embodiment: Islamism itself. Let us use this name for a political (rather than religious) movement that draws on Islam. The bases of current Islamism were laid between the two world wars, on the one hand in Egypt, by the Founder of the Muslim Brothers, Hassan Al-Banna, and on the other in the Indian subcontinent, by the Pakistani Abul Ala Maududi. This movement was born at the end of the 1920s in reaction to the abolition of the Califate by Atatürk in 1924, and thus at the end of the fiction of a state common to all Muslims, and at the beginning of the period of national states. The movement was strengthened thanks to the phenomena of rural exodus and urbanization, industrialization and globalization, which entailed the destruction of traditional cultures. To make up for this, Islamists propose an extremely schematic, hard-line version of Islam, which they set within a political project that is deemed to put an end to all the frustrations and humiliations suffered.

Several features can be identified as common to the scattering of political groups that are attached to Islam.[19] First of all there is their Manicheism: there are only two parties, that of God (theirs) and that of Satan, and they are engaged in a pitiless struggle. All sovereignty belongs to God, and so democracies, monarchies and dictatorships are condemned at one and the same time, since all leave power in the hands of men. The Quran, containing God's word, must be considered as the Constitution of the Islamic state; both law and administrative institutions must submit to it. Social justice will govern the economic relations between people. Current states will meld together into a new Califate, whose vocation it will be to spread, at the same time as the Muslim religion, across the rest of the world: Islamism is internationalist. This project is far from being realized, it needs to be pointed out, but it still represents the horizon guiding the present action of the individual Islamist. It is undermined at the same time by a structural contradiction: this attempt to submit the political realm to the religious leads to the formation of a political movement, to which religion inevitably ends up being subjected.

In the middle of the last century, Islamism took an even more radical turn in the writings of one of the Muslim Brothers, the Egyptian Sayyid Qutb, who was executed by Nasser in 1966, as well as in the doctrine professed by the Iranian (and Shiite) ayatollah, Khomeini. These latter strengthened the warlike side of the doctrine: violence is not merely permissible; it is recommended. The concept of *jihad*, which can be translated as 'effort' or 'struggle', saw its meaning restricted to that of holy war; waging this war was seen as an obligation for every Muslim, just as much as pilgrimage or prayer (which is hardly in conformity with the Quran). Islam and the West, taught Sayyid Qutb forty years before Huntington, were destined to become engaged in a pitiless struggle.

This movement, in particular in its current forms, does not represent any kind of a move back to the past, a resurrection of the Islam of origins, but represents, rather, a reaction to the ever more rapid transformation of the world in which Muslims live today – which is already a reason for giving up trying to find the sources of contemporary violence in the Quran. This 'modernism' will in any case be the reason why the Khomeini's revolution in Iran was to be condemned by the traditional Shiite clergy. It is not by chance that the Islamists recruit their militants essentially in Europe, among Muslims who were born there: their immigrant parents or grandparents had a cultural identity, while they are obliged to construct one for themselves, since they have neither the identity of a country of origin nor that of the country in which they live.

Islamism and totalitarianism

We must not confuse Islamism with terrorism. Not only are all terrorists not Islamists, but the converse is not true either. Islamism is an ideology that leads to violent actions only in certain particular circumstances; contemporary terrorism is a mode of action whose origins and objectives are not in the least religious. It seems rather to follow in the wake of the Russian terrorists of the nineteenth century, from whom it adopted the technique of bombings and individual murders. It probably picked up this technique by the intermediary of small far-left groups active in Europe, in the 1960s and 1970s (who indeed often placed themselves in the service of the Palestinian cause).

Islamists have sometimes been compared to Communists at the time when the latter had not yet seized power, and there are indeed many resemblances. Like the Communists, the Islamists deplore the social injustice prevalent in their countries, the corruption and arrogance of the rich, and they set themselves up as defenders of the poor and downtrodden; on the global level, they support third-world ideals and the struggle against imperialism. Combatants in a cause that they consider just, they do not aspire to personal advantages but are ready to sacrifice themselves for the common good; by their honesty and personal integrity, they stand in sharp distinction to the representatives of power. Pursued by the powers that be, they adopt the same conspiratorial techniques as the Communists, forming a hierarchy that extends from isolated cells to the Guide of the movement. Like the Bolsheviks, they perceive themselves as an avant-garde (in this case, of the religious community rather than of the working class: Muslims have moved into the place once occupied by the proletariat) and, like them, they practise internationalism: ideological unity is more important than the diversity of countries of origin. They also believe in the necessity of a permanent revolution that will last until the final victory. 'To declare that there is no God but God for the

102

whole of the universe means a global revolution against all attribution of power to human beings in any form whatsoever, and total rebellion, across the face of the earth, against any situation in which power belongs to men, in whatever way,' thundered Sayyid Qutb.[20]

Next to these resemblances, the differences are also very clear. The first is obvious, but perhaps less decisive than it appears. Communism denies God and religion; Islamism reveres them, and for this reason fights vigorously against Communism whenever the opportunity presents itself (as in Afghanistan during the 1980s). However, we must bear in mind that Communism is itself a political religion: the borrowings went one way before coming back the other way. Theocracies and Communist states are, in this regard, two species of a same genus, ideocracy; it would not be the first time in history that brothers have become enemies. Nevertheless, the status of the two doctrines is not at all the same. Islamists claim to base their attitudes on a religious doctrine that goes back fourteen centuries and has become a way of life; the Communists draw on a revolutionary (and 'scientific') doctrine which does not care a fig for religion. In the Communist countries, the demand for ideological purity had quickly become a veil thrown over pure struggles for power, and slogans and principles were no longer anything but empty formulae, words devoid of meaning. The Party and its leader demanded absolute submission to their decisions of the moment, while the doctrine was adapted to circumstances. In the purely Islamist state (for the moment hypothetical), political power is deemed to be subject to the (religious) law.

Another difference with major consequences concerns the relationship to state structures in the two traditions. Communism is a movement that tried to seize power and succeeded in so doing, first in Russia, then in other countries; this enabled it to create the totalitarian state. We cannot talk of Communist, or Nazi, totalitarianism outside the machinery of the state. The Muslim religion was born in a country without a state (Arabia) and it makes no mention of it; Islamism aspires to founding a community of believers, not a state. That is why it is wrong to see Islamism and totalitarianism as closely related. Existing Islamic states, Iran or Saudi Arabia or Sudan, do not realize the Islamist project itself, but, by establishing strong states, form compromise regimes.

A third major difference is a consequence of the historic moment in which both movements flourished. Islamism benefits greatly from contemporary globalization and the rapidity with which communication is established, whether we are thinking of the spread of propaganda images, or of recipes for making weapons, or indeed of capital. This ease of movement compensates for the extreme territorial dispersion of the Islamist movement.

On the other hand, Islamism constitutes an almost perfect contemporary embodiment of Manicheism, in which adversaries become the incarnation of evil: all our misfortunes, the movement proclaims, stem from the Small Satan and the Great Satan, Israel and its protector the United States. This does not, however, mean that Islamism resembles the Soviet Empire, a highly hierarchized and centralized institution; nor are the loose networks of Islamists akin to the Comintern. Thus it does not really suit the role that American conservative circles, or Huntington, would like it to play: a candidate for the place of the USSR. The term 'Islamo-fascism' is equally perplexing: this comparison between contemporary Islamist tendencies and the far-right movements from between the two world wars sheds no light on either group. If it does provide us with any information, it concerns only the author who uses this word (he is on the side of good and condemns evil!). Attempts to interpret Islam in the light of European totalitarian movements illustrates in particular the difficulty that we encounter when trying to understand a new fact.

It is important to highlight the differences between past and present, since our reactions to the threat depend on them. In order to contain Soviet aggression, military superiority was efficacious: the danger stemmed from a state, and it did indeed prevent any escalation in the tensions between the two 'Big Powers'. Terrorist attacks, wherever they come from, constitute in their turn a real menace; thus we should not take lightly the demands of Bin Laden or other *jihadist* leaders that Americans should be killed wherever they are found. But in order to neutralize them, military power is a feeble resource: the enemy is not an army, but anonymous individuals whom nothing distinguishes from the rest of the population. So the means needed to combat them are quite different. This combat must be, first and foremost, ideological and political: the public powers should try to demonstrate the unacceptable consequences of this obscurantist ideology, including the consequences for its own supporters; at the same time, and so as to dissuade the broader circles of sympathizers, they should focus on the sources of this sympathy, and thus on the perfectly real injustices that nourish it. To this can be added a more 'police'-type reaction: infiltrating the networks, bugging telephones, shadowing suspects, controlling the flow of capital (which would involve the suppression of 'tax havens'), protecting sensitive information, identifying particularly important terrorists or those who might be tempted to change their minds, discreet surveillance – all acts that require a detailed knowledge of the culture of others.

The risk – a certain one – would be to succumb to paranoia and to transform democracies into so many police states. Here is an example of this possible shift, drawn from recent history.[21] Mouloud Sihali was born in Algeria in 1976; he was a good pupil, and attended university. In 1997, he decided to flee from his country since he risked being called up into the army and having to combat insurgent Islamists. He left with a tourist visa, and then obtained false papers that enabled him to get to London. During the following five years, he led a marginal but happy life: he quickly learned English, easily found a job and, being a handsome young man, had several girl-friends of various origins. In September 2002 his life was turned upside down. He was staying with some Algerian friends who found themselves involved in a terrorist plot; he was arrested and, as he seemed cleverer than the others, was accused of being the intelligence leader of the group. The sentence he risked was a heavy one: thirty years in jail. After two and a half years spent in top security deten-tion, the sentence was quashed in April 2005: in the absence of any proof of complicity, he was acquitted.

However, in the wake of the July 2005 attacks in the London underground, it was decided to put away the usual suspects. Follow-ing the new anti-terrorist laws hastily voted in following 11 Septem-ber 2001, any person on whom falls a 'reasonable suspicion' of terrorist activity can be detained without sentence for an indetermi-nate period – a principle contrary to all liberal and democratic tradi-tions. Arrested in September 2005, Sihali was freed four months later, but still subject to severe control: given an electronic bracelet-tagging, he did not have the right to leave a zone of 2 square kilometres, to possess a telephone or a computer, to leave his place of abode after 4 p.m., to meet strangers in the streets or to receive guests without permission. His new trial took place in May 2007; Sihali was again acquitted. He has since been living in London, waiting to be either expelled or naturalized.

Although recognized as innocent, he nonetheless spent nearly five years in prison, a victim of the atmosphere of fear that was main-tained by the government of Tony Blair and the tabloids; this impris-onment will have left an indelible mark on him and broken his life. However, the origin of the fear is easy to understand: the July 2005 attacks in London cost the lives of fifty-six persons; other attacks, even more murderous, were probably foiled. Such is the complexity of the current situation: the anti-terrorist struggle is indispensable, and yet that does not mean that everything is permitted. The emergency laws, voted in under the weight of emotion, must be abrogated. Once that has been done, it will be the task of the representatives of justice to ensure that the finest conquests of democracy are not sacrificed in the name of the effort to defend democracy. In all these circumstances, even the most serious, we need to keep our heads.

The image of the world as a war of all against all is not merely wrong; it contributes to making this world more dangerous. Rather than seeking an enemy to beat (it used to be world capitalism, more recently Communism, and now it is 'Islamo-fascism'), as is done in particular by the former leftists who have now become hawks, the aggressive defenders of the 'free world', we can try to break out of Manichean thinking itself. One means of managing this is to focus our attention on the act, not on the actor: rather than freezing collective identities into immutable essences, we should endeavour to analyse the situations, which are always particular. Wars oblige people to leave their multiple and malleable identities, and reduce them to a unique dimension, each person committing his entire being to the struggle to overcome the enemy. Situations will not allow themselves to be imprisoned in simplistic oppositions and remain irreducible to the categories of good and evil.

The war on terrorism

Should we talk, in today's world, of an ongoing war, of a permanent war? One can hesitate to accept this idea and all that it implies. To begin with, the anthropology underlying such a vision offers only a partial image of mankind. Whatever Hobbes may say, fear is not, always and everywhere, the feeling that dominates the relations between individuals; much more fundamental is the need to *be with* others, to capture their gaze in order to feel that we exist. Like fear, hatred is a human feeling, of course – but this does not entail that an enemy is indispensable for all affirmation of identity – neither individually, nor collectively. In order to define himself, and, after all, to live, every human being has had to situate himself vis-à-vis other people, but this relation is not reduced to hostility: loving, respecting, requesting recognition, imitating, envying, vying, negotiating – these are no less human than hating. Like every Manichean vision that excluded the middle term, the strict division into friends and enemies excessively simplifies the world of human relations. Its effect is to transform the adverse human group into a scapegoat, responsible for all ills.

The policy to which the American government committed itself in the wake of the attacks of 11 September 2001 illustrates this situation. An expression such as 'the war on terror', used by George W. Bush to designate the current situation, has many disadvantages. It is, to begin with, clear that what we have here is a metaphorical war, like the 'war on poverty' or the 'war on drugs', in this sense: unlike a classical war, it is not a human enemy that is being combated but a wound that risks never being definitively closed.

Now this clumsy metaphor risks entailing other consequences. War has the same objectives as politics, as Clausewitz's famous formula puts it, but at the same time it represents the negation of the political, since all interaction is reduced to a contest between armed forces. It brings death and destruction to the adversary but also to one's own camp, without drawing any distinction between innocent and guilty. Winning a military victory over the enemy does not guarantee that you will win a people over to your cause: this is the lesson of the Treaty of Versailles in 1919, the battle of Algiers in 1957, and the occupation of Baghdad at the start of our own twenty-first century. As Alexis de Tocqueville lucidly noted at the time of the French conquest of Algeria, 'it is not enough to have conquered a nation if one wishes to govern it'.[22] A war on terror, or indeed on evil, has the twofold drawback that it is unlimited in time (that war will never end) and in space (the enemy is not identified; it is an abstraction that can find embodiment absolutely anywhere).

Another drawback of this expression is its indeterminate character. It tells us that this individual or that organization are not acting in the name of a state and that they are attacking and destroying civilians and soldiers alike, buildings and means of transport. But it tells us nothing about the overall objective pursued by these militants, or their particular motivations. This absence of any clue about the reasons for the struggle is not fortuitous, of course: in identifying them by their means of action alone, we block any empathy and, a fortiori, any sympathy for these individuals. With the same end in view, the word 'terrorists' was used to describe the combatants for independence in Algeria, and the enemies of apartheid in South Africa. A designation of this kind, however, is of no help in the struggle against them; in order to know an enemy, it is not enough to name the weapons he is using. Even if we limit its application just to Islamic terrorists, the label remains an excessive generalization which does not allow us to distinguish, for example, between Chechen

107

or Palestinian terrorists struggling for the independence of their country, and international terrorists who draw on the authority of al-Qaeda, and claim to be fighting for the defeat of the Crusaders and the victory of Islam. Now, without taking into account these extremely diverse motivations, it is really difficult to act on the networks of sympathizers who alone ensure that terrorism persists.

To speak of a 'war' in this struggle also risks leading to dubious strategic decisions. War is a matter of missiles and bombs, and the fight against terror requires quite different means. If investments are concentrated on weapons, any detailed study of the adversary risks running out of means. As Holmes reported in 2006, in the American Embassy in Baghdad, out of the thousand employees only six spoke fluent Arabic. The American soldiers often have the impression that the Iraqis understand only the language of force, 'and yet they themselves do not speak a word of Arabic'.[23] On the other side, the American forces of occupation have lost the propaganda war, which is decisive if the sympathy of the population is to be won and the terrorists weakened. The images of the torture carried out in the Iraqi prison of Abu Ghraib that were broadcast throughout the world dealt a heavy blow to the reputation of the United States as a defender of human rights and democratic values.

On the internal level, the damage is no less serious. To declare a state of war means one can suspend liberties and personal guarantees in a country, and strengthen the executive to the detriment of the legislative, not to mention the Manichean education that is inflicted on one's own country in the process. Any criticism of government policy is described as a betrayal of one's native land, a low attack on the morale of the troops; but freedom to criticize is a valuable acquisition of democracy. The effects of a 'war on terror' are particularly dangerous because such a war could never end; the suspension of the laws thus risks lasting indefinitely. One of the most harmful consequences of this situation is the damage inflicted on the status of the truth in the country's public life. The Report of the Baker-Hamilton Commission, published in autumn 2006, states that, ever since the war in Iraq, the American government has often sought to marginalize information that went against its policies, and this refusal to take the truth into account has had woeful results. The Report states it in measured but firm language: 'It is difficult to establish a good policy when information is systematically put together so as to minimize divergences with political objectives.' In other words, in many cases the American government has considered the truth as a negligible quantity, which can unhesitatingly be sacrificed to the will to power.

This finding is not really a surprise, except insofar as it came from an official bipartite commission; there is no lack of examples that could illustrate it. The preparation and unleashing of the war against Iraq rested on a double lie or a double illusion: that al-Qaeda was linked to the Iraqi government and that Iraq possessed weapons of mass destruction, whether nuclear, biological, or chemical. Since the fall of Baghdad, this lax attitude towards the truth has not disappeared. At the very time when the whole world was discovering the images of torture and the narratives of execution in the prison of Abu Ghraib, the American government was claiming that democracy was consolidating itself in Iraq. While hundreds of prisoners had been rotting away for long years in the Guantánamo camp, without being given a trial or allowed to defend themselves, and subjected to degrading treatment, the American government declared that the United States was playing its forces in the service of human rights.

There is cause for worry in this development, since it is being produced not in a country subject to totalitarian dictatorship or a repressive traditional order, but in the world's first democracy. It is thus possible, in spite of the pluralism of parties and the freedom of the press, to convince the population of a liberal democracy that the true is false, and the false, true. Those responsible for this situation are, first and foremost, the institutions in which public opinion is forged: government, parliament, big television channels, newspapers. Political action is becoming increasingly reduced to political communication, and so the majority of the population has allowed itself to be swept away by fear. The need to protect their lives, to ensure the security of one's nearest and dearest, to eliminate the threats that are judged imminent, have all led people to forget the habitual legal or moral precautions. Controlling and evaluating information, arguing and reasoning – all these have been perceived as the evidence of a lack of courage and responsibility.

Hobbes's description of human relations as dominated essentially by fear is not true in general, but it can become true if those who control public communication persuade us that we are surrounded by enemies and thus engaged in a pitiless war; this would be a new example of a prophecy creating the reality which it announces. Faced with the danger of death, all manoeuvres are allowed. But fear is a bad counsellor, and we need to fear those who live in fear. A recent film, *Children of Men*, by the director Alfonso Cuarón, clearly illustrated this danger: if the population thinks that all foreigners represent a threat, it will see no problem in having them sent to concentration camps. One trembles at the idea of what might be the reaction of the American government if a new attack comparable with those of 11 September 2001 were to occur: to drive the country they decide is responsible back to the Stone Age, as they threatened to do for Pakistan? Drop nuclear bombs on those they presume to be guilty?

In totalitarian countries, the truth is systematically sacrificed to the struggle for victory. But in a democratic state, attention to the truth must be sacred: the very foundations of the regime are in danger. The French anthropologist Germaine Tillion had clearly understood this. She was, in Paris, a member of one of the first resistance networks against the German occupation, and in 1941 she wrote a tract in which she called on her companions in the struggle never to compromise on the truth, even if this was not immediately going to lead to victory: 'For our country is dear to us only on condition that we never have to sacrifice the truth to it.'[24]

The end and the means

It is not only on the level of military effectiveness that the results of such a strategy remain dubious; furthermore, the reduction of international relations to the couple 'friends–enemies' is far from ensuring the victory of the ideal we were seeking to defend. Even supposing we have succeeded in eliminating evildoers, how can we rejoice at this, if, in order to eliminate them, we have had to become evildoers too? This is another old dilemma of wars waged in the name of a higher good. To bring the Indians the Christian religion that taught the equality of all and the love of one's neighbour, the conquistadores subjected them in war and taught them to hate and despise their adversaries: Christian morality did not emerge from this enhanced. In order to transmit to Africans the benefits of Western civilization, the values of liberty, equality and fraternity, European colonizers waged war on them and imposed on them an order from outside; they arrogated to themselves the right to command the vanquished and disdained their personal dignity: civilization did not emerge from this enhanced. During the Second World War, the massive bombardments of civilian populations by the German air force aroused indignation, since they illustrated, yet again, the Manichean logic in which all the others are guilty. Came the day when the Allies resorted to the same tactics, in the hope of breaking German resistance: barbarism extended its grip a little more across the world.

When the inhumanity of the one is suppressed at the cost of the dehumanization of the other, the game is not worth the candle. If, in order to beat the enemy, we imitate his most hideous acts, it is barbarism that wins yet again. Manicheism cannot fight against Manicheism. The strategy that attempts to counter the enemy's violence with a comparable violence is condemned to failure.

In any case, it is not unusual for the response to violence to reach a level that is higher and not just equal to the shock that provoked it. 'Violence engenders only violence, in a pendulum swing that increases with time instead of dying down,' wrote Primo Levi.[25] The observation may not be original, but it is correct. Experiments carried out by psychologists show that human beings always tend to reply to aggression by aggression of a higher degree, since the damage inflicted on them always appears greater than the damage they inflicted. Examples can always be found in history to illustrate this amplification. Hitler feared, not without reason, the Bolshevik threat; the means implemented to neutralize it turned out to be, even for the German population, a cure that was worse than the disease. During the demonstration in Sétif, Algeria, in May 1945, some hundred or so French people were massacred. The colonial power responded by a repression in which the number of victims reached – according to the sources – between 1,500 and 45,000, in other words between 15 and 450 Algerians killed for each French person. The bombs of Hiroshima and Nagasaki may have made it possible to punish the Japanese for their militaristic policies and the countless cruelties of which they had made themselves guilty in the war in Asia; they still constitute a war crime of a hitherto unprecedented magnitude.

Another example is the campaign led by Senator McCarthy against the Communist influence in the United States in the 1950s. In order to be sure of beating the enemy, the McCarthyites did not hesitate to imitate certain of the enemy's own practices. Among the most virulent anti-Communists were a number of ex-Communists: after replacing their choice of target by its contrary, they had continued to pursue the strategic habits of the Leninists. In several countries in Latin America, the danger of a coup d'état on the extreme left was neutralized at the price of a military dictatorship – which was responsible for 30,000 'disappearances' of opponents in Argentina, 35,000 proven cases of torture in Chile, and the abandoning of the elementary democratic principles in other countries.

At the start of the twenty-first century, the attacks on the Twin Towers in New York caused some 3,000 deaths. The war in Iraq, unleashed on the pretext (let us not forget that it was a completely

111

specious pretext) of punishing those complicit with the attacks, in four years caused the death of significantly higher number of Iraqis, estimated in 2007 as between 60,000 (by the *Iraq Body Count*) and 600,000 (by the medical journal *The Lancet*), in other words between 20 and 200 Iraqis for every American killed. When the enemy is seen everywhere, there is an unhealthy escalation in the choice of means, which Germaine Tillion had stigmatized at the time of the Algerian War in a book with the revealing title *Les Ennemis complémentaires* (*The Complementary Enemies*); the same scenario is being repeated today. At that time, 'the good conscience of Massu [the French leader of the repression – *Tr.*], is Ali La Pointe [the Algerian who planted the bombs – *Tr.*]. Conversely, the good conscience of Ali La Pointe is Massu. There is absolutely no way out.'[26] The torture practised by the one group is echoed by the blind attacks committed by manipulated, weak-minded individuals and children trained to kill and die – and conversely. Where does the barbarity end? Is bombing the person you consider to be your enemy more – or less – civilized than killing him with your bare hands?

In his *Discourse on the Origin of Inequality*, Rousseau described the threat that hovers over men when they base their behaviour entirely on the way they imagine that others view them. Driven by a 'devouring ambition', by the longing to raise themselves 'above others', by jealousy and rivalry, they acquire 'a dark inclination to harm each other'. The advance of democracy and contemporary globalization have had the effect of rendering the way everyone sees himself and others uniform – and this has enriched the compost of envy, jealousy and resentment. The 'dark inclination' is made even stronger when the initial deed is one of aggression: the cycle of acts of revenge and counter-revenge, which are often presented as acts of justice or of just wars, has no reason to stop. The only way to stop the cycle is, as was done by Tutu and Mandela in South Africa, to give up the idea of punishing the offence suffered by an equivalent or greater offence. Or else, as was indeed the case with Germaine Tillion in Algeria, not to fight in order to enable the one cause or the other triumph, as each of them is considered to be just in the eyes of its supporters, but to break 'the grim stupidity of the mechanism'[27] and save human lives by freeing them from the risk of torture and execution, but also from bombs planted in cafés and supermarkets.

One may doubt whether it is possible to impose good by force. Rather than by the maxim 'The end justifies the means', international relations seem to be governed by another maxim: 'Means are more important than ends'. Karl Jaspers remarked that a democracy inevitably changes into a dictatorship when it seeks to conquer other countries in order to impose its noble principles on it. 'So the French Revolution changed into the dictatorship of Napoleon. Democracy that conquers abandons itself.'[28] At present, the government of the United States and some of its allies desire to bring certain political values to the peoples of the Middle East by occupying and subjecting their countries. Now the long history of relations with this part of the world risks suggesting to the Arab and Muslim populations that this is yet another pretext, another camouflage: are not the invaders really coming into their lands to ensure the control of oil resources or military bases? In any case, it is naive to think that the 'Western' rules of life can be slapped down on any country at whim: the life of a society is a coherent whole, and a change in one place often leads to undesirable consequences in another. Finally, subjugating the country after bombing it, after killing thousands of people and leaving tens of thousands of others homeless, practising arbitrary imprisonments, brutality and torture – these are all means of exporting 'Western values' that compromise them for a very long time to come.

However, there is another way, much more effective, of spreading the values that one cherishes. This is to proclaim them loud and clear, and to embody them fully: ideas and principles have a redoubtable power – witness all the regimes that have been overturned from within a state. Governments always have at their disposal a military and police force far superior to that of the few rebels who defy them. But the latter embody, in the eyes of important sectors of the population, an ideal of freedom and justice, the promise of a worthier and happier life. The wave of a popular uprising thus allows the brute force of those in power to be neutralized. These ideas, when exported to others, can also ensure the victory of the weak over the strong, as happened during the process of decolonization in the twentieth century, often driven by 'Western' ideas of liberty and equality, albeit directed against the Western colonial powers. Unfortunately, the professionals of war-by-all-means habitually underestimate the power of ideas and of values.

Torture: the facts

Nothing better illustrates the damage wreaked by an unlimited combat against the 'enemy' than the adoption of torture as a legitimate practice, as happened in the wake of the attacks of 11 September 2001.

113

Acts of torture have been attested in history ever since antiquity, and it can even be said that this practice has been strengthened in tandem with the affirmation of our human identity. Deliberately to inflict suffering on a creature similar to ourselves means that we have to be able to put ourselves mentally in his place, which is a capacity more greatly developed among humans that any other species. Even if we find the first inklings of this capacity among primates, only human beings can take these representations of the representations of another creature as far as this, and imagine what the other is experiencing.

However, the omnipresence of these acts has provoked a reaction: attempts to make them legally unacceptable. In European countries, torture was banned in the course of the eighteenth century; in the world, by the Declaration of the Rights of Man, in 1948. This banning was given a precise and codified form by the Conventions of Geneva in 1949 and solemnly confirmed by another Convention of the United Nations, in 1984, concerning 'torture and other cruel, inhuman or degrading treatments or punishments'. To torture, in the view of these documents, means to inflict on someone a severe pain or suffering, either physical or mental. The signature at the foot of the Conventions has not prevented the governments of various countries from resorting to torture when they have deemed it necessary; however, they have done their best to disguise these practices and publicly deny their existence. The ban is thus not strictly respected; acts of barbarity have not disappeared as if by magic. But an ideal of civilization has been laid down, one which exerts an effect of moderation and considerably diminishes the number of acts of violence inflicted.

Several forms of torture are part of the repressive arsenal of totalitarian countries, and also of military dictatorships or states that are not particularly bothered about protecting individual freedoms. Other countries resort to them only exceptionally, as in times of war. It is well known that the French Army systematically practised torture during the Algerian War, but, in spite of the considerable amount of evidence that has since 1954 attested to this fact, it has never officially been advocated. Only a few isolated individuals have openly spoken or written in praise of torture, such as the journalist Jean Lartéguy in his 1960 novel *Les Centurions*, Colonel Roger Trinquier in his 1961 work *La Guerre Moderne*, or, much later, General Aussaresses in his work *Services spéciaux*, in 2001. The novelty of the current situation resides in the fact that it is the American government itself that is proclaiming the necessity of torture. This break with precedent has led to the subject being introduced into the public debate, where arguments for and against can now tranquilly be exchanged.

The decisive step was taken on 1 August 2002 by a document, generally known as the *Torture Memo*, a memorandum drawn up by the Office of Legal Counsel of the Justice Department of the United States. In view of the multiplication of protests against the torture inflicted on prisoners by the agents of the American government, and in view, too, of the threat of law suits against the torturers, this memorandum sets out in detail the legal reasons for which the acts committed remain licit and do not constitute torture as banned by the international Conventions and the legal code of the United States, section 2340A. The text is signed by Jay Bybee but it was written by John Yoo, Professor of Law at the University of California at Berkeley. It is addressed to Alberto Gonzales, then legal advisor to the President of the United States.

The document's strategy consists in admitting that the prisoners have been subjected to violence, but to dispute the way this is described as 'torture': so we here have a sort of redefinition in the meaning of this last word, which did not, at first sight, seem problematic. 'Certain acts,' says the *Torture Memo*, 'may be cruel, inhuman, or degrading, but still not produce pain and suffering of the requisite intensity' to be described as torture. 'For an act to constitute torture [...], it must inflict pain that is difficult to endure. Physical pain amounting to torture must be equivalent in intensity to the pain accompanying serious physical injury, such as organ failure, impairment of bodily function, or even death. For purely mental pain or suffering to amount to torture [...], it must result in significant psychological harm of significant duration, e.g., lasting for months or even years.' The technique of 'sensory deprivation', for instance, widely used in interrogating prisoners, is not torture: 'while many of these techniques may amount to cruel, inhuman or degrading treatment, they do not produce pain or suffering of the necessary intensity to meet the definition of torture'.[29]

This purely terminological debate has continued more recently, after Congress banned, in December 2005, not just the use of torture but also cruel, inhuman and degrading treatments. In a new *Memo*, the Justice Department authorized CIA agents to strike prisoners, to expose them to extreme cold and heat, and to simulate their drowning (water-boarding), since such practices, the document declares, are not in the least cruel, inhuman or degrading. This same torture hit the headlines on another occasion: three *jihadists*, including the brains behind the 11 September attack, Khaled Sheikh Mohammed, were captured in 2002, taken to an American military base in Thailand and subjected shortly afterwards to this form of torture. These hardened combatants were able to resist only for a short period of time before begging for mercy; these torture sessions were filmed. In 2005, the director of the CIA responsible for secret operations decided to destroy those tapes so that his subordinates could not be put on trial – which was a tacit admission that they had indeed been resorting to torture.[30] Nonetheless, in November 2007, while being interrogated by a Senate commission, the future Attorney General Michael Mukasey again refused to describe water-boarding as 'torture', since this practice is still one of the methods used in interrogation centres. So the American executive proscribes the word but accepts the deed.

It is not this document which introduces acts of torture; but it does make them licit and thereby incites people to generalize them. President Bush apparently considered it as shedding a useful light on juridical procedures and he expressed his gratitude by ensuring that Bybee was promoted, and by appointing Gonzales, after his own re-election in 2004, to the post of Attorney General. Ever since, it has become frequent to see and hear the commentators of the American media openly defending the use of torture, publishing articles under the alluring title 'It Works!', without bothering any more about the legal justifications. Several Republican presidential candidates in 2008 declared themselves to be in favour of torture. The subject has also entered academic debate, and there are some professors of repute who have come up with juridical, political and moral arguments in favour of torture. A sample of these can be read in the volume of essays published as *Torture: A Collection*.[31] They include, in particular, Alan Derschowitz of Harvard, Jean Bethke Elshtain of the University of Chicago, Oren Gross of the University of Minnesota, Sanford Levinson of the University of Texas and Richard Posner of the Chicago Law School. The condemnation of torture is ceasing to be something obvious, and starting to become a question on which opinions can diverge; witness the title of the volume *The Torture Debate in America*.[32] It is easy to imagine that chairs and departments will soon be created to teach the whys and hows of torture ...

The broadcasting of the photographs taken at Abu Ghraib has made it possible to measure one of the effects of this open acceptance of torture in government instructions and public opinion. What the images reveal is not the mere existence of the torture inflicted by the American prison staff: the information had been known for a long time. The novelty lay in the very fact that photos had been taken and that they circulated quite freely. It reflects, of course, the way digital photos have become so very ordinary; but it has other meanings too. Certain 'photographers' seek to protect themselves in this way from any future punishment and send their images to their superiors (but the latter reassure them: they are doing good work!). Others of these soldiers that have become prison guards would like to be able to remember the most extreme experiences they have had to face, and show them one day to their friends. 'But pictures were taken, you have to see them!' wrote one of the photographers to her friend.[33]

Indeed, the images are far from ordinary. A woman soldier is pulling a naked man along at the end of a dog's lead, another is posing next to the heavily bruised face of a dead man, naked prisoners wearing hoods are piled up one on top of another in a human pyramid, under the cajoling gaze of a man and a woman – and so on. The photos were not taken in secret, far from it: what they show is perceived as normal. It is clear that these soldiers, who often appear in the images, do not in the least have the impression that they are performing acts worthy of reproach; and it is obviously not a matter of individual sadistic transgressions. The way torture has become ordinary, and even more than acceptable, has happened at a remarkable speed (this was 2004).

Here we need to distinguish between the attitude of the apologists for torture in the media or the universities and the attitude of the official representatives of the government. The latter do not wish to accept that acts of torture are being committed on United States territory. That is why they prefer the 'heavy-handed interrogation' of enemy prisoners to take place not in America but abroad, either in the jails of allied countries, such as Abu Ghraib in Iraq or Bagram in Afghanistan, or in the secret prisons of the CIA, or else in American military bases, such as Kosovo (so it is said) or Guantánamo. A sort of sinister irony derives from the fact that the latter base is situated in Cuba, a country known for its transgressions of human rights; it is thanks to this situation outside American territory that the United States can freely infringe those same rights. It also seems that, as has been established by a report of the Council of Europe, secret prisons in which suspects have been tortured have been set up in Poland and Romania. The choice of place is probably due to the recent totalitarian past of these two countries and the greater tolerance towards transgressions of the law that has been acquired there by governments and their functionaries, or else to their systematic alignment with American policies, perceived as necessary in the face of their Russian neighbour (it is hard to imagine that such prisons could pass unnoticed for long in Great Britain or France). But this also means that the American secret services are not reluctant to resort to totalitarian practices.

For the same reason, the American government has invented a completely new juridical category, that of 'illegal enemy combatants'. In general, the perpetrators of violence against the population clearly fall into two groups which, once they have been arrested, come under different jurisdictions, but still possess certain rights. In times of peace, they are criminals, protected in every state of law by habeas corpus, defended by lawyers, and judged in accord with the laws. In times of war, they are enemy soldiers who, if captured, must be treated in accord with international Conventions. In what category are we to classify the terrorists of al-Qaeda? Since they do not belong to the regular army of a country that has signed the Conventions of Geneva, they cannot claim the protection of those Conventions. So do they fall under ordinary legislation? It is here that the formula 'war on terror' shows how useful it is: since there is a 'war' going on, the laws of peacetime do not apply; but since this war is not being waged on another country, international Conventions do not come into it either! And since this 'war' can never end, the government that declares it is placing itself for an indefinite period above national laws, as well as above international norms.

The new category of 'illegal enemy combatants', indeed, makes it possible to take the individuals who have been apprehended out of the reach of any regulation and any norm, and thus to practise torture. The *Torture Memo* took account of this opportunity and, after enumerating the other defences against accusations of torture, concluded: 'In the current circumstances, necessity or self-defence can justify methods of interrogation that violate section 2340A.' The 1948 United Nations Convention had specified, however: 'No exceptional circumstance, whether a state of war or the threat of war, internal instability or other public emergencies, can be invoked as a justification of torture.'

Apart from this (major) exception, the memorandum denies that the acts observed are a form of torture. For there to be torture, it suggests (as we have seen) the prisoner needs to lose a leg or an arm, to be unable ever to stand upright again, to have a ruptured liver or to become incontinent for the rest of his life – or, says the *Memo* without so much as a laugh, he needs to be dead! The torture which consists in making people close to the prisoner (for instance, his wife or children) suffer in front of him, does not qualify as such, since he himself is not losing any vital organ. On the mental level, the madness that is provoked in a prisoner must be there for good: only if it does not lessen after a few years can one retrospectively speak of torture. In all other cases, there is no torture, and the United States will have respected the international Conventions.

Let us briefly sum up the types of treatment inflicted on prisoners that 'do not qualify as torture' as they have been reported in the international press. In the prisons scattered across the various countries of the world, but outside the United States, prisoners are regularly raped, hung from hooks, subjected to water-boarding, burned, attached to electrodes, deprived of food, water or medicine, attacked by dogs, or beaten until their bones are broken. In military bases or on American territory, they are subjected to sensory deprivation or other systematic mistreatment of the senses. A hat is put on them to stop them hearing anything, a hood to stop them seeing anything, surgical masks to prevent them being able to smell, thick gloves to neutralize their sense of touch. Or they have 'white noise' inflicted on them, or else violent noise and total silence alternate at irregular intervals. They are prevented from sleeping, either by having a strong electric light kept on day and night, or by subjecting them to interrogations that can last for up to twenty-four hours at a time, for forty-eight days in succession. Or they are forced to pass from extreme cold to extreme heat, and vice versa. None of these techniques, it will be seen, can cause the 'deterioration of bodily functions'.

An American citizen, a terrorist who converted to Islam, Jose Padilla, was accused of plotting against the United States. He was detained in an American military prison in Charleston, South Carolina. For the first two years, he was deprived of all contact with the outside world. He met neither the members of his family, nor any lawyers (since he was not a criminal but an 'enemy combatant'); nor even his gaolers. He did not see the person who brought his food; he was locked away in a cell two metres by three without any window, with padded walls. For several days and nights, the cell was lit by a dazzling light, and then he was plunged into complete obscurity. He had no watch, and could not measure the flow of time. He had nothing to read, nothing to look at, and nobody to talk to. When he tried to sleep, he was woken by violent noises. He was taken into the interrogations hooded, his ears stopped, and was then forced to remain standing for hours at a stretch, still unable to see anything. It will come as no surprise that his mental faculties now seem badly affected: he is in a permanent state of passivity and fear, 'like a piece of furniture', say his current lawyers. At his trial in summer 2007, to the question whether he had been tortured, he mechanically repeated this reply: 'It is a state secret and I have been forbidden to tell you.' One wonders whether such types of treatment should be considered as physical or mental, or whether it is even possible to separate the two kinds.

Let us add, to end with, that while torture is more or less openly practised by the American government, the leaders of countries allied to the United States, in particular those of the European Union, cannot consider that their own responsibility does not come into it. The secret services of their countries collaborate actively with the corresponding American services, and hand over to them information and contacts that lead to arrests and thus, quite possibly, to torture. This kind of practice, however overt, has not led to any condemnation on the part of the French, or British, or German governments; and silence means consent. Their reluctance, after all, is easy to understand: these allies, whether in Europe, Asia, or in the Americas, rely for their security on the United States; so they do not have any moral right to condemn these methods if at the same time they are benefiting from their results. And the governments are not the only ones involved: insofar as the population of all these countries – you and I – do not react against torture, they make themselves complicit in its perpetuation.

Torture: the debate

People often wax indignant, and rightly so, at the fact that innocents have been tortured. It needs to be pointed out that, in a certain number of cases, the persons tortured are indeed guilty of various crimes or criminal intentions, and have actually killed or sought to kill. As for the death penalty, if we wish to oppose torture as such, we obviously need to start with these cases.

In order to confront the justifications given for acts of torture, we need at first to set aside the subterfuges of the *Torture Memo*. This proceeds – paradoxically for a legal document drawn up by competent lawyers – by a form of magical thinking: it seems to believe that one can act on things by changing their name. It is not because someone says that the systematic destruction of a person such as Padilla will not be called 'torture' that these acts actually cease to *be* a form of torture. If common usage, as well as the texts of international Conventions, designate these practices as a form of torture, the reality is in no way modified by their new label. The same goes for more recent attempts, in other speeches by President Bush, to exclude certain acts from the category of 'cruel, inhuman or degrading treatment'. The excuse which consists in saying that they do not occur on American soil, even when they are the effect of the American government's decisions, is also a purely formal artifice which seeks to conform to the letter of the law so as better to hide the extent to which it is betraying its spirit.

In order to understand the reasons for torture, we thus need to turn not to the legal texts but to the remarks of the defenders of torture, which simultaneously reflect and form the thinking of the political decision-makers. The argument most often encountered, already developed by French defenders of torture such as Lartéguy or Trinquier, has in the United States been called a 'ticking bomb'; it was recently popularized by the American television series *Twenty-Four Hours*. The story goes as follows: imagine that you are arresting a terrorist who has planted a bomb, and you know that it is going to explode in one hour's time, but not where it is. Are you going to agree to allow a thousand people (a hundred thousand in the case of a nuclear bomb!) to die, simply because you were not prepared to torture a single person? If you reply in the negative, you are deciding that torture is permissible, or even recommendable in certain cases. From then on, it is enough to indulge in a calculation of losses and gains: even a single human life is irreplaceable and priceless, so it legitimates torture – especially if it is the torture of someone wicked.

Actually, this case is frequent only in apologias for torture, and barely at all in the real world. It requires the combination of such a set of circumstances that the situation becomes highly improbable: one would need to know of the existence of the bomb and the time of its explosion, know who the guilty person is and catch them at exactly the right time, ensure that this capture remained secret from his accomplices so that they would not move the bomb elsewhere, obtain a truthful confession at the first go, and so on and so forth. This scenario is all right for suspense films or perhaps first-year undergraduate philosophy classes, in which the ethics of utilitarianism are studied. It is a suggestive case of conscience, but it in no way corresponds to the practice of torture as we can observe it. During the Algerian War, the army arrested any person who appeared suspect for any reason at all, not those persons who it knew had already planted their bomb; it tortured them to discover who its enemies were, and where they were hiding.

In the American literature on the question, the case of Abdul Hakim Murad is often cited. He was tortured in Manila in the Philippines, between 7 January and mid-April 1995, and this case supposedly shows how torture allowed a terrorist attack to be prevented – the attack on Pope John Paul II during his visit to that city on 12 January. We can immediately see that this line of argument hardly enables one to justify his torture during the three months following his confession, during which time Murad 'confessed' other plans that were still on the drawing board. Even the attack on the Pope was prevented not thanks to torture, but to the fact that Murad was arrested. And how can this argument from emergency be used in the case of detainees such as those in Guantánamo, who have been rotting away in their gaol for years? Furthermore, the entire argument rests on a future event, and we know that predicting the future is not an exact science. Is there really a bomb? Is it going to explode?

So let us leave this imaginary case to one side, and start with the actual practice of torture. This is used in particular when an army is confronting guerrilla fighters. The aim of torture is to collect information on the enemy – information that cannot be discovered any other way, since it is sometimes impossible to know who is an enemy and who is not. This, in fact, is the main reason given in order to justify it: this is not a war like the others, it is said; it is particularly fierce, and this enemy is so terrible that, if he wins, we risk losing all that we hold dearest. He can be beaten only if we in turn use illegal methods. This, more or less, was the position openly assumed by President George W. Bush who, replying to criticism of the methods of interrogation practised by the CIA, replied: 'The American people expect us to find out information – actionable intelligence – so we can help protect them. That's our job.'[34]

It might be felt that it is inhuman and degrading to enter this debate, as if there no longer existed any intuition common to all human beings that torture is unacceptable. But, since the debate has been opened, let us provisionally agree to argue within the framework it has established.

As Holmes shows in his book,[35] each of the elements in this line of argument can be questioned. First, nothing proves that information obtained under torture is true. As has been noted by philosophers throughout Western history, from Aristotle to Beccaria, via Montaigne and Hobbes, these confessions (or their absence) tell us a great deal about the ability of the tortured person to resist, but are far from reliable when it comes to the contents of the interrogation – witness the countless confessions extorted during the witchcraft trials in the sixteenth century, all of them crazily fictitious. In addition, the confessions were particularly numerous in Germany – not because the Devil had decided to settle there, but because the methods of torture were harsher. The condition presented today as indispensable – to resort to torture only if all other means of collecting information have been exhausted – cannot be clearly defined: the means at the disposal of a large modern state are innumerable, and we can never be sure that they have all been used. In fact, if the information gathered is going to converge, one needs to rake in a considerable number of potential informants, and it is certain that innocents will be tortured among them. But torturing means punishing someone before knowing whether he is guilty, which contravenes the most elementary principles of the law: a suspicion is not a proof, while punishment is real enough.

Let us examine the argument on the ground it has chosen for itself. Torture is necessary – for this is the basic claim – in order to win the war: this is a justification for its usefulness. However, this is far from being conclusive. The French example of the Algerian War speaks volumes here. Torture was practised by the army in Algeria to combat terrorist attacks. It did indeed help the army to dismantle certain networks of the FLN and contributed to the victory in the 'battle of Algiers'; and yet it also, indirectly, led France to lose the war. The stories of the tortures being inflicted stiffened the solidarity of the Muslim population; in the place of each combatant arrested, several new ones rose up, intent on revenge: the part of the native population that had until then remained neutral now become overtly hostile. Opposition to the war in the metropolis itself was largely motivated by these same stories. In its turn, international public opinion and the governments of several influential countries swung round in support of the Algerian independence movement: the French determination to maintain a state of law had been undermined, and the cause of the independence fighters merely appeared all the more righteous.

The illegal methods used these days by the American government to combat the terrorists have not lessened their number or their violence; quite the contrary, they have become an argument for recruiting new *jihadists* who are turning out to be even more dangerous: they know that, if they are caught, they risk being tortured; they prefer to die as suicide fighters. At the same time, the slim advantages obtained thanks to the vigorous interrogations at Abu Ghraib have been reduced to zero by the collapse in America's moral prestige; what was supposed to bring the final victory closer has pushed it even further away. For, to win that particular fight, the government is obliged to gain the sympathy of the populations of Muslim countries – and it is difficult to get this if your reputation as a torturer goes before you. The commander of the American armed forces in Iraq in 2007, General David Petraeus, seems to have understood this; he declared to his troops: 'Beyond the basic fact that such actions are illegal, history shows that they are also frequently neither useful nor necessary.'[36] But his words had little noticeable effect on the politics of the country.

The 'utilitarian' argument fails to justify torture. Are we to conclude that those people who resort to it have not realized as much? Surely not. But then, another reason must be motivating the use of torture – a reason that is more difficult to admit in public or even to oneself. And yet this reason is rather well expressed by the formula 'we need to terrorize the terrorists'. They have inflicted the most appalling damage on us, killing innocents, spreading fear in every quarter, threatening our dearest values; we need to avenge this insult by making them suffer as much as we have, if not more. We need to show them that our democratic habits have not weakened our toughness. We need symbolically to repair the past, inflicting on them this comparable punishment (an eye for an eye), and sending them a message concerning the future, so they know what to expect. Terrorizing the terrorists also means that we are prepared to become their mirror image – to become even more hardened terrorists than they are.

It is this need to punish the perpetrators for the pain we have suffered that explains numerous cases of torture in the course of history, and it is here that we can find the real reason for torture as endorsed by the American government – and, more broadly speaking, for the support it has found among the American population in waging war on Iraq and setting off on a generalized 'war on terror'. These cases can be explained not by the judicial arguments invoked, or by the need to defend the principles of democracy and the gains made by Western civilization, but by the fear that has gripped the country's rulers, a fear which they have communicated to their fellow citizens. The threat of death, real or imaginary, entails the conclusion that 'everything is permitted'.

The decision to use torture as a terror of retribution gives an inner satisfaction to the person who practises it, even if this is difficult for him to accept openly. Having been injured and humiliated by aggression, he can now humiliate in his turn those whom he considers to be his aggressors, and rediscover his self-esteem. As an ex-soldier of the Algerian War explains, forty years after the events: 'You could feel a certain form of jubilation while being present at such extreme scenes ... Doing to a body whatever you feel like doing to it.'[37] Reducing the other to a state of complete impotence gives you a feeling of supreme power. This feeling is one which torture gives you more than murder does, since the latter does not last: once dead, the other becomes an inert object and no longer produces that jubilation which stems from fully triumphing over the will of another, without his ceasing to exist. To rape a woman in front of her husband, her parents or her children, to torture a child in front of its father – these really give you a sense of omnipotence, a sensation of attaining absolute sovereignty. To transgress human rules in this way makes you feel close to the gods.

It is not just a few isolated sadists who enjoy this feeling; very many individuals do so, albeit only in the exceptional conditions of war – which is one more reason for us not to interpret the fight against terrorism as a war, in other words a situation in which all the legal norms are suspended. It is not true that war reveals what had existed before it; it creates something new. The desire to torture, rape and humiliate does not require that we postulate a hypothetical 'torture instinct' (or 'death drive') in order to understand it, but comes from the same source as our other desires. However, it assumes this violent form when (as in war) the other paths to social recognition turn out to be blocked.

The drive which impels soldiers to torture in order to expel the tension that dwells within them, and to enable them to overcome their own weakness, is easy to understand; nevertheless, the calculation by which it is justified to their own eyes is false. The harm suffered in the past is not eliminated by the harm inflicted in the present, and the sense of assuagement sought in vengeance is an illusion. Any guarantee about the future is also illusory: terror does not always scare terrorists; it can sometimes motivate them to strike even harder. So the American government reacted by upping the violence and disappointing the hopes of the terrorists who had imagined they would paralyse it and force it to retreat. Why would the terrorists not react in the same way? That is why the authorization to torture given by the government and the encouragement lavished by those who manipulate public opinion remain without any positive effects.

It is time to leave the utilitarian framework that we adopted for the needs of debate. Torture is not to be condemned merely because it does not produce the effects expected; it is to be condemned, first and foremost, because it is an unacceptable attack on the very idea of humanity. It is the surest index of barbarism – that extreme pole in human behaviour that leads us to ride roughshod over the humanity of the other. Yet again, torture is in this respect worse than murder, since by torturing I do not remain content with eliminating the person to whom I object, I draw satisfaction from his suffering, from excluding him from humanity, and this intense pleasure lasts for as long as he is alive. Torture leaves an indelible mark on the person tortured but also on the torturer.

Institutional torture is even worse than individual torture, since it subverts every idea of justice and right. If the state itself becomes a torturer, how can we believe in the order that it claims to bring or to endorse? Legal torture extends the destructive action which it carries out, which does not stop with the torturer and the victim but affects all the other members of society, since they know that torture is being practised in their name, and yet turn away their eyes without doing a thing to stop it. As a general rule, the citizens of liberal democracies unhesitatingly despise and condemn the violent actions of the states that tolerate torture, a fortiori the actions of the states that systematize it, such as totalitarian regimes. We are discovering today that these same democracies, without changing their global structures, can adopt totalitarian attitudes. The cancer is no longer gnawing away at a single person, its metastases can be found among those who thought they had vanquished it in others and considered themselves to be unaffected. The power concentrated in the hands of our governments is so great that it frightens everyone: the war of the worlds also risks being the end of the world.

— 4 —

Steering between the Reefs

Nothing is black or white, and the white is often a black that is hiding, and the black is sometimes a white that has got found out.

I still wasn't sure if I was going to be in the police or in the terrorist group, I'll find out later, once I get there.

Romain Gary, *La Vie devant soi*

The end does not justify the means; nor does it tell us what means would enable us to reach it. Let us agree, for a moment, that the President of the United States sincerely wanted to weaken terrorism by invading Iraq; we are still forced to accept the fact that, contrary to what he promised, terrorism grew stronger in the wake of this invasion. This failure does not make terrorism more defensible, but it shows that its harmfulness does not justify the use of each and every means of combating it: certain initiatives have a completely different effect from the one hoped for.

That all human beings can live in dignity, whatever their sex, religion or social condition is, in its turn, an end that deserves to be pursued. But we do not know what is the best means for obtaining this. Here we again encounter the difficulty, glimpsed in chapter 1, of escaping dogmatism as well as nihilism, ethnocentric judgements as well as radical relativism. Everyone is led to navigate between two reefs (and sometimes more): the one which consists in remaining too tolerant towards what are often rather disturbing differences of culture, and that which leads us to combat them in such an intransigent way that these differences emerge even stronger. This is illustrated by several episodes in recent public life, presented as conflicts, or 'clashes', between the European lifestyle and that of Muslims from all over the world: the murder of a film director and threats issued to his scriptwriter, in the Netherlands; caricatures of the Prophet Mohammed published in Denmark; a speech made by the Pope comparing Christianity with Islam. Rather than erecting general rules a priori, I will here analyse each of these cases separately before pondering the evolution of Islam today and the reactions that it is arousing.

Murder in Amsterdam

On 2 November 2004, a man riding a bicycle through the streets of Amsterdam was knocked over and then killed by another man, also on a bicycle. The victim's name was Theo Van Gogh; he was a radio and television presenter, and also the author of several films. One of them had the title *Submission. Part One*; it was made on the basis of a project by Ayaan Hirsi Ali, a young woman of Somali origin, who was at the time a Member of Parliament. The film describes the brutality suffered by women in Islamic society. It aroused the indignation of several Muslims in the Netherlands, and one of them, Mohammed Bouyeri, a young Dutchman of Moroccan origin, put his resentment into action by killing Van Gogh and leaving on his body a letter threatening Hirsi Ali with death. Bouyeri was immediately arrested; subsequently, he was sentenced to life imprisonment.

This murder and everything associated with it had a great impact on the Dutch population, as was shown in an opinion poll conducted a few weeks later. To the question of knowing who was the most important personality in their history, a majority of the Dutch replied not, as one might have expected, Erasmus or Spinoza, Rembrandt or Vermeer, but Pim Fortuyn, a politician who had been assassinated two years previously, and whose programme came down, essentially, to expressing his xenophobia and his desire to see Muslims leaving the country (his book was called *Against the Islamization of Our Culture*). So Bouyeri's act was seen as in tune with the spirit of Islam, but not with the spirit, for example, of Fortuyn's assassin himself (a true-blooded Dutchman with a Christian upbringing, a defender of animal rights). Ever since, this theme has remained at the forefront of the public debate in the Netherlands: in 2007, the head of a new extreme-right party, Geert Wilders, eager to pick up the movement where Fortuyn had left off, demanded that the Quran be banned (it was a book as dangerous as *Mein Kampf*, he cried: half the pages should be torn out and jettisoned) and announced that he, too, had made a film on Islam revealing its pernicious influence. The liberal ex-Minister of the Interior, Rita Verdonk, founded another national-ist party, called 'Proud of the Netherlands', with the main aim of tightening immigration policy. The theme of an (anti-Islamic) 'liberal *jihad*' was launched.

Why was the director of the film killed rather than the author of the screenplay, who had dreamt it up? Because the former was much easier to get at than the latter. Hirsi Ali, an ex-Muslim who had become critical of Islam, was regularly threatened but had already for the past two years benefited from police protection. Van Gogh had always refused the idea of such protection and had continued to travel around by bike. He too was used to receiving threats, but he did not take them seriously. In the programmes he presented on television, and in his public statements, he had chosen to play a pro-vocative role: he enjoyed making remarks that were anti-Semitic ('the yellow stars copulated in the gas chambers'), Islamophobic (Muslims were simply, in his view, 'goat-shaggers'), or hostile to the authorities. The real target of Bouyeri's act of murder was, as people rapidly discovered, Hirsi Ali, who had made the struggle against Islam the centre of her public activity.

In 2006, two years after the murder of Van Gogh, Hirsi Ali pub-lished her autobiography, known in English under the title *Infidel*. This is a passionate and fascinating book, which makes it easier to understand her ideas and the path she has travelled. Born in Somalia in a Muslim family, she was brought up by her mother and grand-mother; her father, a political opponent of the government, lived in exile abroad. The upbringing she received was that of traditional popular Islam, mixed up with a great number of superstitions. Against the advice of her father, she was subjected to clitoridectomy: her mother was very devout and beat her mercilessly when she did not obey the rules inculcated in her to the letter. Her teacher of Quranic studies also beat her violently to punish her rebelliousness, so much so that her life was endangered.

As a teenager, she became enthusiastic about the ideas of the Muslim Brothers. This movement, which lay at the origin of con-temporary Islamism, rejected popular Islam and aspired to redis-cover, beyond the concessions successively made to the spirit of the time and place, the original purity of the doctrine. It was a sort of Counter-Reformation and is also reminiscent of the evangelical renewal among contemporary Protestants – the 'born again'. It enjoyed renewed popularity in the 1970s, thanks to the petrodollars that were sent to it by the fundamentalists of the Persian Gulf. It was, indeed, the frenzied consumption of energy characteristic of Western countries that strengthened those who declared themselves to be the deadly enemies of the West (this is a variant of the story of the merchant who cannot stop himself selling the length of rope with which he is to be hanged).

The Muslim Brothers encountered by Hirsi Ali were not merely more sincere in their faith and more intelligent than the traditional preachers; they were decent individuals, people of courage and integrity, who combated governmental corruption, helped the poor and suffering, and convinced young people to quit drugs or crime. As they have at the same time decided that the West is engaged on a Crusade against them, they wish to take part in this war in order to win it, and establish a worldwide Islamic government. The enemies of Islam must perish; in 1989, aged nineteen, Hirsi Ali had no doubt that Salman Rushdie deserved the death demanded by the *fatwa* of the Ayatollah Khomeini.

However, she was also assailed by doubts. While still very young, she had started to read; to begin with, children's books, then sentimental rosewater love stories that circulated among her classmates in Kenya and Ethiopia, where she lived. Later, she discovered the English, Russian or American classics. The complexity of the world revealed by literature contrasted with the schematic nature of the religious thought that she had made her own. Her liking for music and dance, and the discovery of her own sexuality, also contradicted the rigorous teaching of the Muslim Brothers. It was the impossibility of reconciling these two poles of attraction that finally led her to affirming her own personal autonomy; she wished to be financially independent so as to decide on the course her life would take, to think for herself, to be her own woman. She was forced to marry a Somali man who lived mainly in Canada, and left her country to join him in 1992; but, during a stopover in Germany, she fled to the Netherlands, a land of hospitality for refugees.

Thanks to her gifts for languages and to her own efforts, she quickly found work as an interpreter, and her integration into Dutch society passed without a problem. She was dazzled by the quality of life that she discovered in her new country, by the respect for common norms and for individual decisions. The inevitable comparison between the two societies led her to think that all countries are not equal: she clearly preferred the one in which differences of opinion were solved by negotiation rather than a trial of strength, in which individual choices were respected instead of being punished, in which the critical spirit was encouraged, rather than a blind submission to tradition, in which homosexuals were not attacked, and, more than anything, perhaps, in which women were not treated as inferior beings. For this reason, she herself became critical of certain ideas that are widespread in the West on the relativity of values and the equivalence of cultures; she also regretted the way that certain immigrants were imprisoned in their cultures of origin, which transformed society into a juxtaposition of closed cells that did not communicate with each other (she called this 'multiculturalism').

Up until then, Hirsi Ali's career can be read as an eloquent illustration of Enlightenment ideals, emphasizing universality, the rights of the individual and the critical spirit; it recalls the career of various heroes and heroines from the European novels of the nineteenth century who chose to free themselves from the irksome tutelage of religion and family in order to lead their lives as they saw fit. It was the terrorist attacks of 11 September 2001 that induced her to cross a new threshold. Deeply affected by the gravity of the event, she discovered a mission for herself; to open the eyes of Westerners to the harmfulness of Islam. For she was convinced, from the very first day, that the attacks were a pure effect of the Muslim religion. 'It *is* about Islam. This is based in belief. This is Islam,' she said to her friends on 12 September. It was just as if the fact of having had that religion in common with the perpetrators of the attacks was now obliging her to be among the first to denounce it. This suspicion of involuntary complicity and guilt had to be eradicated: 'Did Islam permit, even call for, this kind of slaughter? Did I, as a Muslim, approve of the attack?'[1] Already profoundly shaken in her faith, she now declared herself to be an atheist.

In order to find more justification for her judgement, she turned to the literature dedicated to Islam and terrorism, but wasn't interested in anything that did not endorse her new views. 'Infuriatingly stupid analysts – especially people who called themselves Arabists, yet who seemed to know next to nothing about the reality of the Islamic world – wrote reams of commentary,' she writes. On the other hand, the books of Bernard Lewis and Samuel Huntington, which stigmatized Islam and thus corresponded to her own convictions, met with her approval; she now saw the world through the prism of a war of religions. No other cause lay behind the action of the terrorists: 'This was belief, I thought. Not frustration, poverty, colonialism, or Israel: it was about religious belief, a one-way ticket to Heaven.' The body that was really responsible was not Islamism but Islam; not Bin Laden but the Prophet Mohammed. Islam was contrary to reason and human rights; it was

131

totalitarian and Manichean. 'The inhuman act of those nineteen hijackers was the logical outcome of this detailed system for regulating human behaviour.'[2]

In 2003, Hirsi Ali was elected to parliament as a candidate of the Liberal Party. She dedicated herself in particular to the struggle against the pernicious influence of Islam. Most of the measures that she sought to introduce were aimed at protecting women, as well as drawing up a list of crimes of honour – a first step in the effort to suppress them. Others concerned customs relating to religion: we should break with 'multiculturalism', cease to subsidize separate cemeteries, halal abattoirs or, as Dutch law lays down, the construction of mosques and the maintaining of faith schools. She proposed that liberals should speak out in favour of closing down and banning Muslim schools. More generally, she decided to launch a frontal attack on Islam: 'Mohammed is a pervert, and a tyrant,' she declared during one public debate.[3] It was in this spirit too that, in collaboration with Van Gogh, she made the film *Submission*. In it, we see a woman's naked back, bearing whip marks, with verses from the Quran justifying the punishment of women written on it: women are guilty if they have loved a man outside marriage, or resisted their husbands, or allowed themselves to be raped.

The anti-Islamic combat

What raises a question in Hirsi Ali's action is not its ultimate objective: there is a general consensus in Europe around values such as democracy, individual autonomy, the critical spirit, human rights – and, more specifically, the rights of women. Her way of achieving this object, however, is less convincing. Her description of the world, a description that lay behind the action she took, is strikingly simplistic. It was at the very time of the terrorist attacks, before she had had the time or the opportunity to study all the facts of the case, that she decided that Islam was the sole cause behind this aggression. Subsequently, she immediately discounted any information that went against this interpretation, and retained only whatever confirmed her in her views. The idea of a political motivation, of a form of vengeance aimed at effacing the collective humiliation, did not hold her attention. Her readers were invited to take her word for it that this was the exclusive responsibility of Islam: it was insofar as she was an ex-Muslim that she had to be believed. But neither an author's sincerity nor her past sufferings prove the truth of her argument.

The same goes for her overall judgement on Islam, which is accused of being the reason for the backwardness of the Muslim world and for the sufferings of the women who live in it. Contemporary fundamentalists refuse to situate the Quran and the action of the Prophet Mohammed in history; they want to see it as a divine revelation of eternal value, which needs to be applied wholesale to the contemporary world. But, in her own way, Hirsi Ali is just as reluctant to adopt a historical perspective. Many elements of the Muslim religion that now appear unacceptable to a European do not belong to that religion as such, but were taken over from prior traditions. In her pioneering work, the great anthropologist Germaine Tillion has demonstrated that the inferior position of women was the result of a mutation that occurred at the time of the Neolithic revolution, when human beings started to live in settlements and to master agricultural techniques. Her book *Le harem et les cousins* (in English: *The Republic of Cousins* (1966)) showed why and how endogamy and the sequestration of women were imposed all round the Mediterranean. In relation to the habits of older civilizations, the Islamic doctrine was rather favourable to women: they had had no share in inheritance, but now it taught that a half-share should be reserved for them. Such a prescript is of course shocking if we compare with our own egalitarian legislation; much less so, if we set it back in its context. The same can be said of various other characteristics of Islam.

On the basis of her schematic and monolithic understanding – not altogether different from the Manicheism that she condemns – Hirsi Ali commits herself to an equally problematic action. At the start of the twentieth century, Max Weber had formulated a distinction that has often been used since then, one between an ethic of conviction and an ethic of responsibility. The former is that of the moralist. It consists in defending what one thinks without worrying about the effects these words may have. The latter is that of the politician who adopts the converse point of view: what counts for him is not the sincerity of a person's remarks, but their effectiveness. Now Hirsi Ali's interventions are better justified as an expression of her own feelings than as a political action; she gives the impression of having a personal account to settle with Islam, as if she wished to wipe out, by her present virulence, her own previous commitments.

Depending on the occasion, her interventions waver between a moderate position, as when she incites Muslims to accept democracy, and a radical position, as when she calls for the eradication of Islam, which she holds responsible for every ill. It is now this latter position

133

that is associated with the name and the image of Hirsi Ali. However, expecting that all the Muslims in the world, now over a billion in number, will follow her path and embrace atheism is not really a realistic hope. When people see themselves rejected in what they represent to themselves as their collective identity, they become wary and hostile; they will be more willing to change if they can feel both that they are being faithful to themselves and respected by others for what they are. If renouncing Islam is the necessary condition for this change, and believers refuse to commit themselves to this renunciation, do we need to launch a new crusade to force them to do so? Such a means would destroy the aim sought – making this population more autonomous in its way of thinking, of freeing it from the tutelage of a dogma from elsewhere. We can see in contemporary Iraq the examples of the damage caused by this method: liberty cannot be brought by constraint.

A frontal attack in Islam is, in any case, not necessary if we wish to encourage its integration into democracy; we simply need to defend the separation of the theological and the political which – a point to which we shall be returning – is not foreign to the Muslim religion. In the interpretation of the religious message, we can fall back, among all the statements made in the Quran, on those that are compatible with the democratic spirit and nudge the others in the same direction. Muslims can serenely live their faith within a democracy, but only on condition that they do not reduce Islam to Islamism. This, however, is exactly what the Islamists (who claim to be speaking on behalf of the whole community) do, just as much as their virulent critics (who are thus doing them a great favour). In her most spectacular acts, Hirsi Ali decided to highlight provocation rather than to facilitate adaptation: she cannot really expect her declarations on the perversity of the Prophet to become a subject of debate with believers. The hostile reactions to her remarks seem, in turn, to radicalize her behaviour, as if her aim were civil war. Now to embark on a debate, to get your partner in a conversation to listen to your arguments, you need to have a common framework of references at your disposal.

Should we blame the 'multiculturalist' model for the failure in integration that has afflicted certain groups of Muslims? The answer is less obvious than Hirsi Ali would claim. That all the inhabitants of Western countries do not possess the same culture is a statement of fact, not a value judgement. The United States is a country in which this diversity has been taken into account; and yet it is also the country in which the population proclaims its patriotic (American) sentiments most loudly. The possibility of practising one's culture of origin without suffering from discrimination does not stop one being loyal towards the country in which one lives. Cultural, national and ideological solidarity are not to be confused: 'a same law' does not mean 'a same culture'. The situation in European countries is not the same, but this does not rule out 'multiculturalism' in advance. There is no universal humanity: if we deprived human beings of all particular culture, they would simply cease to be humans.

The interventions of Hirsi Ali raise three general questions that we need to keep distinct, for they require different answers. The first is the question of the threats that have been hanging over her since 2002, and thus of the right to criticize religions or to reject them, a right inherent to every democratic regime. There can be no doubt on this: to utter death threats or to incite violence against a person whose opinions you dislike is a crime that must be punished. In the eyes of law as of ethics, physical violence is of more account than symbolic violence. The second question concerns the status of women in traditional societies, in particular, in Muslim societies, and the violence from which they suffer: the combat in which we need to engage on this point is just and necessary, even if the means chosen by Hirsi Ali do not always turn out to be appropriate. Finally, the third concerns the global, geopolitical and historical explanations that she gives of recent events, and the radical solutions she promotes: on this score, it is possible to find her remarks unconvincing.

For her part, Hirsi Ali recounts that she had established three precise objectives for her action. The first was to alert public opinion in the Netherlands to the suffering of Muslim women, who are locked away, beaten and forced to obey the decisions of their families; sometimes, if they disobey, they are even put to death. It is true that she has managed to draw people's attention to these sufferings, and to remind us of the necessity of opposing them; from this point of view, her action has been effective, even if the struggle is not yet over. Second, she wished to trigger a debate in the Muslim community about the reform of Islam. In this respect, her intervention was a failure, since it was perceived as being exterior and hostile to religion, and thus as constituting an appeal not for the religion to be reformed, but simply rejected; and nobody debates with someone who denies their identity. Third, Hirsi Ali wished to incite Muslim women to denounce their sufferings as unacceptable. On this level, the results are mixed: certain women are grateful to her for her frankness, but many other Dutch Muslims did not recognize themselves in the characters in *Submission*.

In the book he devoted to the recent events in the Netherlands, *Murder in Amsterdam: The Death of Theo Van Gogh and the Limits of Tolerance*, Ian Buruma describes a television programme in which, in the presence of Hirsi Ali, the film *Submission* was shown in a shelter for women who had been subjected to domestic violence. One of them told her, 'You are simply insulting us. My faith gave me strength. That was how I realized that my situation could not go on like that.'[4] This simple woman seemed to understand more clearly than the militant atheists what the use of religion is and how, beyond any imaginary description of the world or any particular anachronistic precept that it might contain, it can provide those who suffer with an existential support. In her own book, Hirsi Ali agreed that it was difficult to gain a hearing from certain women whom she wishes to defend, but she merely explains it as the result of their long practice of submission. Even if this were the case, an invitation to leave one's religion behind risks meeting with no response: yet again, we find that it is impossible to force someone to be free. But Hirsi Ali seems not to be bothered by this: she perceives her own action as a prolongation of the anti-clerical struggle that has been under way ever since the Enlightenment, a war of reason against prejudice, or indeed, following the Leninist model, as the combat of an enlightened vanguard on behalf of the masses who are incapable of freeing themselves.

Unable to find herself accepted as a reformist by the Muslims of the Netherlands, Hirsi Ali has since found other attentive ears. Since 2006, she has stopped working as a member of the Dutch Parliament, and now works for a Washington think-tank, the American Enterprise Institute, close to the neo-conservative milieux who led the American government into its war in Iraq, and thus also to the camp at Guantánamo and the prison of Abu Ghraib, and who will perhaps soon be leading it to bomb Iran. In this framework, words can provoke actions no less murderous than those committed by terrorists. Will this be the final incarnation of this uncommon woman? On reading her autobiography, we may speculate that this will not be the case: the rich and complex personality that emerges cannot long remain satisfied with this simple appeal to a war on Islam.

The Danish caricatures

On 30 September 2005, the premier Danish daily, *Jyllands-Posten*, published twelve cartoons on the theme of the Prophet Mohammed. The Van Gogh affair was present in the background of this initiative: remembering the film director's tragic fate, the country's cartoonists were hesitant to step out into this dangerous terrain, and the newspaper wanted to encourage them to overcome their fear. The reaction of several representatives from the Muslim community in Holland was intense but, initially, without consequences. A few weeks later, the latter appealed to the media, as well as to the religious and political authorities of Muslim countries, and the protests in these countries took an alarming turn: at the end of January 2006, anti-Danish protests were increasing, and the Danish government was being called on to apologize. During these events, several persons were killed, in Afghanistan, in Libya, in Nigeria, and elsewhere; on one account, 139 deaths were caused. The Danish government tried to calm the situation, and other European countries did likewise, as well as several well-known figures within the Muslim community; the controversy abated during February. However, it has left enduring traces: it has become a point of reference every time the place of Islam in Europe comes into question. So let us take a closer look at the facts.[5]

We first need to remember the national context in which this 'affair' occurred. Until recently, Denmark has had very few foreigners living on its soil. The first groups to arrive there, in the 1970s, were supposed to return home once their work period had come to an end; as in Germany, they were 'guest workers'. The slight increase in their numbers led to the rise of parties of the extreme right, who described the immigrants as the perpetrators of a new occupation (after that of the Germans during the Second World War) and as a threat to 'Danish values'. Indeed, as elsewhere in Europe, ever since the death of Communism, the programme of the extreme right has been reduced to two nationalist choices: sending immigrants back home, and opposing European integration. Muslim immigrants are particularly visible, and they thus arouse the strongest sense of rejection. The administration has created the particular category of 'descendants' to include within it the children of immigrants, even if they are born on Danish soil. The opposition to 'multiculturalism' has become one of the main themes in public debate. In addition, Denmark has an official religion, Lutheran Protestantism; those who serve this Church have the status of civil servants, and lessons in Christianity are obligatory in the state schools.

In 2001, a party stood at the legislative elections that had been created a few years earlier following a split in the extreme right: this was the Danish People's Party, led by Pia Kjæsgaard, a straight-talking nurse. Her electoral propaganda presented the blonde Danish women as being threatened by the suntanned brutes from the South responsible for mass rapes, forced marriages and street gangs. Kjæsgaard supported the idea of 'Denmark for the Danish'; Islam was a cancer, she told her compatriots, a terrorist organization; its faithful were awaiting an opportunity to massacre us. She also declared, 'There is only one civilization: ours,' thus putting herself on the side of Oriana Fallaci rather than Huntington. Another party leader stated, 'There are many points in common between Hitler and Islam.' The representative of another extreme-right party asked, 'Do you know what the difference is between a rat and a Muslim? The rat doesn't get any welfare.' These public comments have left their mark.

The elections, held shortly after 11 September 2001, brought to power a coalition formed of liberals and conservatives, with the support of the Danish People's Party. One of the urgent matters that faced the new parliament was adopting a law conceived so as to discourage any applicant for immigration. The conditions of the family grouping were toughened: for a foreigner to be able to live with his or her Danish partner, he or she needed to be able to prove that they had a stronger link with Denmark than with their place of origin, and both of them needed to be at least twenty-four years old. The Minister of the Interior, a former leftist called Karen Jespersen, suggested interning delinquent asylum-seekers on a desert island. As a result, in four years the number of residence permits based on the claim of family reunification fell drastically.

It was within this context, in which the condemnation of Islam often served as a facade for the rejection of immigrants, that the affair of the caricatures occurred. An author could not find an illustrator for his book on the Prophet Mohammed, and complained about this in public; Flemming Rose, editor of the culture section of *Jyllands-Posten*, decided to investigate other cases of what he called self-censorship, and commissioned some drawings. Their publication was accompanied by a text in which the journalist explained that modernity and Christianity fitted together, whereas Islam incarnated darkness; the war of civilizations was inevitable and we needed to overcome our fears, and thus commit ourselves to the struggle of good against evil. In this case, it was important to prove one's attachment to freedom of expression, the first of the 'Danish values' which presupposed, in his view, that everyone should be 'prepared to be despised, derided, ridiculed' – a disposition which he recommended to Muslims. The immediate object was to prove that it is possible to say bad things about Islam without having to be afraid of suffering the same fate as Van Gogh. The editor of the newspaper presented the whole enterprise in a leader, under the title 'The Threat from the Darkness', in which he deplored the 'exacerbated sensitivity' of the Muslims.

The cartoons themselves are not particularly aggressive. Five of the cartoonists avoided doing as they had been instructed, and did not actually represent Mohammed. Two others are mere images, without any suggestion of a value judgement. The five final ones can be described as caricatures: one shows the Prophet with horns, three others make fun of Muslim attitudes to women, and the last, the one most often quoted, shows Mohammed with a bomb in place of a turban. What gives them a particular meaning is the framework in which they were published: these cartoons illustrated less the right to freedom of expression than the right to attack Islam by mocking the Prophet, whom Muslims view as a holy person.

Let us leave to one side the strange conception of freedom of expression as defended by the newspaper editor: he reduces it to the right to derision and mockery (at this price, it is no longer Spinoza who best exemplifies this virtue, but television programmes such as, in France, *Les Guignols de l'info* [roughly the equivalent of *Spitting Image* – Tr.]). Let us start out, rather, from his self-proclaimed goal: to defend freedom of expression by criticizing or ridiculing Islam. Two questions arise. The first concerns the nature of the target: why go for this example of 'censorship' from among all those that are possible? This choice cannot be a matter of chance. If the editor had requested that people make fun of black men or obese women, the response of the cartoonists would have been just as much an example of freedom of expression, since such mockery is generally judged to be in poor taste. If he did not do so, if he began with a book that could not find an illustrator, this was because he also, or in particular, had another aim in view: to cast doubt on the legitimacy of Islamic precepts and, in the final analysis, to demonstrate that Muslims are intolerant.

The second question concerns the place of this theme in the society in which the experiment took place. In a population as permeable to xenophobic language and values as contemporary Danish society, nobody is going to be shocked at the insinuation that Islam is intrinsically misogynist and terrorist. Quite the contrary: this confirms the feelings of the majority of people, who, rather than bowing to the 'multiculturalist' dogmas of the politically correct, can finally see what they think being freely expressed. If the aim had really been to prove that freedom of expression is good in itself, then statements that went against the common opinion and transgressed the prohibitions to which the majority of the population adheres should have been chosen: making anti-Semitic remarks, for example. If the idea of defending freedom of expression in this way does not occur to anyone, this is because – contrary to what we hear in some apologias – that freedom is neither the only one nor the most fundamental among the values of a liberal democracy; it figures among them, of course, but along with others, which it needs to fit in with. Everyone tacitly accepts this hierarchy, and nobody mentions censorship when it is a matter of forbidding incitement to racial hatred.

Freedom of expression is no ordinary value, since it allows us to free ourselves from any other value; it is a demand for complete tolerance (nothing that anyone says can be declared intolerable), and thus a generalized relativism of all values. I demand the right to defend any opinion, as well as to denigrate any ideal. Now every society needs a firm basis of shared values; replacing them all by the idea that 'I have the right to say anything I want' is not enough to sustain a common life. It is perfectly clear that the right to withdraw from observing certain rules cannot be the only rule organizing the life of a community. 'It is forbidden to forbid', a slogan used during the May 1968 events in France, is a pretty formula, but no society in the world conforms to it.

The foundation of liberal democracy is the sovereignty of the people and the protection of the individual. Together with the freedom to choose that it guarantees for the individuals who compose it, the state also has other objectives: protecting their lives, their physical integrity and their property, fighting discrimination, working towards the common justice, peace and well-being, and defending the dignity of all citizens. That the individual has his own rights does not mean that he ceases to live in society. His acts have consequences for the other members of the group; and words are not just an expression of one's thoughts – they are also actions, and take place in social space. More exactly, certain 'performative' words are in themselves autonomous actions, such as slandering or defaming someone: in such cases, saying means doing. Other words are, in addition, incitements to other actions: orders, appeals, supplications that involve the responsibility of the person uttering them. Between having the right to carry out an action and actually carrying it out, there is a distance that you cross when taking account of the possible consequences of that action in the present context. As a result, words or other forms of expression are subject to restrictions that are imposed by virtue of the values to which the society adheres. Thus most European countries have anti-racist laws in place, or else laws that punish the defamation of groups, whatever their character, and even anti-blasphemy laws. So too in Denmark, though admittedly they apply only to the Lutheran Church...

The governments of these countries have no hesitation in resorting to these laws. At the very time the affair of the caricatures was causing the greatest uproar, in February 2006, the English Holocaust denier David Irving was sentenced in Austria to three years' prison for disputing the existence of gas chambers at Auschwitz. During the same period, French bishops managed to ban an advert based closely on Leonardo da Vinci's *Last Supper*; the ad was deemed to be offensive to Christians since it mocked the image of Christ. In the same month of February 2006, the leader of the German Christian Social Union, Edmund Stoiber, demanded that the Turkish film *Valley of the Wolves* be taken off the screens, describing it as a 'hate-filled film, racist and anti-Western'. In June of the same year, the French Interior Minister Nicolas Sarkozy initiated proceedings in the Court of Appeal against a rap group whose remarks were perceived as a defamatory attack on the honour of the national police. In Denmark itself, the decision was taken to suspend for three months Radio Holger which, in July 2005, had incited people to 'exterminate all Muslim fanatics, in other words to kill a large number of Muslim immigrants'. So there are indeed limits to freedom of expression that people choose not to transgress.

Between the legal sphere, which rests on prohibitions, and the personal sphere, where freedom is extensive, there is a public and social sphere, imbued with different values. The legal order does not consist merely of laws, but includes all the regulations and even institutions, insofar as the latter consist of a sedimentation of laws and rules. The grand principle that it obeys is that of equality. Social life, for its part, is played out within this legal framework, but cannot be reduced to it; and *its* principle is not equality (who would like to live in a society where everyone was treated in the same way?), but recognition, which you obtain by showing yourself to be more brilliant, or more loving, or more loyal, or braver than the rest – in short, by showing yourself to be superior, not equal; what people demand here is not equality but distinction, gratification, reward for being exceptional. This social space is not, itself, homogeneous: the image is not the word; the giant poster is not the illustration in a book; the newspaper caricature is not the painting hanging in a gallery. A slogan uttered from a political platform does not need to answer the same requirements as a doctoral thesis. There is also a difference between criticizing a generally shared ideology (which is a brave act) or criticizing a group that is marginalized and discriminated against (which is a hateful act), and a difference between making fun of oneself and making fun of others.

The social consensus that governs this public sphere in turn limits the freedom of expression. Thus we avoid mocking obese people in public, even if no law forbids it, and, in contemporary films, care is taken not to represent all blacks as rapists or all Jews as shady bankers. For this reason, too, certain writings – even if they are not forbidden by law – will have difficulty finding a publisher if they transgress the established consensus: everybody is nervous of a 'media lynching'. This precaution does not, however, seem to extend to Muslim Arabs. When taken to the extreme, it produces the 'politically correct'; when abandoned, it leaves room for what might be called the *politically abject*, presented in the guise of 'honest talk'. Now, if the quest for truth and the ability to demonstrate one's opinions are precious liberties, they are not the only ones to govern our existence.

In short: the caricatures of Islam are not a good illustration of the principle of freedom of expression; and this principle itself does not have, in social life, the force of an absolute which its defenders claim for it. Justifying the publication of *Jyllands-Posten* by invoking this principle alone does not seem sufficient. The suggestion that it was meant to help the Muslim masses emerge from their ignorance and their passive submission to dogmas does not appear convincing either: public stigmatization is rarely a good pedagogic tool. But, in that case, what supplementary reasons motivated this publication?

First and foremost, we should not neglect the benefits that we can obtain for ourselves by assuming the role of a knight in shining armour, defender of freedom, or an apostle of the Good: these are among the allures of Manicheism. We derive a definite satisfaction from feeling ourselves to be righters of wrongs; from being driven by righteous indignation. As we have seen, the editors of the newspaper in question tranquilly gave themselves the gratification of being the representatives of good fighting bravely against the forces of evil, the Light against the Darkness. But there is another possible explanation, suggested the day after publication. According to one of the twelve cartoonists, 'the paper simply wanted, right from the start, to provoke'; this was also the conclusion of the other big Danish dailies.

Indeed, one sometimes has the impression that journalists are convinced of one thing: unlike 'us', who are endowed with the finest virtues, Muslims are unable to adopt a critical attitude towards their religious dogmas; to prove it, you just have to wave a red rag in front of them. If the editors had been aiming to provoke a violent reaction among certain Muslims and, consequently, a rejection by their country of its Muslim minority, already under fire from the extreme right-wing party associated with the government, they would have gone about it in just this way. The result, desired or not, was an exacerbation of the tensions surrounding immigrants, not their conversion to 'Danish values'. This immediately casts doubt on the very formulation of the dilemma confronting those who intervened in the public debate in Denmark. Rather than a choice between defending freedom and the Good on the one hand and caving into self-censorship on the other, the real alternative could be expressed thus: contributing to a heightening of tension in the relations between groups within society on the one hand, or making it easier for them to integrate mutually on the other. Yet again, we find that an ethics of responsibility would be better suited to political action than an ethics of conviction.

The reactions

Reactions to the publication of the cartoons initially came from a few imams in Denmark, who saw them as an opportunity for reawakening the religious sensibility of a population of Muslim origin and bringing it into the mosques, where they preach a fundamentalist version of Islam. They turned first to the newspaper, demanding an apology; when none was forthcoming, they organized a demonstration in the streets of Copenhagen and, in a petition signed by several Muslims, asked the prime minister to intervene. The cartoonists received death threats: the police rapidly identified and arrested their sender, a seventeen-year-old boy considered to be 'psychologically unstable'. The imams then decided to intensify their campaign and turned to the Organization of the Islamic Conference (OIC), an organization with fifty-seven member states, as well as to the ambassadors of Muslim countries at Copenhagen. They had thus clearly decided that international religious authorities or Muslim countries had something valuable to say on the conduct of public affairs within Denmark. In mid-October, the OIC and eleven of the ambassadors addressed letters to the Danish prime minister voicing their disquiet; the ambassadors also asked to be seen by him.

The prime minister categorically refused this last request, referring to the freedom of expression and reminding them that 'the Danish government has no means of influencing the press'. This reply was, to tell the truth, a bit curt. The action of a politician is not limited to applying the law; he has much more room for manoeuvre and nothing obliges him to ignore the other objectives of his action, such as the peaceful and harmonious life of the different components of society. When a significant number of individuals claim to feel offended, he can give them a hearing, show them respect and solicitude, explain to them why he does not wish to interfere with press freedom, and set out the legal form that their protests could take.

In this regard, we need to distinguish between the possible reasons behind the protest: the ban on representing the Prophet is a purely theological (iconophobic) demand, which the European media are not obliged to observe; on the other hand, representing the Prophet with a bomb where his turban should be may offend, not theology, but Muslims themselves, since it is thereby being insinuated that they are all terrorists, or that the practice of terror derives from Islam (which may perhaps be the conviction of Bin Laden, but is certainly not that of ordinary believers). A government reaction of this kind, one that still refused to yield on basic principles, would have made it possible to allay the tensions between the different communities. Indeed, a few months later, non-Muslim voices were raised in Denmark to regret that the government had not intervened in this way. Twenty-two former Danish ambassadors expressed their disappointment; the European Commissioner for Justice, Franco Frattini, voiced his personal disapproval of the publication of the cartoons. Only in his New Year wishes did the prime minister present a more conciliatory position. But two and a half months had gone by, and the damage was done.

The imams denied a hearing had meanwhile decided to appeal directly to the Muslims of their respective countries of origin. They put together a dossier containing the twelve original cartoons and adding another nine that had been published in a different newspaper, together with three particularly aggressive ones they had found on the Internet. At the beginning of December they went to Egypt, Saudi Arabia, Lebanon, Syria and elsewhere; in all these countries they complained to the religious authorities but also to the ministers and other official characters. In each place, their request for help was given a particular spin in accordance with the political needs of the moment. In Egypt, for instance, there was a risk of the Muslim Brothers obtaining a significant number of votes in the elections; the government saw the imams' requests as a good opportunity for demonstrating to its population that it too was concerned to protect Islam. In Syria, where the government was suspected of heavy-handed interference in Lebanese political life, the affair happened at just the right time to turn people's attentions away from this suspicion. In Palestine, Fatah saw this as a way of presenting itself as the defender of popular beliefs, and thus of rivalling Hamas. The delegation of imams also established contact with the television channels; the millions of spectators of Al Jazeera were informed about the cartoons in a highly tendentious way.

By this stage it seemed that nothing could stop the protest movement in Muslim countries, reinforced by a new publication of the cartoons, this time by a little Norwegian magazine. Initially orchestrated by governments and religious institutions, the movement entailed street demonstrations, with a boycott of Danish products being organized, and death threats started flying through the air. By the beginning of February, the authorities were starting to lose control of the movement, but they did nothing to stop it. Danish embassies in several countries were attacked and even set fire to. Violence spread, and the number of dead and injured increased.

The behaviour of the Muslims involved in these reactions is clearly not entirely above suspicion. It is, to begin with, inappropriate to go and put pressure on foreign ambassadors or, even worse, the ministers of foreign countries to intervene in Danish internal affairs: this shows disrespect for the sovereignty of each country and at the same time excludes you from the community you are seeking to reform. The appeal to foreign religious authorities, as on television stations, was a kind of blackmail: if you do not accept our demand, the imams seemed to be insinuating, angry mobs could run riot and cause a great deal of damage; your embassies will be burned, your products will be boycotted. So the imams were showing no respect for the powers of the country in which they lived, while at the same time they were asking the government of that country to treat them with consideration. In the dossier they presented in Muslim countries, the twelve original cartoons were mixed with others from different sources: this illustrated their desire to win a victory rather than to ensure that justice triumphed.

Newspaper and magazine journalists, as well as those of the television, produced the version of the facts that suited them best; a sense for nuance, or for the complexities of the situation, were rarely their first concern. The governments of these countries, in turn, were not taken in by their manoeuvres: under the cover of virtuous indignation, the messages they sent to the Danish government were in reality addressed to their own populations. Finally, the violence of crowds in the streets was all the more paradoxical in that it was deemed to give the lie to the Islamic violence suggested by the cartoons: however, in place of the single bomb replacing the Prophet's turban, the demonstrators brandished a hundred of them, as if they secretly cherished the image they deemed offensive! The consequence was paradoxical: the wounds inflicted on the image of Islam by its zealous supporters were even more serious than those caused by its detractors.

It is clear that the manipulators of these demonstrators, political or religious leaders, found this to their advantage: they were strengthening their prestige among the believers by presenting themselves as their intransigent defenders (they too are apostles of the Good!) and at the same time distracting people from what was going wrong in their own countries, by designating a convenient scapegoat. The exacerbation of the conflict and the impression of an inevitable clash of civilizations were manna from heaven, so to speak: they could now override the borderline between Islam and Islamic fundamentalism. The propagandists of al-Qaeda took advantage of this to strengthen the network of sympathizers they needed to foment new terrorist acts.

At the same time, we must not overestimate the importance of these agitators. If thousands of people were prepared to listen to them, this was not merely, or even mainly, because of the Danish caricatures; it was because they saw this as an opportunity to express their resentment against those they held responsible for their misfortunes, the arrogant Western powers. The humiliation that was the real point of departure for this upsurge of feeling stemmed from several sources: the presence of Western armies on the territory of Muslim countries such as Afghanistan and Iraq (including a Danish contingent), the injustices inflicted on the Palestinians, and the images of torture in the camps and prisons. These events occurred within a precise framework, that of the negative effects of urbanization and globalization on traditional identity, presented in their turn by local governments as if provoked by the West. Let us, finally, bear in mind the display of a certain Western opulence on television screens, at a time when access to the countries in which it is being flaunted, and thus access to this wealth itself, is forbidden. On their side, the virtuous speeches on human rights which the inhabitants of these lands of resentment hear, and which are formulated by those who are responsible for their distress, do not help. In the publication of the caricatures they see nothing but an incitement to violence. All these ingredients, when brought together, form an explosive mixture that owes its vocabulary to religion, but whose causes are political.

From February 2006 onwards, the Western press was engaged in the defence of freedom of expression; European governments and international organizations intervened with the rulers of Muslim countries, urging them to prevent the violence; these rulers, already worried that they were losing control of the movement, quickly put a stop to it. A few red rags would continue to be waved in European countries, who yet again would like to see the theorem established at the time of the affair verified: in order to demonstrate that Muslims are extremists, you have merely to treat their Prophet without due respect: then they will become extremists. A small Danish political group published an image of Mohammed on a dromedary, drinking beer. Another group announced its intention to burn the Quran in public. In 2007, a Swedish newspaper published a cartoon of the Prophet with a dog's body; individuals claiming the support of al-Qaeda immediately uttered threats against the journalists. During the 2007 electoral campaign, the Danish People's Party placed a portrait of Mohammed on its posters, with this slogan: 'Freedom of expression is Danish, censorship is not'; since these elections, this party has cooperated closely with the government.

It is also worth mentioning two final episodes linked to this theme. In autumn 2006, a French professor, Robert Redeker, published an anti-Muslim diatribe in *Le Figaro*; he subsequently received death threats and was forced to ask for state protection. Threatening someone with death for his opinions is, to say it yet again, a crime that must be punished. Once this principle has been restated, it is also possible not to approve of the publication, in a major Paris daily, of that hateful, violent article, which describes the Muslim religion as animated by hatred and violence alone, deemed to be absent from the 'free world'. What could it achieve other than bringing a (risky) notoriety to its author and the proof that, if Muslims are presented as 'a hysterical mob flirting with barbarism', there will always be at least one person among them who will wish to punish the author of the declaration? Is it not the eloquent defence of this posture which, under cover of criticizing a religion (the demand for a 'right to blasphemy', placed under the protection of Voltaire), allows the faithful to be stigmatized? The woman responsible for the corresponding column in *Le Monde* in turn expressed her opinion on Redeker's article in these terms: 'We would certainly not have published it. Our "Debates" pages are not a place for empty insults but for analysis.' These days, in Europe, Muslims are the main community which people take pleasure in provoking with impunity in wide-circulation newspapers and magazines, and these provocations are added to the

147

daily victimization these immigrants, and descendants of immigrants, suffer when their physical appearance or their name betrays their foreign origin.

In this respect, we can draw a comparison with another ethnic group traditionally discriminated against in Europe: the Jews. Their tragic destiny in the course of the Second World War created a consensus in European countries thanks to which any demonstration of anti-Semitism has become intolerable. Holocaust deniers are regularly brought before the courts and sentenced; if they work for the state they also risk losing their jobs. The few people who do allow themselves to make disobliging remarks about the Jews in public are immediately and unanimously condemned. Neo-Nazi or Satanic groups which have profaned Jewish (and indeed Muslim) graves have been punished with heavy sentences each time they are caught. It is true that, in certain suburban districts, teenagers from the Maghreb, identifying themselves in their imaginations with the population of Palestine, have contrived to move from hostility towards Israeli policies to anti-Semitic feelings; but the expression of these feelings in the public space is systematically repressed. This vigilance can even go further and create a climate that is not conducive to public debate, since any local criticism of the Israeli government is considered to be a manifestation of anti-Semitism; witness the recent trial of Edgar Morin, Danièle Sallenave and Sami Naïr, authors of an independent think-piece in *Le Monde*.

In February 2006, the French satirical paper *Charlie-Hebdo* in its turn published the controversial cartoons, together with several others. Sales shot up tenfold, from an average of 60,000 copies to nearly 600,000. Two Muslim organizations issued a writ against it; the affair came before the courts in February 2007. The editor declared at the trial that he had sought both to defend press freedom and to fight fundamentalism: he saw himself as an incarnation of the Enlightenment, scattering the Darkness alongside Descartes and Spinoza. France was in the middle of a presidential election campaign; the big beasts from different parties came to court to declare that they preferred freedom to submission. Nicolas Sarkozy, the then Minister of the Interior, sent the court a letter in which he expressed his clear support: 'I prefer too much caricature to no caricature at all.' To nobody's surprise, the newspaper was acquitted a month later. I am not for my part suggesting it should have been found guilty, but that, on this occasion, justice failed to remain independent of the political power, and lost its own authority.

A few reflections

What conclusions should we draw from this affair of the caricatures? It indisputably established a model for the interpretation of incidents past and, doubtless, still to come. In fact, the 'Rushdie Affair' which it is often compared with bore only a partial resemblance to it: while Khomeini's *fatwa* and the demonstrations in the Muslim world are similar to recent events, the novel *The Satanic Verses* has nothing to do with the publication of the cartoons. In writing his novel, Rushdie was seeking neither to defend press freedom, nor to unmask Muslim fanaticism.

The caricatures revealed a conflict within the European countries between two attitudes towards their Muslim populations and the occasional fundamentalist tendencies of the latter. The authorities can either seek confrontation by exacerbating the conflict, or seek, first and foremost, to take people's susceptibilities into consideration. With all due respect, I feel I cannot unreservedly approve of the first position, illustrated by the journalists of *Jyllands-Posten*. It is quite wrong to present these events as a struggle between censorship and freedom of expression, as was done by the demagogues of the Danish People's Party, without taking into account the content of the words uttered, when what is at stake is the rejection or welcome meted out to those who do not resemble the majority. Today, the demand for total freedom of expression is the usual facade behind which there lurks xenophobia, the common theme of movements such as the Danish People's Party, the Flemish Interest in Belgium, or the Freedom Party in Austria. When the leader of the Swiss extreme right, Christoph Blocher, defends the propaganda of his party, which presents foreigners as black sheep who should be kicked out of the country, he claims he is merely launching a discussion; whoever criticizes him for this is a censor. 'The posters are meant to provoke, to provoke a debate. We need to stop seeing racism everywhere.'[6] A significant precedent comes to mind: at the time of the Dreyfus Affair, the most virulent organ of anti-Semitism, founded and edited by Édouard Drumont, was already called *La Libre Parole – Free Speech*.

It is no less misleading to situate this attitude in the wake of Voltaire, struggling in the eighteenth century against the abuses of the Catholic Church. Those who do so manage to forget a weighty distinction: Voltaire and his companions in the struggle were opposing the dominant institutions in their society, the state and the Church, whereas contemporary militants receive the support and encouragement of ministers and leaders of the parties in power. The amalgam

becomes shocking when those fighters for freedom identify themselves with the dissidents of Communist countries in Eastern Europe:
the latter risked paying for their bravery by suffering several years'
deportation to the gulag, while the former 'risked' seeing themselves
invited to dinner by the Head of State. It is a little excessive, one has
to admit, to seek to benefit simultaneously from the honours reserved
to the persecuted and the favours granted by the mighty.

The native populaces of European countries have become more
intransigent with immigrants, in particular with Muslims. The fear
of these populations is increasing; witness this preposterous proposal: the authorities of Rotterdam expressed the intention of
banning anyone from speaking any other language than Dutch in
the streets! Now one unfortunate consequence of fear is that it reinforces people's reasons for being afraid: discrimination and repression nourish resentment and in turn provoke violent acts. The
xenophobic right wing has grown stronger in Austria, in Flemish
Belgium, in Denmark, in France, in Italy, in the Netherlands, in
Switzerland... The word 'Islamophobia' really does correspond to a
real phenomenon, and it is not merely allowed to speak ill of Islam:
it is good form. In the West, people feel within their rights to do so:
'we' are defending freedom, even if maybe in somewhat irreverent
ways, while 'they' are replying to our words with violence and
murder. By doing so, people forget that our words too can have
disagreeable consequences: if, thanks to them, the movers and
shakers in the political world acquire the conviction that Muslims
are intrinsically violent and unreasonable, they will not hesitate
tomorrow to send bombers and missiles to teach them how to
reason. Violence is not only where people think it is.

On their side, the European fundamentalist imams have acquired
a public notoriety that they did not possess before. In Muslim countries, the Muslim masses have reaffirmed their conviction that Westerners despise and humiliate them, and these masses are ready to
seek any opportunity to take revenge; the grip of fundamentalists on
them has increased. Dozens of men and women have died as a result
of the publication of the caricatures; even if we cannot blame the
journalists for this, we now need to admit that such a chain of
causes and effects has become quite probable. The dictatorial and
demagogic governments of several Muslim countries are taking
advantage of this to push the discontent of their population in the
direction that suits them. It may be concluded that waving a red flag
is not an appropriate way of enabling different communities to
coexist peacefully.

The reaction from Muslim countries, even if it was framed and manipulated by the political authorities, also shows that religious experience there takes a form to which Europeans are no longer used. It goes without saying that, for the latter, religion is a private affair which must not impinge on the organization of social life; in this respect, even Catholic believers behave as individualist Protestants. It is the opposite that is true in Muslim countries. For this reason, to interfere with the place of religion in society comes down to questioning the image that everyone forms of their collective identity but also of their intimate identity – and this is an operation not to be undertaken lightly. Muslim believers live in a mental world structured differently from that of Christian believers, and they feel that this world is at present fragile and threatened. In European countries, both groups are led to live side by side within the framework of a secular state; for Muslims, who often come from traditional peasant families, it is often not simple to adapt to this overnight. Their sense of being marginal leads them to take refuge a little bit more in a traditional identity. In the following generation, the situation gets worse instead of fading away: those born in the West no longer have that identity, and some of them are tempted by the simplistic schemas proposed by Islamist preachers, so that a fantasmatic tradition becomes their mental framework.

Another lesson to be drawn from these events concerns the degree of interconnection between inhabitants of the planet. This is quite unprecedented. A publication in a daily paper in Copenhagen provokes a riot in Nigeria a couple of days later? Who could ever have imagined it? The instantaneous broadcasting of information, with, in particular, the circulation of images on television, is turning our relationship to the world upside down, and having a profound influence on the way everyone behaves. This broadcasting occurs on a planetary scale (thanks to satellite dishes and the Internet); it comes from many different sources, it lies outside any centralized control. Al Jazeera is in competition with CNN, which means that events in Gaza today have an immediate impact on inner-city life in London and Paris. So we discover that our acts can have much more extensive consequences than we had foreseen – it is time for us to interiorize this new state of affairs. This realization is alarming: it means, for instance, that in the billion Muslims living on earth, there will always be some, fanatical or hinged, who are ready to execute anyone who appears as an enemy of their faith. The weapons will not be difficult to find. No police in the world can guarantee to all an immunity against this new threat that crosses frontiers with all the ease of a message on the Internet. We need to get used to living with the presence of this new danger. The free circulation of information paradoxically suggests a restriction of free expression.

The reserves that I have formulated on the affair of the caricatures do not in the slightest imply that one should abandon the founding principles of liberal democracy. The theological should not get mixed up with the political; the freedom and pluralism of the media must be protected; the right of women to free choice and dignity must be defended. Tolerance of other people will be exercised more easily if it is based on a firm foundation of intransigence towards everything that is intolerable. These demands extend to the international sphere: it is unacceptable for ambassadors to be attacked or the citizens of other countries to be 'sentenced to death'; all governments need to be reminded of these rules. So it is not in the least a matter of setting up a censorship or renouncing the freedom to criticize. On the other hand, we need to remember that our public actions do not take place in an abstract space, but inevitably within a historical and social context. That is why we need to take into account both juridical principles and the recognition that the immigrants living in Europe need. We can achieve this by showing our respect – not for the beliefs but for the believers, not so much for the Prophet Mohammed as for the humble immigrant workers Abdullah and Mustafa.

One final remark. The minute anyone exercises public responsibilities, it is no longer enough to justify oneself by one's own convictions and the right to express them; in addition, there is a clear need to do this as a responsible individual who takes the foreseeable consequences of his acts into account. This responsibility is not the same for everyone; it increases as the power at our disposal increases. A decisive role falls on all those who participate in the organization of the social sphere. Politicians are part of this – but even more so, perhaps, are those whose task it is to run and guide the mass media: directors and editors of television channels and radio stations, newspapers and magazines. The man in the street enjoys more freedom than the prime minister, a satirical and provocative paper such as *Charlie-Hebdo* more than an influential daily such as *Jyllands-Posten*, and the ivory towers of academia more than television channels, since responsibility limits freedom. But this rule is a matter of more or less, and there is nothing mechanical about its application; excesses happen, both in provocation and in self-censorship.

And yet one thing is certain: without their power having issued from the popular will, the media influence public opinion decisively. In order to acquire a democratic legitimacy, one path alone is open to them: that of imposing limits on themselves. Unlimited freedom kills freedom.

The Pope's speech

On 12 September 2006, Pope Benedict XVI gave a speech at the German university in Regensburg on the relations between faith and reason. Some passages in this speech, concerning the connection between Islam and violence, immediately aroused strong reactions throughout the world, especially in Muslim countries. One might have thought that the affair of the Danish caricatures was recurring, as an unleashing of violence seemed to confirm the veracity of the papal insinuations. Benedict himself seemed embarrassed at the uproar, and so addressed his regrets to all those whom his initial message seemed to have wounded. His conciliatory remarks in turn aroused the wrath of other circles – those who had approved of the original speech. This was the reaction, in particular, of the American people, if we are to believe the editorialist of the *New York Times*, David Brooks.[7]

What is the truth of the matter? The Pope's speech, 'Faith, Reason and University', has been published since[8] and everyone can read it and ponder it at leisure. The description of Islam occupies little space in it. The speech is essentially, as its title indicates, about the relations between faith and reason. The argument of Benedict XVI is this: the Christian religion has absorbed the Greek heritage of reason and, in this respect, shows the way to be followed by any religious practice in the contemporary world. As one can well imagine, this syncretistic vision of the Christian religion is an affront for two adversaries. On the one side, the defenders of pure reason, who insist on placing questions of faith outside reason. On the other side, the supporters of pure religion, who see no intrinsic relationship between religion and reason, and who, in consequence, also accept the propagation of religion by unreasonable means, such as violence and war.

This is where Islam comes in. Benedict XVI did not formulate his judgements in his own name, but contented himself with quoting two ancient authors. The first was the Byzantine Emperor Manuel II Palaeologos who, at the end of the fourteenth century, wrote a book in which he depicted himself in dialogue with a Persian scholar on

153

the relative merits of religions. 'Mohammed only ever brought bad and inhuman things, such as the right to spread by the sword the faith he preached,' he said. The Christian God, however, 'does not like blood, and not to act in accordance with reason is contrary to the nature of God'. The soul is reasonable, so we need to approach it with the means of reason – words, not weapons. The second commentator was an Arabic-Andalusian commentator of the eleventh century, Ibn Hazm, who apparently wrote that God has no relation with this world, that he is absolutely transcendent, above all category, including that of reason. So Islam is simply being cited here as the example of a religion that refuses to come to terms with reason; and even so, the Pope is not expressing his personal opinion on the matter.

Let us first ask – even if this is clearly not the point that provoked the controversy – to what extent these images of the Christian and Muslin religions correspond to reality. Serious doubts immediately arise as to the correctness of the description. Islam has been spread sometimes by war, and other times by words; some of its representatives have rejected any relation between faith and reason, while others, on the contrary, have wished to defend the solidarity between them. As all commentators on the controversy have recalled, it is difficult within this context to ignore the figure of the man known in Europe as Averroes, the twelfth-century Arab thinker whose manifesto had the title *The Decisive Discourse on the Agreement between Religion and Philosophy*. Indeed, it is thanks to Averroes and to other Muslim scholars like him that the heritage of the Greek world was transmitted to European theologians and philosophers, notably Thomas Aquinas, who in the thirteenth century formulated his own synthesis between (Aristotelian) philosophy and (Christian) religion. Benedict XVI was inspired by Thomas Aquinas, but Thomas Aquinas was not unaware of the thought of the Muslim Averroes.

Nor can it be said that Christianity has always promoted the unity of faith and reason. The Greek critics of the new religion, in the first centuries AD, rebuked it precisely for trying to keep God outside any relationship with the laws of nature and reason. In the second century, Galen wrote, 'Moses thinks that everything is possible for God, but we Greeks claim that there are things that are by nature impossible.' And Porphyry, a century later: 'God cannot do everything. He cannot make two times two equal a hundred and not four. For his power is not the sole rule of his acts and his will.' So the Greeks were criticizing the Christians precisely for what Benedict accuses the Muslims of.

154

Without going into the detail of a complex question, to which numerous volumes have been dedicated,[9] we can point out that the harmonious fusion between faith and reason among Christians is far from being self-evident. It cannot be claimed, on the basis of a single word, that Plato's *logos* is the same as St John's, or that St Paul chose to preach in Greece out of love for philosophy; what if it was merely because he had been prevented from bringing the divine word to Asia? There are many Christian authors, apart from the Protestants and modern positivists mentioned by the Pope, who have renounced reconciling God with human reason, stating that this would be to diminish him. 'I believe because it is absurd,' said Tertullian. Christianity is a religion of universal aspirations which has emphasized human love; this does not mean that the divine creation of the world, or the arrival of the Man-God, or the Immaculate Conception, or the Trinity, or transubstantiation, or the resurrection are beliefs that are founded in reason.

The relation between Christian doctrine and Greek philosophy is more complex than Benedict XVI allows, but the Pope needs to present it as harmonious in order to put forward two disputable arguments: first, among the great religions, only Christianity is intimately bound up with reason; and second, the identity of Europe stems from the encounter between the Greek tradition and the Christian tradition, with the later addition of a Roman ingredient. Now, in order to support his first argument, the Pope is obliged to play on the meaning of the word 'reason', sometimes restricting it, sometimes broadening it (the reason of scientists is judged to be too narrow, and that of other Christians too loose; it is reason in the Christian doctrine which has the correct range of meanings – and which just happens to coincide with the reason of the Greek philosophers). As far as the second argument goes, it is the Pope's idea of collective identity that is problematic: this is not fixed once and for all; it is made of encounters with the exterior and of interior conflicts; in both cases, these processes will end only with the death of the collective. The Greek and Christian ingredients are of course present in the European identity, but they are not the only ones, and, for as long as Europe lives, she will continue to absorb others.

Christ's original teaching did not glorify the promotion of the faith by war; the struggles that it announces are purely spiritual. But Christians have not always left things there. The formula in the Gospel,[10] 'Compel them to come in' (into God's house), has served as a justification for many acts of violence. One hardly feels one has any right to remind the Pope of the long centuries of history during which war, and even holy war, was considered as a perfectly legitimate, and even reasonable, means for spreading the teaching of Christ, or one version of it as against another. There are too many examples to choose from: Crusades, colonial conquests and wars of religion.

Peaceful means and warlike means are well represented in both of these two great monotheistic religions. We can even, without too much difficulty, discover in what circumstances people incline towards the peaceful or the warlike. Remember that the Emperor Manuel, so admired by the Pope, composed his dialogue at a time when his capital was under siege by the Ottoman army and the fall of his city seemed imminent. It seems as if men become reasonable when they no longer have any opportunity to impose themselves by force. If Christ's apostles did not promote the use of weapons, this was also because they knew they stood no chance against the legions of Rome; so they preferred the spoken word, and peaceful persuasion. Things became quite different in the Middle Ages. And the situation changed yet again when kings appropriated all secular power in Europe: then the Christian Church again favoured the spiritual path.

The same probably applies to Islam. The exegetes have long since shown how, while he was living in Mecca, the Prophet was peace-loving, whereas once he had settled in Medina, he called for holy war. But other events have happened since then, and the context is no longer the same. As a result, he was merely a preacher in Mecca; in Medina, assuming religious authority at the same time as political power, he became a warlord. But the Pope is wrong when he attributes a peaceful verse in the Quran, 'No constraint in religion' (II.256) to the Mecca period; on the contrary, it dates from the time in Medina, which gives it its full significance: even when you are in a position of strength, you must not impose conversion.

The Pope could have drawn his examples of violence or non-violence just as much from Christians as from Muslims. The two groups are comparable on the historical level, but not on that of ethics – for the Pope himself is a Christian. The moral demand, as is well known, is formulated only in the first person. There is merit in behaving virtuously (for example, in renouncing violence), but there is not merit in demanding that others do so. Such, after all, is one of the teachings of Christ: 'And why beholdest thou the mote that is in thy brother's eye, but considerest not the beam that is in thine own eye?'[11]

In the explanations provided in the wake of the Muslim protests, the Pope pleaded that he had spoken in good faith: he had not been expressing his own feelings; he had contented himself with quoting two old authors, one from the eleventh century, the other from the fourteenth. But this is hardly convincing: there was nothing to prevent Benedict XVI from pointing out that he disagreed with the authors he was quoting. One rather has the impression that he preferred to use this indirect method in order to protect himself, in case he was rebuked for holding this opinion (rather like Brooks who, in the column quoted above, does not give his opinion directly, but hides behind 'the way ordinary Americans view the Arab world'). The subtlety of the procedure was however overridden by the simplification proper to the media world: it was, of course, the Pope who was attributed with the opinions of these authors from the Middle Ages! Had Benedict XVI forgotten that he was not merely addressing the participants in a university seminar but that his words, abbreviated and simplified, would immediately be broadcast around the world?

It is in any case rather difficult to imagine that the Pope, quoting the Byzantine Emperor, did not envisage in advance the hostile reaction that would follow his depiction of Islam ('Mohammed brought only bad and inhuman things'). It is, of course, not to a war between civilizations that he was inciting us, but his speech, by its simplifications and omissions, contributed to the 'clash' that intransigent Muslim preachers also promote.

The Pope is right to condemn violence placed at the service of ideas, even if the latter are the most correct ideas in the world; he is also right to address this appeal to Muslims, since some of them are currently being tempted by holy war. But his argument would have been much more convincing if, instead of recalling the Muslim violence of the fourteenth century, he had started by referring to the violence perpetrated by Christians: we have renounced the violence that we used to practise, he might have said – why don't you do the same? It is true that Mohammed was a violent warrior, but he was not always one, and the supporters of other ideologies have been violent too: the statement needs to be so severely qualified that it loses its *raison d'être*. This is especially true if we remember that while, these days, Christians no longer propagate their faith by means of war, the states in which they live have not renounced the use of force to impose their ideas and the social order that they view as the best: thus in the Iraq War, justified in the name of democratic values (often expressed, it must be said, in a religious vocabulary).

So we can feel some doubt as to the correctness and usefulness of the papal intervention. Should we, for all that, judge as legitimate the reaction that it aroused in certain Muslim countries? Yet again we heard the preachers, those professional agitators and manipulators, uttering threats, provoking physical violence, and calling for holy war. It was exactly as if they were seeking to defend by violence the idea that Islam is not intrinsically violent! In their turn, they see only the wrongs committed by others and avoid asking themselves about their own failings. They prefer to drape themselves in the role of the victim to legitimate the violence that they themselves inflict on others. Admittedly, an appeal to violence is present in other great religions too, and not just in Islam; but these days, Islam alone is invoked as a religious justification for acts of murder. If this is (as I believe) an abuse of the religion, it is the responsibility of Muslims themselves to condemn it and prevent it from happening in the future.

However, it should be pointed out that another reaction has also arisen in the Muslim world. This took the form of an open letter to the Pope, signed by thirty-eight ulemas (or Islamic theologians) from several Asian, African and European countries. Written in a tone of polite deference, the letter highlights the numerous historical mistakes in the Regensburg speech, tries to present a much more peaceful image of Islam (is not the most frequent attribute of God 'the Merciful'?) and promotes a 'frank and sincere dialogue'. However, it is to be regretted that, in their letter, the ulemas do not explain how we are to reconcile these peaceful verses in the Quran with other verses that preach conversion by force or even murder in case of a refusal (they do not mention these latter). It is even more unfortunate that they do not address their words with at least as much, if not more, insistence to those who daily trample on their interpretation of Islam – the Islamists, those 'agitators,' as Abdelwahab Meddeb puts it, 'who have changed a tradition open to the experience of the Absolute and the Invisible into a bloody ideology that gathers together all the excluded and frustrated people of the world'.[12]

The Pope's speech was a clumsy mistake, perhaps even quite the wrong thing to do, but the reactions that it aroused crossed the boundary into the criminal. The speech does not excuse the reactions, even if it shows, yet again, that a peremptory declaration that the others are irrational and violent is not the best means of bringing them round to a little more reason and a little less violence.

By way of Islam

It is possible to find a common terrain for those who, in Europe or elsewhere, wish to establish a constructive exchange between Muslims and non-Muslims. All that is needed is to accept two postulates, which in Europe belong to the heritage of the Enlightenment. The first is juridical and political in nature. It presupposes that human societies are governed with the aid of laws established by their citizens and that, in public life, the latter are more important than any other constraint. This is the very principle of democracy, or the sovereignty of the people (disputed by Sayyid Qutb and the Islamists in the name of the 'sovereignty of God'), the corollary of which is the recognition of an equal dignity between all those who comprise the people, consequently their equality before the law, whether they be men or women, black or white, of this religion or that. In such a state of law, it is forbidden to carry out justice for oneself: no attenuating circumstance can be recognized for 'crimes of honour', or for acts of violence committed for religious reasons. By the force of this same argument, nobody has a right to impose a type of behaviour on the inhabitants of other countries: Khomeini's *fatwa* 'sentencing' a British citizen to death itself flouts the code of the nations. So this principle consecrates the separation of the political and the religious.

The second postulate is anthropological in nature. It affirms the diversity of human societies and cultures, even when all men and women belong to the same species and share in one common humanity. This plurality is deployed in both time and space. This means that we need to accept a historical view of the past and take account of the transformation of mentalities. Anthropology and the study of cultures complement the contribution made by history: they show us that the peoples of the earth organize their existence in many different ways, each of them cherishing their own religion, customs and practices. Since this is the truth of our species, the society that gives a favourable welcome to this plurality enjoys an advantage over the others. Not by chance did the golden age of Muslim culture also correspond to a period of maximum openness to other cultures: Greek and Roman, Persian and Indian, Jewish and Christian. Persecuting the followers of another religion, whether they be 'People of the Book' (monotheists) or pagans, or condemning the apostates who change religion, or atheists, amounts to a failure to acknowledge this constitutive characteristic of humanity.

In order to accept these two postulates, that must come before any dialogue that would not be a mere exchange of polite meaningless words, there is no need at all for Muslims to renounce Islam. This is, first and foremost, because the fact of being a believer does not imply that your other identities need to disappear and that you cease thereby to be the citizen of a country, and to respect its laws.

159

Unlike what fundamentalists claim, religion has never governed the whole of existence. And unlike what the media experts on Islam who have newly sprung up in the West proclaim, Muslims are not an exceptional species in the human race, whose least little move is dictated by their religious affiliation, thus their religion, to the exclusion of any other determining factor. Quite unlike what people of different persuasions believe, moral and religious norms, when they exist, do not mechanically engender acts. 'A religious dogma never has a direct effect in politics,' as Olivier Roy has judiciously remarked.[13] Like all other human beings, Muslims model their behaviour under the pressure of a host of factors – including principles drawn from religion. Throughout history, the citizens of Muslim countries have, like everyone, obeyed the – very diverse – laws of the countries they lived in.

So, to begin with, we need to stop thinking that the Quran provides anyone with the sole key to explaining the behaviour of today's Muslims. This obviously does not stop us asking what the message of Islam's founding texts actually is. But the answer to this question is far from being simple. Like every text that lies at the origin of a world religion, the Quran and other sacred Islamic texts contain statements that lead in different directions, or lend themselves to several interpretations. Many different exegetical schools have been confronting each other on this ground for centuries: there is no single Islamic doctrine – any more than there is one single version of Christianity – but rather a plurality of traditions. It is certainly not for someone who, like myself, is unversed in this domain to formulate an authorized opinion on the matter; at best I can merely summarize the impressions I have drawn from my reading.

I am probably not going to raise many objections if I set out from this initial basis: among the Quran's readers today, there are two major opposed tendencies. The first is the fundamentalists, who would like the literal meaning of the texts to be established as true and correct for all eternity; so they refuse to see that these texts appeared at a certain period from which they have preserved many traces. Consequently, engaged as they are in their own Counter-Reformation, they aspire to subject the way live people now to the principles of bygone days. These fundamentalist exegetes, whether they are conservatives or reformers, should obviously not be confused with the Islamists, whose programme is properly political. The second tendency is the liberal current of interpretation, open to modernity, and more generally to the passing of time, and so to the plurality and mobility of human societies. Within this perspective, the Quran and other sacred texts contain formulae whose meaning appears only in relation to the historical context of the period; consequently, in a different context, this meaning needs to be reformulated.

Various specialists in Islam have shown how it is possible to read the Quran while taking into account the circumstances of its creation. In his work *Islam and Liberty*, Mohamed Charfi has presented a synthesis of their arguments and an apologia for modern Islam. He reminds us of the state of the society that preceded Islam, and this helps to understand the general spirit of the Quranic innovations, such as that concerning inheritance. Sometimes you simply need to read what is written, and read it properly. Thus the unity of the theological and the political, demanded by Islamists but also severely criticized by a considerable number of Orientalists, is not affirmed by the Quran. One of the first representatives of this liberal current of interpretation, the Egyptian Ali Abderraziq (1888–1966), has launched a debate on this subject – a debate that is still going on today. In his book *L'Islam et les Fondements du pouvoir* (*Islam and the Foundations of Power*) (1925), he starts out from the statement, a recurrent one in the Quran, that the revelation brought down by the text is complete and leaves nothing unsaid; but it never mentions a caliphate or any kind of Islamic state. The subsequent state structures have no basis in religious doctrine, but are the work of governments pursuing their own interests. 'What is called a throne is set in place only on men's heads, and it is maintained only by weighing down on their backs.'[14] The difference between final aims explains this separation: the (Muslim) religion is universal; the state is inevitably particular. If the caliphs, or modern heads of state, base their claims on Islam, this is because they are seeking the advantages of divine legitimacy: we have here an example of the subjection of the religious to the political, rather than of the converse. Religion is a facade, not the reality of these regimes.

Charfi goes on to quote several verses of the Quran that can be read in this sense, such as these injunctions addressed to Mohammed by God: 'Your mission is not to force them into the faith' (L.45). 'You are here merely to remind them of the word of God. You have no authority to enforce over them' (LXXXVIII.21–2). This is easy to understand: the society contemporary with Mohammed did not have any state – just a religious community of the faithful. It is the Imam Khomeini and other Islamists who are imposing an anachronistic and, it might be said, heretical reading of the sacred texts, treating the Quran as if it were the Constitution of a modern state. The entire history of Muslim states illustrates how Islam has been turned into

161

a mere instrument by heads of state pursuing their own aims before all else, whether they be hereditary monarchs or dictators. Another symptom of the way that the political and the religious remain distinct is provided by the attitude of present-day parties of Islamic allegiance, placed in front of a radical choice: either they preach the fusion of the two, but thereby condemn themselves to remaining marginal (as in Pakistan, where religious parties have never gained more than 10 per cent of the popular vote), or else they gain power, but at a heavy cost: they have to give up the desire to Islamize the law and the institutions of the state (as in Turkey).

Not only did the Prophet Mohammed require the separation of the political and the religious: he accepted the plurality of peoples and the distinction between what is just (in the human here-and-now) and what is in conformity with the faith (in our relations with God). Justice consists not in spreading Islam, but in not mistreating others, even if they are non-Muslims. 'God does not forbid you to be good and just towards those who respect your religion and do not chase you away from their hearths' (LX.8). Peaceful coexistence is perfectly acceptable, and even recommended. 'Do not commit an injustice by attacking first, since God does not love the unjust' (II.186).

Interpreting the text of the Quran beyond the literal sense of the words, it is sometimes necessary merely to bear in mind an element of the context. Thus the time of day at which one's fast is to be broken was decided in accordance with the geographical conditions of Arabia. 'But what are we to do about the inhabitants of the polar regions where the days are sometimes interminable?' Charfi innocently wonders.[15] It goes without saying that the prescription needs to be adapted to the circumstances; actually, this adaptation is demanded by a great number of precepts. On other occasions, the texts contradict each other. The fundamentalist school suggests deciding on these cases without taking any account of the meaning but resorting to chronology alone: the later suras are deemed to abrogate the more ancient ones. Now, as we have seen, the Prophet was peaceloving in the first years of his preaching, and became a warrior in the last part of his life. So the fundamentalists choose to stick to the military interpretation of his teaching. Charfi recalls and defends the different suggestion of a Sudanese specialist of Islam, Mahmoud Mohammed Taha: a more universal recommendation is deemed to be more important than a less universalist one, since the ultimate horizon of Islam is humanity as a whole.[16] In this case, it is the peaceloving suras which win the day, since only peace has a universal allure.

162

Taha is the martyr of the liberal school of interpretation: this co-founder of the 'Republican Brothers' was accused of apostasy for his conceptions. Having refused to abjure them, he was hanged in 1985, at the age of seventy-five. So the spirit of this interpretative school is at once more historical and more universal than that of the fundamentalists – a conjunction that brings him close to the spirit of the Enlightenment, affirming simultaneously the plurality of cultures and the unitary nature of civilization.

It is not necessary to abjure Islam to enter modernity, accept democracy and enjoy a fruitful exchange with people who are different from you. Being a believer does not stop you carrying out your duties as a citizen. But it is also possible to abandon fundamentalist literalism in the reading of the sacred texts, as Abderraziq, Taha and so many contemporary authors originally brought up in Muslim culture require. In its turn, the struggle against the ideological bases of Islamism can be led on the basis of a non-dogmatic reading of Islam itself. There is no need to force the meaning of the tradition; it simply needs to be taken on in all its breadth and depth. This choice is the one to be preferred, in every way: this is a much more promising way of fighting the extremists than any amalgam between Islamism and Islam. To bear real fruits, it must be defended – more than is currently the case – by the intellectual, spiritual and political elites of countries with Muslim majorities, in preference to Western personalities. It is time for us to hear the voice of the silent and peaceful majority in those countries more clearly, rather than the calls for war and intolerance issued by Islamist agitators. If television channels such as Al Jazeera called on the services of preachers open to the contemporary world and to dialogue with those who are different from them, they would contribute greatly to the favourable evolution of the parts of the world to which they are addressed.

Evolution towards a liberal Islam can be brought about only by Muslims themselves, and cannot be imposed on them from without: the identity – positive this time – of the person bringing the message is an essential factor in the way it is to be received. In France, rivalry and conflict with Germany have lasted for hundreds of years, leading to repeated wars and countless sufferings; it was easy to imagine that the hatred would never be extinguished. And yet it has been overcome, thanks to the identity of the man who assumed the message of reconciliation, General de Gaulle. The same message, defended at the time by a former collaborator or merely by someone who had shirked his duties would have been indignantly rejected; coming as it did from the great war hero, from the man who from the very first day had said 'no' and had more reasons than anyone to keep up his grudge with the old enemies, this message, taken up by other ex-combatants, members of the resistance, and deportees could hardly be ignored. The result, inconceivable a generation earlier, was the establishment of an exemplary understanding between the two peoples; and yet nationalist passions arouse a fervour hardly less intense than religious piety. So, analogously, those whose faith cannot be doubted have the best chance of leading Islam towards its reconciliation with the modern world.

Such an evolution of Islamic doctrine is desirable; however, nobody should see in it a necessary condition for the transformation of Muslim countries. The real source of tension does not reside in the dead ends of theological exegesis, but in the sense of frustration and humiliation felt in many places by the population. The remedy for this lies neither in religion nor in culture, but in politics – and this implies that these countries can manage to negotiate their entry into modernity. In reality, this modernity is not, these days, to be confused with the European and North American West, and Muslim countries doubtless have an interest in emerging from this painful tête-à-tête with their brother-enemy, one who arouses their wrath even more in that he possesses the good things that they desire. Japan, certain countries in South East Asia, India or Brazil now offer other ways of gaining access to a more prosperous and more democratic existence. China and Russia are committing themselves with rather more difficulty to the path of political reform, but they too escape the grip of resentment and are increasing the wealth of their populations.

The states with majority Muslim populations might draw inspiration from these other models and thus leave behind what René Girard calls 'mimetic rivalry'. But this would entail the leaders of the wealthy countries of this part of the world making better use of the immense revenue brought in by the natural resources that they possess, such as gas and petrol. Rather than investing them into the sole defence and promotion of Islam, and thus of their traditional cultural identity, they should be encouraging high-quality education, both in the natural sciences and in the social sciences, an education open to all – men or women, believers or non-believers. If they desire the well-being of their people, they should make it possible for them to learn more about other cultures, and thus more foreign languages, with many translations both scientific and literary, and frequent travels and periods spent abroad. We are far from this situation at present.

Becoming aware of this multipolar world that is now coming into being would also enable people to stop attributing all their difficulties to the wrongs committed by the West in the past or the present, and to turn a critical gaze on oneself. As Charfi writes, 'It is so much easier to accuse other people, to make others bear the weight of responsibility, especially when they are indeed not actually innocent.'[17] But it would be much better not to take this easy way out. Rather than focusing entirely on the external causes of a deplorable situation, over which, most of the time, we have no control – vocal protests against injustice have never dinted the egocentrism of the powerful – we need to attack the internal factors of the malaise in every society, which bear a no less great responsibility: blatant social inequalities, lack of education, absence of a free press, the failure of any opposing powers, police states, and embezzlement from the state by those who are deemed to be serving it. The blame needs to be laid first and foremost at the feet of the cynical and corrupt political leaders who busy themselves increasing their personal wealth while preaching virtue to others, and who manipulate the perplexed masses by getting them to think that everything is the fault of the West.

The humiliation that nurses the resentment of these Muslim populations stems from more than one source. It is not merely the presence on their soil of foreign armies which lies behind this humiliation, or other strong-armed interventions; it is also the necessity of living in a world formed, materially and conceptually, by experiences that are not their own. Western countries can withdraw their armies from Muslim countries or conduct a more equitable policy towards all the states in that region. But it is the responsibility of the Muslim population itself to emerge from the confusion between modernity and the West, to give a serene welcome to democratic values while ceasing to interpret them as the sign of an allegiance to Western countries, on the pretext that its values were born in the West: the origin of a practice is not to be confused with its meaning.

In a passage of his book *Aveuglantes Lumières*, Régis Debray describes a journey that took him to Cairo, on the occasion of an encounter that was meant to favour 'dialogue between civilizations'. He points out, regretfully, that everyone present had preferred the warmth and comfort of their own convictions, and expressed amazement at the mistaken opinions of everyone else. 'Each side strikes camp on its certainties, and demands that the other bows down before them.' People thus grow drunk on their own virtue and reassure themselves as to the potential danger represented by their enemy. 'There is day (us) and night (them). Who would be so bold as to seek for lice in the hair of the Crusaders for Good?' Furthermore, Debray notes how, since he himself cannot fully recognize himself in any cut-and-dried opinion, he shifts his position depending on the people he is talking to. 'Faced with imams, I charge headlong, change into a wild-eyed Voltairean, am reborn as a fighter for free thought. In Paris, faced with my own kind, whose certainties irritate me, I immediately do a volte-face.' Or, seeing himself through the eyes of others: 'A muddle-headed Orientalist, eager to please, dropping my pants to the ulemas in the eyes of the orthodox reader of the *Nouvel Obs*, I find that in the eyes of the Orthodox Sunni Muslim of Cairo I am an arrogant and obstinate westerner.'[18]

Abandoning the role of a knight in shining armour does not mean that you have to hold all opinions as equivalent. You may have severe reservations about the film by Van Gogh and Hirsi Ali, or about the actions of the Danish newspaper; but there is no doubt that murder and collective violence are much more serious acts. However, we have nothing to gain by presenting 'others' as enemies and meetings with them as acts in a war; representation always has an effect on what it represents, and we then risk reinforcing the ill that we wished to fight against.

So that integration into a single whole can be easily accomplished, we need to recognize that all the different members of society have the same dignity. Feeling respected in what you consider as your collective identity leads to opening up to others, not to defensive withdrawal among one's own kind. The educational principle at stake here is well known: a child progresses more quickly if he is encouraged rather than told off; adults are not very different in this respect. It is not enough to denounce discrimination with regard to the law and official norms, whether in the quest for a job or for accommodation; we also need to take positive measures to encourage people. For this reason, it is extremely useful to see in the political world and the media the faces and names of minorities in the country, since those two spheres of activity are exposed to the gaze of all.

It is possible to imagine such symbolic measures: they may help to highlight that dignity equal to all, in the most diverse domains of social life. It would not be scandalous, for instance, in a secular country such as France, where we have six holidays linked to Catholic countries (Easter, Ascension, Pentecost, Assumption, All Saints, Christmas), if there were one linked to the country's second religion, Islam; there is nothing shocking in the rules of common life taking the changing nature of the population into consideration. Nor in suggesting that Arabic be more widely taught in schools, not to keep the children whose parents speak it trapped in this one language, but to make it a language like others. If women really request it, why not set apart non-mixed times in local swimming pools? The promiscuity of the naked bodies of both sexes is admittedly a characteristic of contemporary Western culture, but it is not an intangible consequence of democratic principles. This does not mean that we need to change the laws, but nor is it enough to say that everyone can do as he pleases in his own private sphere: between the legal and the personal, there is a third zone, that of social life, governed by norms adopted by consensus rather than under constraint. So we need to discuss the problems that arise on a case-by-case basis.

— 5 —

European Identity

He knew only too well of those crimes committed in Europe, whose obscenity, whose odious pornography had for the first time, in 1945, enlightened the world as to what was a mere lie, and crudely demonstrated the implacable duality, the total separation so cunningly concealed through the centuries, between Europe and the very fine story it told about itself.

Romain Gary, *Europa*

Today the European Union constitutes a reality that is as much economical as it is juridical and administrative. And yet we all know that, at present, this group of nations does not play a major role in the world stage and that most of its political life is reserved to the countries that comprise it. Several voices have already expressed their disappointment at seeing how European politicians are happy to ponder the lifting of customs barriers and the consequences thereof, or to debate the various bureaucratic rules and regulations, but have lost sight of the European project itself. So they have wondered if the Union's political activity might not receive an added boost from a highlighting and reinforcement of its cultural (or 'civilizational') identity, with culture becoming the third pillar in the European construction, next to economy and juridico-political institutions. They also hope to find rather more soul – a spiritual and affective dimension that is missing elsewhere. This task is imagined to be easy, since it is known that, these days, it is easier to reach a consensus in Europe on its great cultural monuments than around administrative regulations or economic decisions. All Europeans are proud to belong to a part of the world which has given birth to Montaigne and Michelangelo, Shakespeare and Cervantes, Mozart and Goethe, or indeed to the social and political principles now known by the expression 'human rights'. (We have seen, too, in the case of Oriana Fallaci, that this pride could verge on caricature.)

It is easy to understand the reasons for such an appeal: the sense of a common identity would strengthen the European project. Using the vocabulary of the eighteenth century, one might say that a political idea increases its efficaciousness if it is borne not merely by common interests, but also by shared passions; but passions are unleashed only if we feel that our very identities have been affected. So, to begin with, we should specify the content of this identity: here we come up against the question of the plurality of cultures and of the forms of their coexistence.

In search of an identity

There has been no lack of attempts in the past to make Europe's spiritual and cultural dimension explicit. Thus, in the wake of the First World War, the poet and essayist Paul Valéry had suggested an interpretation of this identity that caused something of a stir. I call 'European' – Valéry basically said – the peoples who in the course of their history have undergone three great influences, which can be symbolized by the names Rome, Jerusalem and Athens. From Rome comes the Empire, with organized state power, law and institutions, and the status of citizen. From Jerusalem, or rather from Christianity, Europeans have inherited subjective ethics, the examination of their own consciences, and universal justice. Finally, Athens has bequeathed to them a taste for knowledge and rational argument, the idea of harmony, and the idea of man as the measure of all things. Whoever can lay claim to this triple inheritance, Valéry concluded, can rightly be deemed a European.[1]

Valéry's interpretation, which has the advantage of elegance rather than of originality, has given rise to various comments. One of them was the work of an ardent European, the Swiss intellectual Denis de Rougemont. In several writings dating in particular from the 1950s and 1960s, he promoted the European cause, and in turn asked himself about European identity. His suggestions for improving Valéry's definition are of two kinds. On the one hand, the heritages identified by Valéry are richer and more complex than the latter said. Rougemont especially draws our attention to two additional consequences of the Christian doctrine. This breaks with the cyclical conception of time, which predominates in most pagan cultures, and

169

replaces it with an idea of irreversible time, thereby giving birth to the notions of history and progress. In tandem with this, Christianity cultivates an interest in material reality – another characteristic of the Western world. Unlike Judaism, Christianity is a religion of incarnation; God has become man. This means that the world of the here-and-now is not considered as cursed, and deserves to be known. This historical particularity allows us to understand why, several centuries later, men were able to scrutinize the world around them with close attention, turning it into an object of analysis and scientific knowledge.

On the other hand, Rougemont reminds us that these three sources of influence were not the only ones to mark the continent's history. Europeans took their doctrines of good and evil from the Persian tradition; their idea of love from Arab poets; their mysticism from the Celtic peoples who inhabited the continent at the same time as the Greeks and Romans.

It would be easy to follow Rougemont's path and add new elements to the portrait sketched by Valéry. We would need to insist especially on the contributions of the modern period, which seem no less essential for the cultural identity of Europe. The age of the Enlightenment, which synthesized and systematized the thought of the previous centuries, would here occupy a major place. One of its contributions would be the idea of autonomy, which means that every human is able to know the world by himself and to influence his own destiny. Just as the people are sovereign within a democracy, the individual can become so, to a degree, within his personal sphere; as a result, the very idea of democracy is transformed, since it simultaneously guarantees the power of the people and the freedom of the individual, including his freedom from that power. The eighteenth century also witnessed the advent of humanism, in other words the choice that consists in making man into the final aim of human action. The aim of human existence on earth is no longer to seek the salvation of his soul in the beyond, but to attain happiness here below. The acknowledgement of a legitimate plurality, whether it be that of religions, cultures or indeed powers within a state, is also part of the legacy which the Enlightenment has bequeathed the history of humanity: pluralism becomes a value within itself. For all these reasons, the names of Athens, Rome and Jerusalem, invoked to symbolize the European identity, need to be supplemented by those of London and Paris, Amsterdam and Geneva, Berlin and Vienna, Milan and Venice.

Having come so far, we may however feel some doubt at such a benevolent, indeed euphoric interpretation of European identity. Let us bear in mind, to begin with, that a culture cannot be reduced to the works created within it, but that it also includes the set of collective modes of life. And from this point of view, what is individual to the cultures of the different countries and regions that make up Europe is of more significance than what they have in common. The first ingredient in the culture of a group is language – and there is more than one language in Europe! This plurality is not without meaning: every human being comes into the world in a particular country, not in some uniform environment. Brought up in the ideal of modernity, which consists of thinking of ourselves as free subjects, we do not like to recognize the extent to which we are governed by this tradition – but that does not stop it existing.

The difference between languages is not the only one. These days, most European cities are one or two hours away from each other by plane, and you can get from Paris to Milan in a morning; however, every time I travel to a country near France, I am struck more than anything by its singularities: you enter a different linguistic universe, and at the same time you discover ways of moving about, of organizing time and space, in short of living, that are proper to each country. Italians live in the street in a way different from the French, who in turn are quite different from the Germans, and so on. Traditions are more enduring than people are prepared to say, and the impermeability of languages contributes to this.

The collective memory that a country builds up for itself does not coincide with that of its neighbour, even when it involves one and the same event. In this respect, the memory of the Second World War constitutes the exception rather than the rule, since the German survivors have basically espoused the point of view of their vanquishers. Other conflicts, in which the rights and wrongs are not shared out so clearly, on the other hand, created irreconcilable interpretations. If people in Europe are unanimous in condemning Hitler, this unanimity vanishes if you talk about Napoleon, a hero for some and a tyrant for others. Two hundred years after the events, the Battle of Waterloo is not commemorated in the same way in Paris as it is in London; nearer our day, Communism cannot be judged in the same way by those who lived in the countries where it was in power and those who could only imagine it from afar.

The great works that we love to identify, these days, as constitutive of European culture were born within particular traditions. It is true they quickly became known beyond the frontiers of their countries of origin, but this influence did not stop at Europe. And reciprocally, right from the start, European creators absorbed traditions from far horizons: Egypt and Persia, India and China. Today, European cultural characteristics are found far away from Europe; non-European inventions have spread throughout Europe too. For example, it is sometimes said that the novel is a specifically European genre – which no doubt corresponds to a situation in the past, but not in the present: how can we imagine the novel these days, without thinking of its Russian representatives, or those from Latin America or North America or, more recently, Asia and Africa? The same goes for painting, philosophy, religion and every other ingredient of culture: what was born in Europe returns, transformed by its sojourn elsewhere, and at the same time Europe hastily absorbs foreign influences, from African masks to Chinese calligraphy, from Buddhist traditions to the magical realism of the Caribbean. It could not be any other way: the works of the mind have a universal vocation, everything is grist to their mill and they seek to travel everywhere; born within a particular tradition, they aspire to be received by all.

The plurality of national and regional traditions is one of the reasons why European identity lacks coherence; another comes from the very length of the history of the countries in this part of the world. The characteristics noted by Valéry, Rougemont and others do of course exist, but other, more negative traits could also be identified. The idea of equality between all human beings comes to us from European history, and yet the idea of slavery is far from foreign to it. Religious proselytism and secularity belong to it equally, just as do the revolutionary spirit and conservatism. Tolerance is European, but fanaticism and wars of religion are no less so. Respect for the autonomy of each person is a European acquisition, and yet much more visible conquests (the subjection of foreign peoples to the will of the strongest, and imperialism itself), belong equally to the European inheritance. Liberalism is part of the European tradition, just as Communism is. Actually, those voices clamouring for Europe to repent of its shameful past of slavery and colonialism are these days more numerous than those which simply trumpet out its fame.

Maybe in Europe each doctrine has also given rise to its opposite, since one of the characteristics of the European tradition is precisely the exercise of critical thought: here all values can be subjected to examination. This characteristic may be a source of pride, but it does not make it any easier to identify what is essentially European. If we choose from the past only what suits the present, we are indulging in a highly selective reading of the past and betraying real history by replacing it with a pious history in conformity with the demands of the 'politically correct' of our age.

The over-partial character of this reading of history, reduced to the collecting of brownie points, is not the only thing for which we can criticize the image I mentioned at the start. The very idea of founding European identity exclusively on the history of this continent could be put in question. Can collective identity be reduced to mere fidelity to the past? There is not – as we have seen – any immutable collective identity, fixed once and for all. Those who claim the opposite are habitually involved in a precise political project: they wish to give a substantial content to our identity in order to legitimate the exclusion of all those who do not share it. This strategy is adopted, these days, by extreme European right-wing parties. They are fervent nationalists on the institutional level (they are fiercely opposed to any strengthening of the European Union), and yet they discover that they are pro-European on the level of culture, which they define as a pure heritage of the past. For them, saying that Europe is Christian becomes yet one more argument for forbidding this territory to Muslims. They are even happy to appropriate the thought of the Enlightenment, which they understand as a mere rejection of faith: this is a new means for excluding believing Muslims, since other religions do not these days arouse so much devotion.

By choosing, from Europe's rich past, the characteristics that suit them best, and refusing to see the necessarily shifting nature of cultures, all those who identify its stable and substantial kernel are in reality projecting on to the past a judgement anchored in the present, and reiterating their contemporary ideal by seeking prefigurations of it in times gone by. But if it is the present ideal that is leading people to read the past selectively, why should they take the trouble of looking backwards? Why not content themselves with frankly affirming their current vision of the world? Probably because they then confuse European culture (which is particular) with moral and political values that, as we have also seen, have a universal vocation. The same goes as much for the idea of democracy and human rights as for scientific and technical rationality, which today is the prerogative of the whole of humanity.

So on the one side, that of cultures and works of art, national or regional traditions are more important than the European tradition, and diversity more than unity. The idea of constituting a European cultural canon, common and immutable, is indefensible. In addition, the European Union does not have any ambition to eradicate the specific nature of the states that comprise it, neither on the economic and social level, nor on that of juridical and administrative structures: its project is not to form a European state, or a European people, but to unite those which already exist. On the other side, that of values, this tradition dissolves into universality. The very quest for an irreducible kernel turns out to be problematic. So are we condemned to abandoning the idea of a European identity?

Plurality as the basis of unity

My hypothesis will be as follows: the unity of European culture resides in the way it manages the different regional, national, religious and cultural identities that constitute it, granting them a new status and benefiting from this very plurality. The spiritual identity of Europe does not lead to the eradication of particular cultures and local memories. It consists, not in a list of proper names or a repertoire of general ideas, but in the adopting of the same attitude towards diversity.

It was in the period of the Enlightenment, as I have just mentioned, that plurality, in Europe, started to be systematically perceived as a value. In his *Persian Letters* (1721), Montesquieu's evaluation of plurality is positive, in that he pleads for religious tolerance. Not only is unity not something to be aspired to, but plurality is to be encouraged, since in turn it stimulates competition. The faithful of a minority religion, 'kept far from all honours', are all the more inclined to work hard and thus contribute to the general well-being. The zeal shown by each of them to prove that they are the best is spurred on by the multiplicity of groups. Civil wars are the product not of this plurality, but of the intolerance of the dominant group. In short, it seems 'a good thing for a state to have several religions'.[2] A few years later, in his *Philosophical Letters*, Voltaire fully shared this viewpoint. 'Were there only one religion in England, despotism would be a threat; were there two, they would be at each other's throats; but there are thirty, and they live happily and at peace with one another.' He extends his judgement to other nations, comparing English, French and Italians. 'I do not know which of the three countries deserves the greatest honour; but happy the one who knows how to recognize the merits of each!'[3]

The idea of plurality was most clearly associated with the idea of Europe by the Scottish philosopher David Hume in an essay entitled 'On the Rise and Progress in Arts and Sciences', published in 1742. Before Hume, those who pondered the existence of a European

174

identity sought it in one common characteristic: the heritage of the Roman Empire or the Christian religion. Hume was apparently the first thinker to locate it less in a characteristic shared by all than in the plurality of countries forming Europe. From time immemorial, human groups have sought to ensure their internal cohesion, and thus their cultural unity, since this gives them strength and enables them better to fight their enemies. For the first time in history, the old adage can be replaced by its opposite: here it is division that is strength!

Hume's aim in this essay is to explain what appears to him as a remarkable cultural development, that of the Europe of his time. So he investigates the conditions that have made it possible and identifies one of them as the existence of 'a number of neighbouring and independent states, connected together by commerce and polity'.[4] The states forming Europe have a number of characteristics in common, as well as economic and social bonds, but at the same time they are sufficiently similar in size and power for none of them to be able to subject the others: each of them remains independent. It is this balance between unity and plurality that thus becomes the characteristic of Europe.

The advantage of plurality resides in the way it favours everyone's freedom to think and judge. Anyone who knows only the norms of his own country is impelled to submit to them; when someone has the opportunity to compare between several norms, it is easier for him to distinguish prejudice or fashion from what is right and true. The jealousy between states drives each of them to perform better than its neighbour and to exercise a critical spirit at the same time. Descartes was subjected to a close investigation outside France, and Newton outside England. How has Europe preserved this plurality of states, all comparable in power, on its territory? Hume saw the explanation, as did Montesquieu in the same period, in the continent's geographical conditions. 'If we consider the face of the globe, EUROPE, of all the four parts of the world, is the most broken by seas, rivers, and mountains.'[5]

In support of his view, Hume cites one parallel example and two counter-examples. The first is ancient Greece. As in Europe, this country had a common framework for all city-states, formed by 'the ties of the same language and interests'. At the same time, thanks to comparable geographical conditions, every city-state maintained a high degree of autonomy and refused to recognize the supremacy of the others. 'Their contention and debates sharpened the wits of men.' The first counter-example is Europe itself, at the time when it was

175

dominated by the Catholic religion alone: this uniformity had entailed the 'utter depravation of every kind of learning', from which the continent was able to emerge only thanks to the divisions between Catholic and Orthodox to begin with, then Catholics and Protestants, and finally Christians and free thinkers. So Europe has become the same kind of land of pluralism as Greece was in the past – which is why both of them managed to cultivate freedom and learning. Hume's second counter-example is China, which witnessed the blossoming of a brilliant culture, only to see its evolution come to a halt at a particular moment. Hume explains this by the absence of inner plurality: 'CHINA is one vast empire, speaking one language, governed by one law, and sympathizing in the same manners'[6] – which has made it easier for its rulers, as well as public opinion, to become tyrants.

Modern historians are not far from granting that Hume is correct on this point. In his book *The European Miracle*, E. L. Jones in turn concludes that one of the main conditions of this 'miracle' (the process of industrialization at the start of the nineteenth century) was the right balance between plurality and unity. 'Limited diversity [...] gave Europeans some togetherness and some freedom of thought. This was a better result than religious totalitarianism or an infinity of splintering.' On the one side, then, there is a common heritage and a certain awareness of the way our neighbours behave, which mean that, in the terms of Edmund Burke in the eighteenth century, 'no European can feel himself a complete exile in any country of the continent'.[7] In spite of their great linguistic diversity, Europeans have also had common languages at their disposal: for many centuries it was Latin, in the modern period it was French, and these days it is English. The result is that a novelty introduced into one of the European countries rapidly spreads to all the others.

At the same time, the existence of several states of comparable size prevents any empire or centralized power from being set up. This division is explained, yet again, by the geographical conditions of the continent and the way its fertile lands are scattered piecemeal across it. It can occasionally be a brake on development, but in general it creates more advantages than disadvantages. Remember how Christopher Columbus managed to set off on his inaugural journey: this man from Genoa was turned away by a first prince (in Portugal), and made his way to a second (the King of England), then a third (the King of France) and a fourth (in Spain), before finding in Queen Isabella of Castille a suitable patron for his expeditions. If Europe had been a unified empire, the refusal of the first prince and sole prince would have spelled the end of his plans. Likewise, Galileo was obliged to stop his research because of the persecutions of the Catholic Church, but their results were immediately taken over and developed in Protestant countries. If the same religion had held sway everywhere, scientific inquiry would have stopped. The censorship imposed in one country can be evaded by publication in a neighbouring country: the leaders, temporal or spiritual, are fortunately never in agreement between themselves.

For centuries, Europeans have been led to coordinate and adapt between themselves ideologies of different origin. Greek thought reached them via Roman civilization, a process that already involved a labour of reinterpretation. Christianity, for its part, was grafted on to a previous religion, Judaism, which it took over and hijacked for its own use. We are back with Valéry's intuition, but without reducing European identity to this or that heritage: it is their very plurality that is revelatory. When, during the Renaissance, an increasing number of attempts were made to amalgamate and harmonize these two great trends (which were already hybrids: Greco-Roman and Judeo-Christian), yet another activity of conversion and conceptual adaptation took place, one that could not, however, conceal the multiplicity of origins. Furthermore, next to these two great trends, many other sources continued to nourish the continent's cultural identity. Thanks to this labour of absorption, Europeans became able to adapt rapidly to changing circumstances. The advantage they drew from this was clearly revealed when they made contact with the native populations of America: much more quickly than their adversaries, they understood the way the others' society was organized, as well as their mental universe, and this allowed them to complete their planned conquest and colonization.

This inner plurality goes with the openness to external influences. Europe has always borrowed an enormous number of things from its neighbours (as well as giving them others). As for the contributions of those populations that lived in the southern shores of the Mediterranean, we can hardly speak of 'external' influences. The lands of North Africa were part of the Roman Empire, and the Berbers living there provided the latter with several emperors and, later, with several Fathers of the Church. In the Spain occupied by the Moors, a tolerant Muslim civilization flourished, and through this intermediary a good part of the classical Greek inheritance passed. From the fourteenth century onwards, the Turks occupied the south-east of Europe and started to interact with their neighbours; they conquered Byzantium, but also absorbed its heritage.

At the same time, Muslim countries became the obligatory stop-ping-off point for more distant influences, Indian and Chinese; on their side, the Crusades enabled Europe to benefit from the progress made by an East that was more literate than the West. What Francis Bacon, at the start of the seventeenth century, called the three great-est inventions known to men – the compass, gunpowder and printing – all had their origin in China. Paper also came to Europe from China, thanks to the existence of Arab channels of communication. But Europeans were not content with being passive recipients: thanks to the emulation that exists between different countries, inventions of foreign origin spread everywhere rapidly. Fifteen years after Gutenberg's death, all the major European countries were using printing, whereas in China the procedure remained the preserve of the centralized power.

The notion of 'barbarian', found in Europe but not in other great cultures such as China, is telling. Over and above the pejorative judgement it carries, it has the merit of naming the external *others*, turning them into an entity, and thus encouraging people to take a closer look at them. This curiosity served the colonial and imperial ambitions of the Europeans, but cannot be reduced to them: exchanges with those others assumed many different forms.

Jones provides evidence for Hume's hypothesis (which he does not mention) when he pursues a comparison between Europe and China. The Ming dynasty was hostile to mechanical inventions, and ordered the destruction of the astronomical clocks invented in the eleventh century. On the eve of the great voyages, at the start of the fifteenth century, Chinese vessels were able to sail the seas much better than the ships of the Portuguese and the Spanish; their instruments of navigation were superior, and their sea charts more precise. The Chinese reached Kamchatka as well as Zanzibar. However, a conflict at court led to the defeat of the party that was supporting the seafar-ing expeditions and, in 1430, the decision was taken to bring them to an end. Trade by sea was declared illegal. An attempt to re-establish it failed in 1480, following which the court ordered the destruction of all documents concerning the previous voyages. The art of building big ships was lost, and the coast was deserted. These measures could be imposed in China because it was a unified and centralized empire. In Europe, the wrong decisions made by any particular government would have been compensated by the action of all the others.

The recent development of China provides us with an argument that tends to prove the same thing. After years of isolation and ever-stronger central power, thanks to Mao's dictatorship, the country decided, in 1992, to open up to the external world, sending its students abroad and opening its borders to visitors; at the same time, the government ceased trying to control every aspect of social life, leaving room for local initiatives, and also relaxing the grip of the political sphere on the economy. As a result, a dose of pluralism within the country could be introduced. In addition, thanks to the Internet, there is now greater freedom in the circulation of information. The results of these movements of opening up and pluralization have been a spectacular economic take-off and the increasingly high profile of China throughout the world.

A particular debate had caused quite a stir among Europeans in 2003, when the Constitutional Treaty was being prepared for the countries in the European Union: should any mention be made, in the preamble to the Constitution, of Europe's 'Christian roots'? The decision was finally taken to omit it, not because these roots did not exist, but because such information belonged in history textbooks rather than in a legal text. It might have been pointed out, in support of this argument, that it is not the responsibility of political authorities to evaluate the relative weight of the Christian religion, of Greek thought, and of humanist principles in the history of Europe. But what we must bear in mind above all is the fact that the European Union was made possible solely thanks to an acceptance of the diversity of its members. Now the positive vision of pluralism was imposed only during the Enlightenment, because of thinkers such as Montesquieu and Hume. For this reason, if we wished to remember only one decisive tradition for the emergence of present-day Europe, it would be the heritage of the Enlightenment.

The European continent bears the name of a young girl, Europa. In the story, she was ravished by Zeus who had transformed himself into a bull, and then abandoned on the island of Crete, where she gave birth to three sons. But Herodotus recounts a much more realistic version of this legend. According to him, Europa, daughter of King Agenor of Phoenicia (a land corresponding to present-day Lebanon) was ravished, not by a god, but by perfectly ordinary men, Greeks from Crete. She then lived in Crete, giving birth to a royal dynasty. So it was an Asian woman who had come to live on a Mediterranean island who was to give her name to the continent.[8] This act of naming seems to announce, from the dark, backward and abysm of time, the future *vocation* of Europe. A doubly marginal woman becomes its emblem: she is of foreign origin, uprooted, an immigrant against her will; and she lives on the edge, far from the

179

centre of the land, on an island. The Cretans made her their queen; the Europeans made her their symbol. Pluralism or origins and openness to others: these thus became the distinguishing feature of Europe.

Forms of coexistence

If the only characteristic of European identity were acceptance of the other or of the different, it would be a very feeble identity, since it could incorporate absolutely any foreign ingredient. In reality, identity resides not in diversity itself, but in the status accorded to it. In this way, a purely negative and relative trait is transformed into an absolute positive quality; difference becomes identity, and plurality unity. And it really is a unity, however paradoxical this may seem: in such a way as to give differences the *same* status. In this sense, European unity can be assumed by the European Union and contribute to the reinforcement of its project.

Actually, until the end of the Second World War, while benefiting from its inner plurality, Europe also suffered greatly from it. We cannot forget that the continent's history is riven by wars: the names of these wars may change, but not their disastrous effects, from the struggle between the Roman Empire and the 'barbarian' populations of the North to the worldwide conflicts of the twentieth century, via – and here you can take your pick – the Hundred Years' War, the Thirty Years' War, the Seven Years' War. It needed the trauma of the Second World War for the European Union to come into being; it set out from the desire to eliminate wars between the member states, and the renunciation of the use of force in case of conflict (for conflicts themselves have not disappeared). Thanks to the acceptance of this principle, the Union's countries now enjoy in their relations a peace that they had never known previously.

Now that they have set a firm limit to the effects of diversity, European countries have been able to explore to their advantage the different forms of coexistence. We might say that the minimal form of this is tolerance: we do not 'approve of' others; we do not borrow anything from them; we merely refrain from persecuting them. This represents a definite progress, the logical conclusion of the struggles of the seventeenth and eighteenth centuries for religious tolerance, and it implies that disagreements between groups are no longer regulated by resorting to force, but simply by negotiation and persuasion.

The countries or cultures that cohabit in Europe, however, have not remained content merely with mutual toleration, but have engaged in more vital interactions. As we have seen, Montesquieu insisted on the beneficial effects of coexistence: it provokes emulation and competition, and everyone involved tries to prove that he is as good as, or better than, his neighbour. Hume thought there was yet another benefit here – the development of the critical spirit. Thanks to the distance separating the observer from the country he is observing, the former does not share the same 'prejudices'. With the aid of the other's gaze resting on us, or of our own gaze turned on to ourselves and imaging ourselves as an other (it is Montesquieu who invents the gaze of the Persians on the French), it becomes possible to distinguish between 'custom' and 'nature', to separate out arguments founded on the authority of tradition and rational arguments. The comparison between particular identities teaches us to examine every doctrine with critical eyes.

Pluralism also leads to another consequence: it prevents one of the participants assuming a hegemonic position and setting himself up as a tyrant over the others. That is why Voltaire was so glad to find that there were thirty religions in England: none of them could possess a 'plenitude of power', as they said of the time of the conflicts between popes and emperors wielding sole dominion. It was this same principle that Montesquieu set at the basis of a 'moderate' (and thus benevolent) government: so that power can block power, all powers must not be concentrated in the same hands.

The principle of secularism, adopted these days in one form or another by almost all European countries, enables us to take another step: not only must religions tolerate each other mutually, but a non-religious authority, the state, is entrusted with the task of ensuring that they are fairly situated within the public space and guaranteeing that every citizen also has a personal sphere that lies outside the control of the state itself, as well as outside that of the religions.

We also need to remember the idea of 'general will', as defined by Rousseau, and distinguished from any hypothetical 'will of all'. The latter corresponds to the unanimity of all the citizens within a state, a highly improbable unanimity in the absence of any constraining measures; the former corresponds to a 'sum of differences',[9] to a point of view that takes the disagreements into account but proposes to act in the name of the general interest. Kant would take up this idea from Rousseau in his argument on behalf of 'common sense' which, as we have seen, merges into what we call civilization. The relation between cultures, societies and states within a larger whole can be conceptualized in accordance with this same model. This general interest will not appear clearly to all, but it can be established at the end of a properly argued, well-informed debate. At the end of the eighteenth century, Condorcet formulated his careful conclusion on the possibility of reaching consensus: 'If I examine the current state of enlightenment in Europe, I see, despite the diversity of governments, of institutions, of usages, of prejudices, the enlightened men of the whole of Europe agreeing on what is true.'[10] People will never agree about everything; 'enlightened men' (and we should add women!) *can* agree.

In the current process of European construction, the question has often been raised as to whether, in order to reach a common identity, Europeans would be able to adopt, to begin with, a common memory. The model of the 'general will' as distinct from the 'will of all' could be useful here, since such a common memory is really possible only if it takes the form of a 'general memory'. The 'memory of all' would require particular memories becoming identical: this is an unrealizable and in any case undesirable task. A European 'general memory' would, on the contrary, be a 'sum of differences', taking into consideration national or regional points of view. To demand of each French, German or Polish person that they have the same memory of the past would be as futile as asking them to give up belonging to their community. However, what *is* possible is to ask them to take others' points of view into account, to highlight resemblances and differences, and to place them within a general framework; indeed, this is already happening – not among everyone, admittedly, but among sufficiently 'enlightened' men and women of goodwill. It is also, as we have already seen, a horizon for the education of all.

Thus the Europeans of tomorrow will be, not those who share the same memory, but those who can acknowledge, in the 'silence of passions', as Diderot put it, and yet with a certain fervour, that their neighbour's memory is just as legitimate as their own. By comparing their version of the past with that of people who were only yesterday their enemy, they will discover that their people has not always played the convenient role of hero of victim, and will thereby escape the Manichean temptation of seeing good and evil divided out on either side of a border, the first identified with 'us', the second with the others. Nor will they be lured into the more general trap of reducing the past to massive moral categories, such as 'good' and 'evil', as if the many-faceted and complex experience of millions of people through the centuries could be contained within them.

182

The cosmopolitan model

European identity thus consists of a way of accepting the plurality of the entities forming Europe and benefiting from it. Europe is not a nation, but a form of cohabitation between nations. This is both a cultural characteristic – the countries and regions of this continent have, in the course of their history, accepted the need to acknowledge the alterity of others and to cope with it – and a political value, which now appears in the programme of the European Union. In the way it is managing this plurality, Europe is distinguished from other great political groupings across the world: multinational states such as Russia or India, or states with variegated populations, such as China or the United States.

The German sociologist Ulrich Beck recently suggested designating the path taken by the European Union as *cosmopolitanism* and placing it at the heart of a conceptual model that integrates different ways of experiencing cultural alterity. In two works published in 2004, *Der kosmopolitische Blick* (in English, *Cosmopolitan Vision*) and *Das kosmopolitische Europa* (in English, *Cosmopolitan Europe*), he analyses at length the social and juridical reality of contemporary Europe, and suggests a set of categories that enable it to define its project. The meaning Beck gives to the old term 'cosmopolitan' is linked to three conditions. First, it describes a set formed of smaller entities that obey a common norm. Second, the differences between these entities in turn possess a legal status. Third, and finally, the latter are endowed with equal rights.

When one of these characteristics is missing, this absence gives birth to other forms of coexistence between political or cultural entities. If the different ingredients in the whole are not treated equally, what we have is an *empire*. An empire possesses common norms and acknowledges the diversity of its constituent parts, but treats them in a hierarchical and hegemonic fashion, rather than equally – witness the British or French Empires, or the Austro-Hungarian or Ottoman Empires (each in its own different way). The metropolis possesses a number of privileges refused to the colonies, or provinces, or satellites. The dominant culture tolerates minority cultures, but does not admit them on the same level as itself.

If the differences between the parts that constitute the whole are not recognized, what we have is more like the model of the nation, as in the case of China or the United States: individuals can be quite different between themselves, but the nation is one, with a single government and a single parliament. Beyond the frontiers of the state, this attitude melds into *universalism*, as it is sometimes imputed to the French political tradition, which seems to refuse to recognize the existence and relevance of cultures. 'The universalistic approach replaces the multitude of different norms, classes, ethnic identities and religions with one unified norm.'[11] As for the cosmopolitan approach, it does not abolish differences but gives them a common framework and the status of equality of rights.

If, on the other hand, the plurality of the constitutive elements is recognized and they are granted equal rights, but without any common normative framework, what we have is a *postmodern* model, which favours differences alone. Cosmopolitanism, for its part, 'requires a certain fund of universal norms in order to regulate the treatment of difference'.[12] Postmodernism, in this sense of the word, absolutizes relativism and essentializes the differences of all involved. Within a single state, it promotes communitarianism (or what is sometimes wrongly called multiculturalism), demanding that the difference between communities be recognized, but refusing to acknowledge any differences between the individuals in each community or any necessity for a unique framework for all the communities within the state. Cosmopolitanism, however, promotes cultural plurality on the basis of a universal norm concerning the equality of all human beings, and imposes a regulation of differences.

The idea of a cosmopolitan Europe is complementary to that of a Europe of the nations: the one presupposes the other and at the same time provides it with a framework. A good example can be found in the relation between law and public force (the police): all European states have integrated into their jurisdiction elements of 'European' law, and this enlargement makes it possible to attain a higher level of justice – but none of them have given up their national police. Without the member states there can be no application of the law, as Beck rightly puts it. It is not by altruism that people ever learn to see themselves through the gaze of others, but because they find it to their advantage. 'Those who integrate the perspectives of others into their own lives learn more about themselves *as well as* about others.'[13]

Today the European Union has turned its back on attempts to impose unification by force, such as those of Charlemagne and Charles the Fifth, Napoleon and Hitler, and draws its inspiration rather from the pluralist model bequeathed by the Enlightenment. The European miracle, writes Beck, shows 'how enemies can become neighbours'.[14] The singular path which has led to the creation of the European Union out of a plurality of autonomous and consenting states has produced a unique and at the same time complex identity.

184

It implies that not only individuals have rights, but also historical, cultural and political communities, i.e., the member states of the Union. Its spiritual identity, in turn, cannot be reduced to the sum of its ingredients, any more than it can be defined purely negatively, by their variety or their differences. This identity comes from the fact that it has learned to convert the negative into positive, in other words plurality into unity.

European identity is founded on the renunciation of violence; this principle can be considered, today, as irreversibly attained. However, the recognition of inner plurality does not stop at the absence of armed hostilities. Not only does the proximity of others no longer constitute a threat: it becomes a source of benefits. Within the Union, all states do not carry the same weight, but they all obey the same principles of justice. That is why the most powerful states see themselves as obliged to help the weaker: rights do not depend on force.

So there really is a European cultural identity, one that is original and worthy of respect. However, this identity is obviously not enough to start the political engine of the Union and to ensure its action in the several domains of common life in which unity is preferable to plurality. Why would it be desirable for the political leadership of the Union to be strengthened? Because the integration of the European states is already too advanced for the measures carried out by a single powerful state to be effective, and also because its words will carry much more weight than those of each of its individual members. In short, it would be to the advantage of everyone.

The areas in which this unified action would be beneficial are numerous. Ecology is one: threats to the environment ignore borders, and the cloud from Chernobyl did not stop at the Rhine, any more than do waves of microbes or chemical substances. Neither does scientific research: expensive projects require the collaboration of all, whether they concern the struggle against disease or global warming, communication or technology. Or immigration: those who have entered any country belonging to the Schengen zone can settle in any other, and the borders that need to be kept under surveillance are now those of Europe, not of the countries that comprise it. Or economy: the European Union, whose population is nigh on 500 million, has means of action that none of the members states have, and it can ensure that its inhabitants benefit from the advantages of globalization and are protected against its drawbacks. The big multinational enterprises these days lie outside the control of states; concerted action on the part of the Union may have more impact on them. Or security: terrorists and criminals seem to circulate from one country to another more easily than do police forces and judges. Or energy: since it is possible to draw on the resources of a neighbouring state, isn't it clear that the question needs to be treated at the European level? The list could easily be lengthened.

Now, in all these areas, and in many others too, the power of decision remains in the hands of national governments. In addition, one needs merely to compare the passion aroused by national, legislative or presidential elections, and the oratorical jousts to which they give place, with the relative indifference in which the European elections occur, to see where the nerve centres of political action lie. In European initiatives themselves, the predominant influence is wielded not by the elected parliament, but by the council that brings together the heads of member states. And this situation is unlikely to change any day soon: the political elites of every country prefer to keep their local power, even if limited, rather than risking not regaining it at the European level. The different peoples would do well to become more integrated into the European Union, but they cannot promote this directly, and there is little chance that they will rise up in rebellion. So the different kinds of conservatism are destined to last.

One of the negative effects of this weak degree of integration is the absence of solidarity between the European peoples. And yet such solidarity is indispensable to the functioning of any political project. Thanks to solidarity, the men and women of each country will be ready to accept the privations and sacrifices that belonging to a greater whole might entail. We are familiar with this dependency on the national level: in times of peace, everyone makes a financial contribution today, so that they can be helped tomorrow; in times of war, certain will risk their lives so that all may continue to live in freedom. But this solidarity cannot come into being without the peoples feeling a sense of solidarity for each other, and this feeling comes in turn from democratic participation, from the common choice of a destiny. The French will feel responsible for what happens to the Slovaks (and vice versa), and one group of people will be ready to risk their lives in order to defend another on the day when they have decided together on the direction their lives are to take. Nobody wants to die so that customs barriers can be lowered, and nobody willingly parts with some of her income if she doesn't feel she has anything in common with those who will benefit from her contribution. Now the European peoples do not have the impression that they have a common democratic life; so everyone simply looks after herself.

The Union of European States has been given a decisive impetus as a result of the threats that have hung over them. The plans for an understanding that would eliminate the risks of conflict in Europe go back a long way, but they would have remained a pipe dream if the traumatic memories of the Second World War had not been in the minds of the survivors. The second fairy who leaned over the cradle of Europe was just as menacing: after Hitler, it was Generalissimo Stalin who was ready to send his divisions across the forests and fields of Europe. Today Europe no longer faces any enemy of his stature: Russia is pacified, China is far away, Islam does not represent a credible threat, and the United States is an ally. As a result, the construction of Europe has run out of steam.

Europe in the West

Until recently, the European question has always been set within a broader framework, that of the West, an entity comprising Western Europe and North America, more specifically the United States. After all, the United States is linked by its origin to the European heritage and the 'Founding Fathers' drew inspiration directly from the spirit of the Enlightenment; the country's political and cultural identity has absorbed entire swathes of European history. In the wake of the Second World War, the idea of the West had even acquired a new currency, insofar as Americans and Europeans were opposed to the same enemy, the triumphal Communism of the Soviet Union and its satellites. For those who, like me, came from those so undemocratic 'people's democracies', the West constituted a homogenous bloc and an ideal political order, a model that was the inverse of the totalitarian regime in which we lived.

However, with the collapse of the Berlin Wall and the disappearance of the Soviet project, this latter interpretation of the idea of the West has become outmoded. Indeed, these days, the West no longer has one single antagonist. It still has adversaries, admittedly, but these are spread across different parts of the world and no longer automatically arouse the same reactions. As a result, a fissure has opened up within the West (that orphan of the Soviet threat), between the European Union and the United States. The contrast between these two entities has existed for a long time, of course, and has frequently been analysed by historians and sociologists; but, for some fifteen years, it has assumed a new form, both on the level of political action and on that of the ideals that underlie it. True, when measured by the

187

centuries, fifteen years do not amount to much; but measured by a human life, they do. This muddling of the concept of the West can be interpreted in many different ways; it cannot be ignored.

Certain differences in the reactions to recent events can be explained by the forms taken by the inner plurality of the populations on both sides of the Atlantic. The United States is home to an even more heterogeneous population than Europe, but on the level of foreign policy it forms, unlike the Europeans, a single state, a nation-state. This gives rise to several consequences. Many observers have been struck by the fact that, initially, the war in Iraq was given a rather different treatment in the American and European media, whereas those parts of the world to a large extent share the same values and the same preoccupations. The journalists' professional competence could not be impugned. On the other hand, the contrast between unity and plurality counts for something. American journalists produced uniform information, in agreement with the declarations of their government. It was not so much because they were subjected to direct pressure from it; rather, not having to deal with information from any other source, they remained the prisoners of what the eighteenth century called national prejudices, the opinion common to the society in which one lives. On its side, Europe benefited from what, in other circumstances, is a source of weakness: its diversity. The European Union is composed of several countries, each in turn divided into several opposed political forces. A piece of information that is revealed in Italy does not risk passing unnoticed in France or Germany, and vice versa. Here, plurality serves competition and, as a result, truth.

Another significant difference stems probably from the relation both have with history. Europeans seem to have a national consciousness that is less proud of itself than the Americans', thanks, *inter alia*, to the stronger presence of the past in their memories. They know that their states were responsible, in the past, for catastrophic political decisions, with the establishment of dictatorships and the exploitation of subject peoples. This may explain why the self-critical reflex is more widespread in European countries than in American society. This might be one of the reasons why the European Union and the population of its member states no longer nurse dreams of empire. They were indeed tempted by this posture in the nineteenth century and at the start of the twentieth, but they returned from the imperial venture with their tails between their legs and bloody noses. (The unconditional support of Great Britain for American policies is at present a sign not of domination but of submission.) The explanation for this European choice should thus be sought less in a greater attachment to virtue than in the stronger presence of the past and its consequences. It is true that a worry about efficacity was also involved: Europeans were convinced that an occupation of Iraq would intensify terrorism instead of lessening it (and they were right).

However, we cannot say that this contrast between European and American public opinions, this divergence between the two societies, is reflected in government policies. This is understandable: the leaders' point of view differs from that of the masses. While it is true that armed conflicts between the member countries of the European Union have become unthinkable, the same does not apply to relations with the rest of the world. The recent attacks in Madrid and London were a reminder of how illusory such a vision was. Not all dangers have miraculously quitted the human world, and they never can: dormant volcanoes can always reawaken. Russia, which is neutral today, risks becoming hostile again. Now European countries have for the most part renounced ensuring their defence, preferring to shelter behind the shield of NATO, placed under American control. Occasionally they have shown some reluctance to follow United States foreign policy but, being unable to take full responsibility for their own decisions, they have had to fall in with American policies, even if only with extreme reluctance. They have even taken part, admittedly discreetly, in the 'war on terror' (as we have seen with regard to torture) and acquiesced in the transformation of NATO: having been a force designed to ensure security in Europe, the organization has become an army promoting Western interests throughout the world, as in present-day Afghanistan.

However, if a conflict between Europeans and Americans is excluded, it is not true that their judgements and their interests altogether coincide. Since the disappearance of the USSR, the government of the United States seems to have drawn its inspiration from a hegemonic and imperial model. It considers that the interests of its country are concerned by whatever happens in absolutely any part of the world, and that the use of force is a legitimate means for maintaining what is deemed to be the best international balance. This decision is made explicit in the latest version of the United States' strategic doctrine, presented to Congress by the government in May 2006. It contains two major principles. The first: the 'supreme aim' of American action is to 'put an end to tyranny in our world'. The second: to ensure its defence, the country must not remain content with reacting to sudden aggression, but must conduct a policy of protection on all

189

sides, 'even if uncertainties remain as to the time and place chosen by the enemy to attack'. The aim is thus a new world order, and not just the defence of a country's interests; the means is armed intervention, which presupposes that the enemies in question cannot be led to cooperate and change without being forced to do so; in short, evil is part of their very identity.

Another path may be open to the European Union, on condition that it manages to reconcile the choices made by its population with the realism of its leaders. The young Europeans of our time find it difficult to imagine that these countries, between which they circulate so freely, could have been waging war on each other in the recent past, and they tend to project this situation on to the rest of the planet. For this reason, an appeal for the protection of peace no longer has much motivational force among Europeans: the absence of war strikes them as self-evident. True, in most cases, European governments can intervene in situations of conflict by economic, juridical and diplomatic, but not military, means, and they can favour negotiation rather than force; and this makes it possible for the interests of all parties to be observed. So they could embody a different policy, allying a renunciation of hegemonic projects with firmness. But resorting to armed force cannot be excluded on principle. Europeans ought to know that they do not live in a world from which any reason for violence or aggression has by miracle disappeared.

The policies of the European Union towards countries in the rest of the world cannot have strict equality as its principle, but it can aspire to an ideal of equity. This is a 'qualified equality', a justice in the moral rather than legal sense. Unlike equality, equity takes the past and future of a relation into account, as well as its present context, and the needs and aptitudes of the participants. On the European territory, those who come from foreign countries cannot have the same rights as citizens, but it must not be forgotten that they are human beings like the others, driven by the same ambitions and suffering from the same lacks. If it succeeds in steering in this direction, the European Union will serve as an example to other regions of the world, by the way in which it governs relations between its several different members.

The demonization of the enemy that underlies the American choice, and the desire to be purer than the pure sometimes present in the European debate, appear an inadequate response to the challenge posed by the plurality of human societies. As far as the United States is concerned, their hegemonic temptation should be tempered by the acceptance of the plurality of the world, its inevitably multipolar character. It would be to their advantage if they were to seek a state of coexistence and equilibrium: the different powers should be strong enough to prevent any attempt at aggression but insufficiently influential to maintain situations of domination. Their objective should be the stability of compromises, made visible by the signing of agreements, respect for international treaties and the renunciation of the preventive use of force. On its side, Europe would to a greater extent than at present accept its identity as what I call a 'tranquil power', in other words a power lacking in any imperial project but in no way renouncing the ability to strike the enemy in order to defend itself (see my *The New World Disorder*, published by Polity). It should have a military force at its disposal, since the world will never be definitively pacified, and this force should belong to it alone, since its interests do not coincide with those of any other part of the world.

Such a movement, on both sides, would be a real contribution to the consolidation of peace on earth.

The frontiers of Europe

If we accept that the European identity is based on its inner plurality, we might be tempted to conclude that its limits cannot be determined: no alterity can be too foreign to it, so long as the bearers of that alterity agree to the formal procedures of cohabitation. Understood in this way, Europe would be the seed of a new League of Nations, destined to absorb all the countries of the earth. This seems to be the wish of Ulrich Beck, who sees *Europeanization* as a process that should never end. I will, for my part, reformulate the question of limits in a rather more concrete way, namely: what could the *optimal* frontiers of the European Union be?

The frontiers between countries have never played the same role. During a long initial period, what might be called the religious phase in the history of humanity, the decisive frontier is that which separates heaven from earth, not that between different countries. The sacred is defined by a relation to God, not to other people. Admittedly, everyone lives in a particular country, but the frontiers of the latter evolve in accordance with marriages, inheritances or transactions between princes, without the inhabitants immediately feeling the consequences of this in their daily lives. For a while, the Netherlands and Spain formed a single country; then they separated. Burgundy constituted part of France, then became independent, to the point of plotting against it with England in the Hundred Years' War;

finally, it returned to France. France sold Louisiana as if it were a private domain. When the dealings between princes were not the deciding factor in where frontiers were to be drawn, these were decided by the hazards of the actions of war, and the positions occupied by armies at the time of armistice.

This first long religious period was succeeded by a national phase. The prince's subjects were then replaced by the nation's citizens, who were the living embodiment of it; as a result they were far from indifferent to the limits of its extent. From this time on, it was the nation that defined the sacred. Duty no longer called on you to die for your faith, but for your country. For this reason, the first theoreticians of the modern nation, such as Rousseau, thought that good Christians would be bad citizens: their solidarity extended to all men, whereas the solidarity of a citizen stopped at the frontiers of his country.

Ever since the end of the Second World War, Europeans seem to have entered a third, post-religious and post-national phase. It is not that they have lost all relation to transcendence and the sacred – something which, in any case, could not be conceived of without a radical mutation occurring in the nature of the species. But the object of their devotion is now constituted by other individual human beings, those close to them, those they love: children, parents, lovers, friends. Everyone constructs his own hierarchy of values. In this context, the frontier again loses a great deal of its importance. What counts above all is the quality of the individuals I cherish and that of the life that ties me to them, not the colour of the passport that I have to show to customs officials. If there are indeed frontiers, it is now felt preferable to think of them not as walls, but as bridges or thresholds, interfaces that permit mediations and connections. It is also in this spirit that any attempt to settle on frontiers for Europe can only be provisional, and that any country can be imagined as one day becoming 'Europeanized'.

We can still wonder, however, if such a vision of the contemporary world is not too utopian. A political entity needs frontiers, in other words a distinction between those who are its citizens and those who are not. This is indeed the essence of any political perspective: unlike the humanitarian point of view, which is formulated in the name of all human beings, politics is always the politics of a group, a state, a set of states or of forces within one state. And yet this perspective is not incompatible with the universalist and humanitarian attitude. Being hospitable, or generous, or charitable to foreigners does not mean that we ignore the difference between citizens and foreigners; the two points of view may be complementary. The humanitarians' viewpoint sets a horizon and safety railings for the politicians': there are limits that no *raison d'état* should ever cross. On its side, humanitarian action needs a political framework and human rights become a palpable reality only when states themselves take over their defence – in other words, when human rights also become *political* rights. We have seen this already: frontiers, whether they be those of each nation or those of the European Union, remain indispensable.

The explicit criteria for joining the Union come down to three demands, none of which permit anyone to fix the definitive frontiers of the whole set. The first is formal and juridical in nature: the candidate state must accept all that the community has achieved in terms of laws, norms and treaties. The second is political: it must be a state of law, a liberal democracy, in other words it must simultaneously guarantee the rigorous equality of the rights of all, without any racial, ethnic, religious or sexual discrimination, and thus also effective universal suffrage. It must also safeguard both the freedom and the security of individuals, against any interference from other individuals, or indeed from the state itself. This freedom is to be guaranteed by the pluralism not just of parties, or of means of information, but also of spheres of life – public and private, political and economic, and so on. The third and final criterion is economic: only states with a market economy and a certain level of development can seek to join the European Union, and a state that is too poor compared with the others cannot be part of it. Other demands can be added as and when they arise (for example, for the states that have emerged from the former Yugoslavia, the need to collaborate with the International Tribunal).

Together with these explicit criteria, others, unformulated but quite self-evident, are also applied. This includes the demand for geographical continuity: even if it satisfies all the conditions that define the European project, Canada cannot be part of it – if only because of the Atlantic Ocean! Greece's joining was in this respect an exception, before the entry of the countries of Eastern Europe into the European Union, but this is to be explained by the, as it were, interior nature of the Mediterranean Sea. Another unspoken criterion concerns the size of candidate countries. Even if Russia satisfies the other criteria for joining, its place will never be within the European Union: its surface area is twice as big as that of the European Community, and its politics is that of a great power.

Should a cultural criterion be added to this list? The suggestion was made at the time of the Turkish candidacy: the idea of a 'Christian

193

club' was mentioned, either to blast it or defend it. But that would be to confuse history and law. The Christian religion has left, as I said, an indelible mark on the cultural identity of Europeans, but what the European Union demands is, rather than the imposition of unity, the acceptance of plurality. As we have seen, the specifically European value lay precisely in refusing to formulate such a demand for substantial unity. If Europe is a club, it is, rather, a 'secular club': the demand it makes is for freedom of conscience and the equality of all citizens before the law. The question of Turkey's joining or not cannot be decided on the basis of a cultural criterion; all we can ask here is for Turkey to adhere to a secular politics (as it is already doing).

However, it would be possible to draw on yet another criterion to decide on this case, or other similar ones: it would be the criterion of strategic interest. Most of the time, politicians remain faithful to their national traditions, and do not think in terms of the European interest, even though the latter certainly does exist. It is far from absurd to reformulate the initial question in this way: who are the neighbours that the European Union would find it advantageous to have? The ideal neighbour ought to be a relatively close country in political, economic and administrative terms, a country destined to be a partner and friend, rather than a hostile country or one that is already engaged in another sphere of alliances.

From this point of view, it would be in Europe's interest to have Turkey as a neighbour, rather than countries that are much less close, such as Iran, Iraq and Syria. This would be the case if Turkey were to be part of the European Union. Likewise, further north, desirable neighbours would be Ukraine or, one day, Belarus, rather than Russia itself. Morocco might play the same role in relation to the Maghreb, and the latter in relation to Africa. These states would have the far from contemptible status of transitional states, threshold states, which would ensure for them a key role in the relations between the European Union and other groups of countries, in the Middle East, the Maghreb or indeed with Russia. Individual treaties would guarantee this, in many regards privileged, status. A Europe with these limits can still admit new members, such as the ex-Communist countries to the East or, in the West, those who have never displayed much enthusiasm for joining, such as Norway, Iceland or Switzerland; but these inclusions would not modify its identity.

The right policy would consist not in choosing realism against idealism, or vice versa, but in appealing to both: setting up an ideal (here the well-being of the European peoples), and giving ourselves the means to achieve it.

We saw at the start that barbarism, in the absolute sense, consisted in not recognizing the humanity of others, whereas its contrary, civilization, was precisely this ability to see others as others and yet to accept at the same time that they were as human as ourselves. If European identity, in its turn, is defined by a judicious managing of plurality – that of member states, that of political opinions and cultural traditions – could we not claim that the idea of civilization merges into that of Europe? Certain people have not hesitated to do so, but I will not follow their example. It must be stated that the history of Europe is also that of conflicts, persecutions and wars – not that Europeans have been any more barbarous than the other peoples of the world, as they sometimes claim in an access of self-denigration, but because human history has always been like that. On the other hand, the project of a European Union is indeed an attempt to make the way the world works a little more civilized. In order to approach this still distant ideal, Europeans must now take an additional step and overcome the fear that still too often hampers them.

Civilization is not the past of Europe. But, thanks to the actions of Europeans, it might be its future.

Conclusion: Beyond Manicheism

If it is to be effective, dialogue must satisfy a twofold requirement. On the one hand, it must recognize the difference of voices engaged in the exchange, and must not presuppose that one of them constitutes the norm while the other can be explained as a deviation, or as backward, or as evidence of bad will. If you are not ready to question your own certainties and self-evident beliefs, to adopt provisionally the standpoint of the other – even if this means acknowledging that, from his own point of view, the other is right – the dialogue cannot take place. On the other hand, however, it cannot lead to any kind of result unless the participants accept a formal framework common to their discussion, and unless they can agree on the nature of the arguments admitted and on the very possibility of seeking justice and truth together.

This dialogue between people who have come from different countries and different cultures does not occur in a vacuum, and the centuries of history that have preceded it cannot be erased – centuries in which the current 'countries of fear' have dominated the current 'countries of resentment'. So we can see what demands can be addressed to the political and intellectual elites of Western countries if they desire to take part. A first requirement here would be that they cease to consider themselves as an incarnation of the law, of virtue and universality, of which their technological superiority would seem to be the proof; so they should immediately stop setting themselves above the laws and judgements of others. The right to military intervention that certain Western powers have arrogated to themselves is not only without any basis other than force; it risks suggesting that the ideals defended by Westerners – liberty, equality, secularism, human rights – are merely a convenient camouflage for their will to

196

power, and thus are not worth consideration. We must say it again: freedom cannot be promoted by constraint, or equality by subjection. If Western politicians wish these ideals to remain active, they must begin by withdrawing their troops from the countries in which they are intervening (at present, Iraq and Afghanistan), close down illegal prisons and torture camps, and help set up a viable Palestinian state. For the Muslim population of these countries to turn its attention to the internal causes of these disasters, the most blatant external causes must be suppressed – those for which the West is responsible.

In parallel, within the Western, and in particular the European, countries, people would have to stop believing that we contribute to the spread of human rights around us if we assume the roles of valiant righters of wrongs and irreproachable teachers. The facile dichotomies between Light and Darkness, free world and obscurantism, sweet tolerance and blind violence, tell us more about the overweening pride of their authors than the complexity of the contemporary world. No merit lies in preferring good to evil when we ourselves define the meaning of these two words. If those champions of the just cause desire to draw the lost and perplexed towards their own ideal, they would all do well to adopt the converse attitude, and show that they are able to be self-critical, highlighting what, in their interlocutors, is already bringing them towards this ideal. It is more virtuous – and more cunning – to dissociate the precept from the person who formulates it. In the present case, that of Islam, it is enough to remember that the demand for justice or the acknowledgement of plurality are values that also belong to its tradition.

It does not ensue that these Western countries would need to renounce the principles that they have chosen as the basis of their common life. So that others can be treated fairly, the sovereignty of the people, the liberty of the individual, the affirmation of equal rights for all and the recognition of the plurality of human societies should be, not abandoned, but reinforced. What needs to be renounced, on the other hand, is the reductive vision of those others that is spread (if not exclusively, at least predominantly) by the media and official discourse.

The reduction in question is threefold. Firstly, the Muslim population, with some billion people spread across many countries, is reduced to Islam, as if (unlike all other human groups), Muslims allowed the least actions of their lives to be dictated by religion, which thus becomes the sole cause behind their decisions. Then, secondly, Islam is reduced to Islamism: a religion that is fourteen centuries old and describes a path of spiritual progress is interpreted

197

as the political programme of a few contemporary militant groups. Finally, Islamism is reduced to terrorism, even though it can take many paths of political action that do not break the laws in force. Now Bin Laden does not express the truth of Islam any more than Hitler expressed the truth of the West – even less, the truth of all Muslims. If we practise these successive reductions of meaning, we are playing into the hands of contemporary extremists who are most willing to be considered as the spokesmen of a vast community of believers. These reductions are not merely false; they are pernicious: they mean that we drive a billion Muslims into the arms of a few thousand Islamists, and suspect them all of being terrorists.

The way different groups are melded together and, without distinction, seen as all tarred with the same brush, fans the flames of hostility rather than extinguishing them, and makes the end sought become ever more remote. The medical vocabulary used when people talk about Islam should be dropped, and reference to 'Islamic contagion' or 'contaminated Muslims' be abandoned: the temptation to carry out surgical excisions inevitably looms in the background. In order to stop new Bouyeris from arising, we need to stop seeing his act as the truth of Islam: whatever their perpetrators may say, such criminal acts do not stem from any religion, or from any culture. The two participants in this dialogue would do well to draw a very clear line between cultural identity and political choices, between forms of spirituality and civic values as embodied in law. It is thanks to a distinction of this kind that other non-Western countries have managed to adopt the principles of democratic government without having to renounce their traditions and customs. The separation between laws and values, on the one side, and culture and spirituality on the other, can become (in the West too), the point of departure for a politics adapted to contemporary society.

Every society, as we have seen, is pluricultural. The fact remains that, nowadays, the contacts between populations of different origins (especially in the cities), migrations and travels, and the international exchange of information, are all more intense than ever before; and there is no reason why the tendency should be reversed. Good management of this growing plurality would imply not that we assimilate others to the culture of the majority but that we respect minorities and integrate them into a framework of laws and civic values common to all. That objective is simultaneously important (since it has to do with the life of the whole collective) and accessible (insofar as it does not affect customs adopted in earliest childhood, constitutive of a basic identity, but concerns rather rules of life that can easily be accepted as varying from one country to another).

It is not a matter of enclosing Muslims in their religious identities, but of treating them with as much respect as all other members of the community. For the separation and enclosure of cultures or communities is closer to the pole of barbarity, while mutual recognition between them is a step towards civilization. Public funding should go to what unites rather than to what isolates: to schools open to all, following a common syllabus; to hospitals that guarantee a welcome to all patients without discrimination on the grounds of sex, race or language; to modes of transport – trains, coaches, planes – where you can be sitting next to anybody. Individuals can never be prevented from feeling happier among their own kind, but that preference is really part of private life: the state's job is neither to make this easier, nor to forbid it.

None of us will ever be entirely 'integrated' into the society in which we live – and that's a good thing; but, without a basic integration into the social pact, the individual is condemned to distress and pushed towards violence. As for society, its interest lies in doing everything to ensure that the path of violence is not followed.

Societies marked by fear, like those imbued with resentment, are today at a crossroads. They can foster these passions even more or try to contain their perverse effects. If these societies remain enclosed within a dual relation, of rivalry and confrontation, there is a risk that they will illustrate yet again the law we glimpsed earlier: every blow dealt by one of the adversaries provokes an even harder blow from the other. The fear of some people, due to the acts of aggression they have suffered, leads them to strengthen their blows; the resentment of others, nourished by past and present humiliations, leads them to even more violent and desperate acts. And nowadays technology has placed in the hands of both groups a means of destruction with a power and an ease of use never attained before. If we do not succeed in breaking this fateful head-to-head confrontation, life on earth itself will be under threat. To ensure we do not fall prey to barbaric acts of a terrifying magnitude, our best hope lies in freeing ourselves from the grip of fear (on one side) and resentment (on the other), and trying to live in this plural world in which self-affirmation does not need to involve the destruction or submission of the other. There can be no hesitation about the choice we need to take. The time has come for each person to assume his or her responsibilities: we must protect our fragile planet and its inhabitants (however imperfect), human beings.

Afterword, 2010

The book you have just read was in all essentials completed by the end of 2007. Though it does not comprise an analysis of events on a day-by-day basis, it does refer frequently to current affairs. Now in the course of the two years that separate the time of completion from the present, several things have occurred that shed additional light on the questions discussed here. So the aim of the present afterword is to update some of the preceding analyses, without modifying their overall tenor in the slightest.

Bush's willing torturers

The actual existence of torture in American jails was well known at the time I was completing my book. Nonetheless, the publication on 16 April 2009, by the new United States administration, of documents that had hitherto been kept secret revealed details concerning the actual way in which torture was being carried out. I will briefly summarize these facts.

One is struck, first of all, by the incredibly pernickety regulations that were formulated in the CIA manuals and taken over by the legal authorities in the government. Up until then, it had been possible to imagine that the practices of torture were what are called 'blunders', involuntary transgressions of the norms, occasioned by the urgency of the situation. On the contrary, it is now clear that these were procedures fixed down to their least details, to the nearest inch and the nearest second.

Thus there are ten forms of torture, and subsequently thirteen. They are divided into three categories, each of which comprises several degrees of intensity: preparatory (nakedness, manipulated feeding, sleep deprivation), corrective (blows), and coercive (being hosed with water, locked in boxes, or subjected to torture by immersion). Slaps on the face must be administered with fingers spread out, halfway between the tip of the chin and the bottom of the earlobe. Hosing a naked prisoner with water can last for twenty minutes if the water is at 5°C, forty if it is at 10°C, and up to sixty if is at 15°C. Sleep deprivation must not last longer than 180 hours, but, after eight hours' rest, they can begin again. Torture by immersion can last up to twelve seconds, no more than two hours per day, for thirty consecutive days (a particularly tough prisoner underwent this torture 183 times over, in March 2003). A prisoner should not be locked in a box for more than two hours, but if the box allows the prisoner to stand upright, he can stay there up to eight hours at a stretch, eighteen hours per day. If you put an insect in with him, you cannot tell the prisoner that its sting will be extremely painful or indeed deadly. And so on and so forth, for page after page.

We also learn how torturers are trained. Most of these tortures are copied from the programme followed by American soldiers who are preparing to face extreme situations (this allows those in charge to conclude that these ordeals are perfectly tolerable). More importantly, the torturers themselves are chosen from among those who have had 'a prolonged educative experience' of these extreme ordeals; in other words, the torturers have themselves initially been tortured. Following which, a four-week period of intensive training is sufficient to prepare them for their new job.

The indispensable partners of the torturers are the government's legal advisors, who are there to ensure that their colleagues are immune from prosecution. This, too, is new: torture is no longer represented as an infraction of the common norm, regrettable but excusable: it *is* the legal norm. With this in mind, lawyers resort to another series of techniques. To get around the law, interrogations need to be conducted outside the United States, even if this means American bases. According to the official legal definitions, there is torture when the intention to produce intense suffering can be attested; so it will be suggested to the torturers that they deny the presence of any such intention. So slaps on the face are given not to produce any pain, but to cause surprise and humiliation. Being locked in a box is not meant to lead to sensory disorientation, but to make the prisoner feel uncomfortable! The torturer must always insist on his 'good faith', his 'honest beliefs' and his reasonable premises. Euphemisms must be systematically employed: 'reinforced techniques' instead of torture; 'expert interrogator' for torturer. Care must also be taken to avoid leaving any material traces, and for this reason mental destruction is preferable to physical damage; for this reason, too, any visual recording of sessions is to be destroyed afterwards.

Several other groups of professionals are involved in the practice of torture; the contagion spreads far beyond the limited circle of torturers. Apart from the lawyers who legitimize their acts, the following are regularly mentioned: psychologists, psychiatrists, doctors (obliged to be present at every session), women (the torturers are men, but subjection to degrading treatment becomes even more humiliating when women are watching), and university professors able to produce moral, legal or philosophical justification.

Who, these days, can be held responsible for these perversions of the law and of the most elementary principles of morality? Those who willingly carry out torture are less responsible than the senior legal figures who have justified and encouraged them; and the latter are less responsible than the political decision-makers who have asked them to do it. Does this mean they should be put on trial? In a democracy, politicians are condemned by depriving them of power – we refuse to re-elect them. As for other professionals, one might expect them to be punished by their peers, for who would wish to be taught by such a professor? Or brought to court before such a judge? Or treated by such a doctor?

If we want to understand why these fine Americans have so easily agreed to become torturers, there is no need to think the reason might lie in some ancestral hatred or fear of Muslims and Arabs. No, the situation is much more serious. These practices of torture remind us, first and foremost, of a fact that psychological lab experiments had long since established: there is nothing at all unusual about those who perpetrate acts of violence; anyone, or almost anyone, would have behaved the same way if placed in the same circumstances. If we wish to gain a better understanding of the astonishing ease with which ordinary people are transformed into torturers, it is on these circumstances that we need to concentrate, rather than on the supposedly unusual character of the individuals involved. I do not intend to go into a large-scale study of the torturers of Abu Ghraib (or of Guantánamo, or of Bagram, or of other secret CIA prisons scattered around the globe); but a few details of use to our analysis can already be drawn from the published information.

First of all: such practices, which seem to go against both the laws of any country and against widely shared human feelings such as empathy or compassion, become much easier in times of war than in peacetime, since war is, by definition, a suspension of all legal or moral norms. The most reprehensible act there is, killing one's fellow man, becomes the most valorous of acts once it is renamed 'eliminating an enemy'. Once the foundations of common life have been shaken, the transgressions of particular rules cease to appear as such. The situation of war has a decisive impact from yet another point of view: it is universally accepted that, in wartime, subordinates owe their superiors absolute obedience. When you are faced with the danger of immediate death, when bombs are exploding all around you, it is not the right time for discussions and prevarications. Even in a country that worships free initiative, the circumstances of war force people to obey orders without thinking. So we see yet again what pernicious consequences the idea of a 'war on terror' can have.

Another revealing circumstance can be found in the ideological frame that governs such acts. For none of us perceives purely material facts deprived of any meaning; facts always come to us accompanied by a sort of 'instruction manual' that guides the way we interpret them. In this case, torturers have been well indoctrinated: if they wish to be good soldiers, and thus give meaning to their lives, they need to imbue themselves with a 'sense of duty' and be ready to suppress their spontaneous reactions, since this is required by the 'defence of the homeland'. And this comes on top of feelings that are easy to understand and share: fear for one's own life or, even more, for the well-being of one's nearest and dearest, threatened as they are by those bloody beasts we are fighting against. So the soldiers will be reminded, over and over again, of the damage caused by terrorist attacks.

We also need to remember a more particular circumstance: the harsh training that the future torturers have undergone before going into action. It may be (as Alice Miller suggests in her research) that many of them were beaten or abused as children; but at all events, they have all been subjected to a hard apprenticeship that can be seen as akin to torture. And anyone who has been humiliated will find it easy to agree to humiliate others in turn.

The new American administration, which came to power at the start of 2009, declared loud and clear that it was abandoning the use of torture. There is no reason to cast doubt on its good intentions. But nor is there any reason to say that the question has been settled once and for all: what has once happened can happen again, at any moment. I for my part feel some disquiet on seeing that certain French authors from the time of the Algerian War still enjoy a good reputation with the American military – authors who theorized the struggle against guerrillas by any means possible, including torture, such as Roger Trinquier, already mentioned in my book, or David Galula, whose work *Counterinsurgency Warfare: Theory and Practice* has been republished in several editions recently, including in French – *Contre-insurrection: Théorie et pratique* (Economica, 2008) – with a new preface by General David Petraeus, leader of the American military action in the Middle East.

Obama's election and the war in Afghanistan

The Bush administration that led the United States was directly responsible for several transgressions of international legality as well as of American legal traditions. So it was with unreserved solidarity that I greeted the election of Barack Obama as president, since, in his electoral speeches, he defended another vision of the world. How are we to assess his policies one year later? I will obviously set large swathes of his activities to one side – those that concern the international or domestic economy, American health care, or interracial relations – to focus on just one part of the global scene: the conflicts that are still troubling the Middle East.

I cannot fail to approve of the overall perspective adopted by Obama, which is also that of my book. After all, the Democratic candidate had decided to reject policies based on the widespread feeling of fear among the American population, and to appeal to other political passions, in particular the hope of a better future, the appetite for a self-affirmation that would no longer lead to the destruction of the other. I cannot fail to agree, either, with a vision of humanity that recognizes that human beings in every country are alike insofar as they are essentially motivated by the same aspirations and the same anxieties, and simultaneously acknowledges that they belong to profoundly dissimilar cultures, none of which is in itself, a priori, bad and reprehensible. And how can anyone not approve of the conclusion that Obama draws from this, namely, that we should try to talk to everyone, to our friends, of course, whom we will treat with respect, but also to those who are very different from us, or even to those who are at present our enemies, hoping to find mutually advantageous solutions to the ongoing conflicts?

The Obama administration has initiated several actions that illustrate this programme, such as: forbidding torture, closing the camp at Guantánamo, withdrawing military forces from Iraq, and proposing a dialogue with Iran. Even if it is taking a long time to realize these hopes, we can agree that they are a step in the right direction. In other regards, it needs to be said that the overall political thrust of the United States remains unchanged, apparently subjected to what is considered to be in the country's immediate interests. The US has shown little desire (or little ability) to alter the Israeli policy of colonizing and dominating the Palestinian territories, and thus has failed to eliminate this permanent source of unrest, nourished by humiliation and resentment. At the same time, the US has pursued its support for the anti-democratic (but pro-American) regimes of neighbouring countries such as Saudi Arabia or Egypt.

The most serious test case for assessing, not the quality of Obama's programme but the quality of his action, is the current war in Afghanistan. The American president has recently devoted two important speeches to this, one on 1 December 2009 at West Point Academy, where he set out his new war strategy; the other on 10 December 2009, in Oslo, where he received the Nobel Peace Prize, and presented his theoretical justifications for this strategy.

Once again, there is no problem about the latter. Obama reminds us that he is not a pacifist: that, in the world as it is now, he cannot renounce the use of force. He thus invokes, to legitimize his decision to intensify the combat in Afghanistan, the concept of the 'just war'. However, he adds, the decision to go to war does not mean that everything is permitted. The use of torture remains forbidden, and respect for international Conventions and treaties is still obligatory. Finally, Obama emphasizes that war is, in every circumstance, a tragic event, and that for this reason even the victors should abstain from glorying in their victory.

I largely share this point of view. However, I prefer to speak of 'inevitable wars' rather than 'just wars'. No war is just or good; but it is sometimes impossible to evade war – either because war has been imposed by an invader who threatens your most cherished values (as with the Second World War unleashed by Hitler's Germany and the other Axis countries), or because our consciences, as human beings, will not leave us in peace, given the intensity of the suffering being imposed on other peoples (as with genocides). Wars of this latter type have been waged in preceding decades, not by Western countries but by countries adjacent to those in which the massacre occurred: the Vietnamese army put an end to the genocide in Cambodia, and the Rwandan army in exile, supported by Uganda, stopped the genocide in Rwanda. Nonetheless, we still need to remember that, precisely because any mention of genocide provokes strong reactions, it can be used as a means of manipulation that enables other objectives to be realized. There was no genocide in Kosovo in 1999, any more than there was in Darfur in 2009.

But the difficulties start once Obama applies this doctrine to the current situation in Afghanistan. To begin with, he sets aside certain justifications of the military intervention that are frequently put forward: the United States no longer sees it as its task to build up a solid nation in Afghanistan, or to promote democracy throughout the Middle East by military means, or to defend everywhere the rights of the oppressed, men and (above all) women. The sole justification he accepts concerns the security of the United States: we were attacked by al-Qaeda on 11 September 2001; we need to eliminate all those who took part in this attack or who support those criminals.

The weakness of this argument lies, not in the theoretical construction that supports it, but in the fact that this line of reasoning is applied to a situation that does not correspond to it. It is simply not true that the forces of al-Qaeda who carried out the 9/11 attacks have maintained a presence in Afghanistan since 2001. Following the attacks, intervention on the part of the Afghan forces, supported by American forces, eliminated al-Qaeda fighters from the country, as well as the Taliban who were protecting them. However, without the least thought for the consequences of their acts, the American military, backed up by allied soldiers, occupied the country and supported the government they had helped to set up. Ever since then, the presence of the military forces of occupation has produced the opposite result from the one expected: the more these generals reinforce their manpower, the more unanimous the opposition to them becomes. In other words, Obama's action in Afghanistan is reprehensible not because of its aim (ensuring the security of the United States) but because of the means chosen, the occupation of the country, which not only fails to contribute to achieving the aim, but risks making its realization an even more distant prospect.

Let us look at these two levels of inadequacy in a little more detail. On the ground, American soldiers and their auxiliaries are attacked by those they harass; to defend themselves in this hostile ambience, in a little-known terrain, where any road may be mined and where an enemy may be lurking behind every bush, they respond with bombings. To avoid the risk of dying, they are prepared to kill innocent people – the civilians who are at the sides of the fighters they are pursuing. The result is that their enemies are forever increasing in number. 'In Afghanistan,' a high-ranking French officer said recently after serving in the field, 'killing enemies does not diminish their number, and over there 10 minus 2 does not equal 8, but 16: for every person killed, four others come to take his place, his cousins, friends or neighbours. With every passing day, there is one more anti-Westerner in Afghanistan.' It is an oversimplification of language when the Western press designates as 'Taliban' all those opposed to the occupation; in reality, the latter are a mixed set of people – religious Taliban, local warlords, traffickers of every kind, producers and dealers of opium poppies, and conservatives who, in a Western-style democracy, risk losing their prerogatives. The unity of all the insurgents resides simply in the identity of their common enemy, the foreign army of occupation.

The Western public remembers the declared aims of the occupation: the support for democracy, the defence of human rights, the hunt for terrorist criminals. But the Afghan population remembers the lived reality: the indiscriminate bombings, the centres of detention and torture (such as Bagram, the prototype of Abu Ghraib), and the support for corrupt leaders. Should it surprise anyone that it does not harbour friendly feelings for the occupier? One example among others: in August 2008, a French detachment ran into an ambush, which caused the death of ten soldiers. Such an operation could not be mounted without the local population being aware of it; but nobody warned the French of the danger. In the days that followed the ambush laid for the French, an air raid caused the death of ninety-two civilians, mainly children. How could the occupiers, who were responsible for these deaths, be loved, or their presence desired, by the population?

The West hopes that, before very long, the Afghan army will take over their security tasks, which will enable them to withdraw. At the same time, they are forced to realize that, in spite of the subsidies paid them, every year 30 per cent of Afghan soldiers desert, often taking their weapons with them, and sometimes go over to 'the enemy'. They also know that positions of leadership can be bought: the men who become officers are not those who are the most competent, but those who can pay the price demanded. Western governments pay out huge sums to help development in the country, but these funds are of only marginal profit to the population: they go mainly to foreign enterprises (also Western), which make a clean sweep of these new markets; much of the money is used to buy the good will of local leaders.

The presence of an army of occupation is not merely ineffective, it is harmful to the security of Westerners. The main threat to the latter comes not from armed Afghan peasants, but from all those who, outside Afghanistan, feel a sense of solidarity with its population for political, religious or cultural reasons. Today's terrorist is not carrying out directions issued by some secret base; he is aware of the humiliation suffered by those to whom he is close, and he spontaneously commits himself to act on their behalf. Trying to eliminate a decision-making centre of al-Qaeda, a base from which all the orders for terrorist actions are issued, is a futile daydream derived from an outdated set of parameters inapplicable to the new situation. The mountains of Afghanistan (or any other country) do not play a role comparable to the KGB centres in Moscow during the Cold War. It is a different context to which people now need to adapt, one marked by technological developments and globalization. In the West, there is a great deal of talk about the danger represented by Islamism for the countries of Europe or North America; but, for the time being, it is Western armies which are occupying Muslim countries or intervening militarily in them. The propaganda of the enemies of the West that exploits this fact is now spread by the Internet; as for explosives, it is easy to procure them on the black market, or even in the supermarket.

In order to fight terrorism, the West has two means at its disposal: one is policing (gathering information, surveillance, cutting off financing); the other is political in nature (not leaving oneself exposed to the accusation that the values being defended are a mere camouflage for the will to dominate, that 'democracy' is an excuse for occupation). Neither of these is military: the presence of an army reinforces terrorism instead of weakening it.

Today the occupation of Afghanistan has become a cause of aggressions, instead of being a remedy for them. At the same time, this military engagement requires such a high price to be paid that it ought to shock the population of Western countries, in particular in times of economic and financial crisis; if this does not happen, it is because such enormous sums fail to speak to the imagination. Obama relates that, before he came to power, the war in Afghanistan had already cost a trillion (a thousand billion) dollars; at present it requires 1 billion per week. The new commitments represent another 30 billion for the year 2010. The allies also have to contribute: the war is costing the French 1 million euros per day. Is it really not possible to find a more productive use for such colossal sums?

These arguments against American military engagement in Afghanistan, already formulated by several commentators, cannot be ignored by Obama and his advisors. Nor can they fail to notice the vulnerability of the way this intervention is equated with 'a just war'. In his

Oslo speech, Obama enumerates three conditions for a war to be just: 'if it is waged as a last resort or in self-defence; if the force used is proportional; and if, whenever possible, civilians are spared from violence'. Now none of these conditions is satisfied in present circumstances: the security of the United States is not being endangered by the Afghan insurgents; an army of 100,000 men cannot be judged 'proportional' when faced with 500 al-Qaeda fighters; and air strikes make civilian losses inevitable. But in that case, why persist in getting entangled in this dead-end situation?

The sole rational answer that I can find is that the declared aim is not the aim being pursued. We can gain some idea of the latter if we read between the lines of some of the statements that Obama slipped into the same speech. The United States, he claims, are obliged to bear a 'burden' – not the white man's burden, as in Kipling, but that of a people entrusted with a particular mission: to 'underwrite global security', and thus act as mankind's policeman, and contribute to the promotion of freedom throughout the world; such is the 'enlightened self-interest' of the American people. Now this is a collective belief that, although not of religious origin, has the same absolute character as divine commandments and seems not to fall within the purview of rational argument. Otherwise, what could be the origin of such a mission?

In the same spirit, Obama openly envisages the usefulness of war 'beyond self-defence or the defence of one nation against an aggressor', to protect a population against its own government, or to stop a civil war; in short, 'force can be justified on humanitarian grounds'. Such interventions, he goes on to point out, can be carried out preventively. With principles such as these, you can go a long way! As the French author Charles Péguy wrote at the start of the twentieth century: 'There is enough in the Declaration of the Rights of Man to wage war on everyone for as long as everyone is still around'! But does anyone wish this? Obama finds it necessary to assure us that 'evil does exist in the world'. Indeed; but should we not insist rather on the fact that the temptation of good (what he calls 'the temptations of pride and power') has caused much more damage in the world than the 'temptation of evil'? If we resign ourselves to imposing good by force, this is because we have abandoned the principle to which Obama at the same time appeals, namely, that all peoples are impelled by the same basic needs: 'we're all basically seeking the same things'; henceforth, one group of people decides for the others. Finally, while the notion of 'just war' could meet with some reservations, that of 'humanitarian war' simply makes us think of Orwell and the doublespeak slogans of the Party in *1984*.

Waging this war is thus in the interest of the American nation, since it proves and illustrates its military superiority (we know that the latter is incontestable, and that the United States is prepared to pay the price: the military budget of the US, 600 billion dollars per year, equals the sum spent on military budgets in all other countries in the world). Aspiration to power needs no justification beyond power, even if such reasons do exist on an ad hoc basis, for instance the need to ensure one has a strategic sufficiency of oil supplies; power is sought for itself. Avoiding losing face is essential from this point of view; and acknowledging that intervention in Afghanistan was not justified would inevitably produce this result. But does this not mean that the present error is being legitimized by a past error? It is difficult to see how Obama could reverse this line of action, whatever his intimate convictions, without committing political suicide: it seems to flow from his very function as president of the most powerful country in the world.

Renouncing the use of military force in relations between countries in no way means that we are resigned to suffering the way the world is, whatever this may involve: countries as powerful as those in the West have numerous other means at their disposal to influence the course of affairs in other countries. They can act through political and economic channels or help the NGOs that are trying to build schools and hospitals; perhaps, more than anything, they can proudly and faithfully embody the principles which they claim to follow: the force of ideas is much greater than military leaders believe. History teaches us that they can bring walls crashing down and even topple empires.

Identity crisis?

It is true that national identities in European countries are changing, under the pressure of increased integration within the European Union and of globalization. But the nature of the reactions to this change does not strike me as likely to quieten the anxieties it has aroused. In France, as in the other European states, the question of national identity tends to be reduced to that of the way immigrants are received; and the question of immigrants tends to be reduced to that of the possible or undesirable toleration of Muslims in a 'Christian' (or 'secular') land. In a 2009 referendum, the Swiss made it illegal to build minarets in their lovely country; the French are preparing to do the same for the wearing of the burka in any public space, including the streets – so women who wear one will need to remain shut away in their homes.

As a reminder of the rise of ordinary Islamophobia, I will choose this little *fait divers* which occurred in Belgium, in a prison in Brussels, when police had taken over from prison guards who were on strike that day. 'On 30 October,' as *Le Monde* reported on 20 November 2009, 'four or five policemen in balaclavas beat a prisoner, took him to a solitary cell and forced him to strip, before bludgeoning his back and testicles. Then he was forced to recite "The Prophet Mohammed is a paedophile" and "My mother is a whore", as the report of the commission of surveillance records.' The Flemish press in Belgium spoke of an 'Abu Ghraib in Forest' (the name of the district in which the prison is situated): Europeans have no wish to lag behind the Americans.

As the public debate on national identity that was opened in France in October shows, membership of a cultural community, citizenship, and support for certain moral and political values still get mixed up – a confusion I warned against in my book. Rather than reiterate the arguments for or against this blurring, I prefer to illustrate my point by narrating one particular case of a change of country, and thus of national belonging: my own! The idea of coming to France came to me for the first time in 1962 when, having recently graduated from the University of Sofia, I learned that it was possible for me to spend a year in a Western country. There was no question at all of emigrating for good, but rather of staying in another country to continue my studies, and to immerse myself in the world of foreign academia. The reasons for my choice of France and Paris were that I was seduced by the (obviously superficial) image of a city that was a crossroads for arts and letters. I was of course not the only one to think this – and it didn't make a Frenchman of me.

By the end of this first year's stay in Paris, I had learnt a great deal, I had been able to read many books that were inaccessible in Bulgaria, and I had improved my French considerably: it was the language of my day-to-day life. I had also made friends in France – several of them foreigners who had settled in Paris – and, thanks to them, I had discovered something of the French countryside. Like many other foreigners in my situation, I prided myself on the way I had become a connoisseur of French customs: I wanted to taste every type of cheese and, insofar as my modest means permitted it, every kind of wine! So I decided to stay on for another two years to gain a new degree. But this did not make a Frenchman of me.

Those years, too, went by, and in the meantime I got married and started to earn my living in France. My professional interests were also evolving, and I felt myself increasingly drawn into the ongoing public debate in what had become my country of residence. I started to pay more attention to the principles of moral and political life – a subject that we could not discuss in Bulgaria, since all public life there was subject to the ukases of the Communist regime. The principles that I saw operating in France, even if in practice they were often transgressed, struck me as preferable – by far! The rule of law was superior to the reign of arbitrariness and corruption, the protection of individual freedoms was better than the permanent and inescapable surveillance, and respect for the dignity of all was to be preferred to the old patriarchal spirit or the new political castes. But this, too, did not make a Frenchman of me: the citizens of many other countries were in the same situation.

And yet the question 'when did I become French?' can be given a very clear answer; it is a simple matter of my citizenship – which, unlike my political choices or my cultural inclinations, is a matter for the competence of the government and parliament. This change occurred on the day when, ten years after my arrival in the country, by a decree of the Republic, I was naturalized as a Frenchman. From that moment on, my civic duties have tied me to this country in preference to any other – in return for the new rights it has granted me. As for my private identity, it has, to be sure, become French, but not only or merely French. In changing nationality, one does not change childhood! I cannot forget the first twenty-four years of my life, decisive years which mean that, inside myself, I still look on France from the outside, and attribute to culture what, for others, is seen as natural. Rather than being French, I sometimes feel that I am the inhabitant of a single city, or even district; on other occasions, however, I am the inhabitant of the entire continent of Europe, or even of the world! Of one thing, however, I am sure: I would not like any ministry or its officials to decide on my behalf what I should be, think, believe or love.

January 2010

Notes

INTRODUCTION: BETWEEN FEAR AND RESENTMENT

1 Montesquieu, *The Spirit of the Laws*, trans. and ed. Anne M. Cohler, Basia Carolyn Miller and Harold Samuel Stone (Cambridge: Cambridge University Press, 1989), book III, ch. 1.
2 Dominique Moisi, 'The Clash of Emotions', *Foreign Affairs* 1/2 (2007) – now expanded into a book: *The Geopolitics of Emotion: How Cultures of Fear, Humiliation, and Hope are Reshaping the World* (New York: Random House, 2009).
3 Desmond Tutu, *No Future without Forgiveness: A Personal Overview of South Africa's Truth and Reconciliation Committee* (London: Rider, 1999), p. 95.
4 Blaise Pascal, *The Provincial Letters*, trans. and with an introduction by A. J. Krailsheimer (Harmondsworth: Penguin, 1967), letter 12, p. 192.

CHAPTER 1   BARBARISM AND CIVILIZATION

1 See the recent work by R.-P. Droit, *Généalogie des barbares* (Paris: Odile Jacob, 2007), with bibliography; and, from a different point of view, Tzvetan Todorov, *On Human Diversity: Nationalism, Racism and Exoticism in French Thought*, trans. Catherine Porter (Cambridge, MA, and London: Harvard University Press, 1993).
2 Euripides, *Iphigenia among the Taurians*, ed. and trans. David Kovacs, Loeb Classical Library (Cambridge, MA, and London: Harvard University Press, 1999), p. 275, line 1174.

3 Strabo, *Geography*, trans. Horace Leonard Jones, Loeb Classical Library (London: Heinemann; Cambridge, MA: Harvard University Press, 1969), vol. 2, IV.4.5 (pp. 247–9), and IV.5.4 (p. 259).

4 Herodotus, *History*, trans. A. D. Godley, Loeb Classical Library, vol. 2 (London: Heinemann; Cambridge, MA: Cambridge University Press, 1963), III.101 (p. 129).

5 Edith Hall, *Inventing the Barbarian: Greek Self-definition through Tragedy* (Oxford: Clarendon Press, 1991), p. 196.

6 Euripides, *Helen*, ed. and trans. David Kovacs, Loeb Classical Library (Cambridge, MA, and London: Harvard University Press, 2002), p. 41, line 276.

7 Herodotus, *History*, vol. 4, IX.79 (p. 253) (translation modified).

8 Strabo, *Geography*, vol. 1, I.4.9 (pp. 247–9), and vol. 6, XIV.2.28 (p. 305).

9 1 Corinthians 14: 10–11.

10 St Jerome, *Letters and Select Works*, trans. W. H. Fremantle (New York: Christian Literature Company; Oxford: Parker and Company, 1893), LXXV. 2 (p. 155); quoted by Droit, *Généalogie*, p. 165.

11 Bartolomé de las Casas, *Apologetica Historica Summaria*, 2 vols (Mexico City: UNAM, 1967), vol. 2, III, p. 254.

12 Montaigne, *Essays*, trans. M. A. Screech (Harmondsworth: Penguin, 1991), III.9 (pp. 1114–15) and I.31 (p. 231).

13 Romain Gary, *Les Cerfs-volants* (Paris: Gallimard, 1980), p. 265.

14 Rousseau, 'Lettre sur la vertu', *Annales de la société Jean-Jacques Rousseau* XLI (1997): 25; Frans de Waal, *Our Inner Ape* (New York: Riverhead Books, 2005).

15 Kant, *Critique of the Faculty of Judgement*, trans. James Creed Meredith (Oxford: Clarendon Press, 1952), § 40, pp. 151–2.

16 Goethe, 'Epochen geselliger Bildung', in *Werke*, Berliner Ausgabe, 23 vols (Berlin: Aufbau, 1960–78), *Kunsttheoretische Schriften und Übersetzungen*, vols 18–22, vol. 18, pp. 458–60.

17 Freud, *Civilization and Its Discontents*, trans. and ed. James Strachey (New York: W. W. Norton and Co., 1961), pp. 66–71.

18 Bronisław Malinowksi, *A Scientific Theory of Culture, and Other Essays* (Chapel Hill, NC: University of North Carolina Press, 1944), p. 36; Claude Lévi-Strauss, *Entretiens avec Georges Charbonnier* (Paris: 10/18, 1961), p. 180; Clifford Geertz, *The Interpretation of Cultures* (London: Hutchinson, 1975), p. 49.

19 Geertz, *Interpretation*, pp. 49–50.
20 Lucien Febvre, 'Civilisation, évolution d'un mot et d'un groupe d'idées', and E. Tonnelat, '*Kultur*, histoire du mot, évolution du sens', in: *Civilisation, le mot et l'idée* (n.p.: La Renaissance du livre, 1930); Émile Benveniste, 'Civilization: A Contribution to the History of the Word', in *Problems in General Linguistics*, trans. Mary Elizabeth Meek (Coral Gables, FL.: University of Miami Press, 1971), pp. 289–96.
21 Montesquieu, *The Spirit of the Laws*, vol. I, Preface, p. xliv.
22 Johann Gottfried von Herder, *Another Philosophy of History*, in *Philosophical Writings*, ed. and trans. Michael N. Forster (Cambridge: Cambridge University Press, 2002).
23 Herder, *Ideas for a Philosophy of the History of Mankind*, in *J. G. Herder on Social and Political Culture*, ed. F. M. Barnard (London: Cambridge University Press, 1969), p. 48.
24 Montaigne, *Essays*, I.25 (p. 151).
25 Strabo, *Geography*, vol. 2, IV.5.2 (p. 255).
26 Jean-Jacques Rousseau, *A Discourse on the Origin of Inequality*, in *The Social Contract and Discourses*, trans. G. D. H. Cole, revised and augmented by J. H. Brumfitt and John C. Hall (London: J. M. Dent & Sons, Ltd, 1973), p. 83.
27 *Vie de Voltaire*, quoted by Febvre, 'Civilisation', p. 22.
28 *De la religion* (Arles: Actes Sud, 1999), p. 498.
29 Rousseau, *Émile, or On Education*, trans. Allan Bloom (Harmondsworth: Penguin, 1991), p. 187.
30 Kant, *Gesammelte Schriften* (Berlin: AK, 1934), vol. XX, p. 44.
31 Quoted in Febvre, 'Civilisation', p. 47.
32 *Civilisation, le mot et l'idée*, pp. 141–2.
33 Walter Benjamin, 'Theses on the Philosophy of History', in *Illuminations*, ed. and with an introduction by Hannah Arendt, trans. Harry Zohn (London: Fontana/Collins, 1970), p. 258.
34 Published in 2001. An English translation of the article originally published in *Il Corriere della Sera* can be found at: <http://www.giselle.com/oriana1.html> (accessed 7 May 2009).
35 Jared Diamond, *The Rise and Fall of the Third Chimpanzee* (London: Vintage, 1992), p. 171.
36 Ernest Renan, *Oeuvres complètes*, 10 vols (Paris: Calmann-Lévy, 1947), vol. I, p. 901.
37 Élie Barnavi, *Les religions meurtrières* (Paris: Flammarion, 2006), pp. 135 and 137.
38 'Race and History', 1952 text, reprinted (with corrections) in *Anthropologie structurale deux* (Paris: Plon, 1973), pp. 383–4;

English translation in *Structural Anthropology*, vol. 2, trans. Monique Layton (Harmondsworth: Penguin, 1978), pp. 323–62. Passage cited from pp. 329–30.

39   Alain Finkielkraut, *The Undoing of Thought*, trans. Dennis O'Keefe (London: Claridge Press, 1988), p. 25.

CHAPTER 2   COLLECTIVE IDENTITIES

1   M. Conche, *Les Fondements de la morale* (Paris: Éd. De Mégare, 1990).

2   Durán's narrative is translated in *The Aztecs. The History of the Indies of New Spain*, trans. Doris Heyden and Fernando Horcasitas (New York: Orion, 1964). Cf. Todorov, *The Conquest of America: The Question of the Other*, trans. Richard Howard (New York: Harper and Row, 1984); S. Gruzinski, *La Colonisation de l'imaginaire* (Paris: Gallimard, 1988), and *La Pensée métisse* (Paris: Fayard, 1999).

3   See Tzvetan Todorov, *Life in Common* (Lincoln and London: University of Nebraska Press, 2001).

4   Desmond Tutu, p. 35; Auden, quoted by H. Arendt, 'Remembering Auden', in Stephen Spender (ed.), *W. H. Auden: A Tribute* (London: Weidenfeld and Nicolson, 1975), pp. 181–7 (p. 183).

5   Voltaire, *Annales de l'Empire*, *Oeuvres complètes* (Paris: Garnier Frères, 1877–85), vol. XIII.

6   Benjamin Constant, *Journal*, 2 May 1804, *Œuvres* (Paris: Gallimard-Pléiade, 1979).

7   A. Maalouf, *On Identity*, trans. Barbara Bray (London: Harvill, 2000), p. 36.

8   Matthew 5: 46–7.

9   Cicero, *De Legibus*, trans. Clinton Walker Keyes (London: Heinemann; Cambridge, MA: Harvard University Press, 1970) vol. 16, II.2 (pp. 375–7).

10   Benjamin Constant, 'On the Spirit of Conquest and Usurpation', in *Political Writings*, trans. Biancamaria Fontana (Cambridge: Cambridge University Press, 1988), p. 141.

11   Amartya Sen, *Identity and Violence: The Illusion of Destiny* (London: Allen Lane, 2006), p. 156.

12   Élie Barnavi, *Les Religions meurtrières*, p. 132.

13   Ulrich Beck and Edgar Grande, *Cosmopolitan Europe*, trans. Ciaran Cronin (Cambridge: Polity, 2006), p. 263.

14 Ernest Renan, 'Qu'est-ce qu'une nation?', pp. 903–4.
15 Samuel Huntington, *The Clash of Civilizations and the Remaking of World Order* (New York: Simon and Schuster, 1997), pp. 50–1.
16 Yasmina Reza, *L'Aube, le soir ou la nuit* (Paris: Flammarion, 2007), p. 130. Ségolène Royal was candidate for the Socialist Party in the 2007 presidential election in France; she lost to Nicolas Sarkozy. Jean-Marie Le Pen, leader of the Front National, came fourth in the same election.
17 Brice Hortefeux, 'Ma vision de l'identité nationale', in *Libération*, 27 July 2007, p. 20.
18 See Peter Schneider, 'The New Berlin Wall', in *The New York Times*, 4 December 2005.

CHAPTER 3 THE WAR OF THE WORLDS

1 Samuel Huntington, *Clash of Civilizations*, p. 20.
2 Ibid., pp. 253–4.
3 Oriana Fallaci, *The Rage and the Pride*, quoted from: <http://www.giselle.com/oriana1.html> (accessed 7 May 2009).
4 Élie Barnavi, *Les Religions meurtrières*, p. 79.
5 Stephen Holmes, *The Matador's Cape* (New York and Cambridge: Cambridge University Press, 2007), p. 65.
6 *Le Monde*, 7 September 2007.
7 Ibid., 6 June 2007.
8 *International Herald Tribune*, 1–2 March 2008. Ali Ghufron has since been executed in prison.
9 Élie Barnavi, *Les Religions meurtrières*, p. 79.
10 Orhan Pamuk, 'The Anger of the Damned', in *The New York Review of Books*, 14/18 (15 November 2001).
11 Samuel Huntington, *Clash of Civilizations*, pp. 109–21.
12 Oriana Fallaci, *The Rage and the Pride*.
13 Romain Gary, *Chien blanc* (Paris: Gallimard, 1970), pp. 97–8. Originally published in English as *White Dog* (also 1970).
14 Pascal Bruckner, *La Tyrannie de la pénitence* (Paris: Grasset, 2006), p. 33.
15 Élie Barnavi, *Les Religions meurtrières*, p. 108.
16 Samuel Huntington, *Clash of Civilizations*, p. 14.
17 Ibid., p. 20.
18 Élie Barnavi, *Les Religions meurtrières*, p. 113.
19 See also O. Roy, *Généalogie de l'islamisme* (Paris: Hachette, 1995); A. Meddeb, *La Maladie de l'islam* (Paris: Le Seuil, 2002).

20 *Signes de piste*, quoted by Mohamed Charfi, *Islam et liberté* (Paris: Albin Michel, 1998), pp. 52–3. For an English translation of Sayyid Qutb, see *Milestones* (Beirut: Maktabah Publishers, 2007).

21 See also W. Langewiesche, 'A Face in the Crowd', *Vanity Fair*, February 2008, pp. 72–83 and 133–41.

22 Alexis de Tocqueville, *De la colonie en Algérie* (Brussels: Complexe, 1988), p. 39.

23 Stephen Holmes, *The Matador's Cape*, p. 81.

24 Germaine Tillion, *A la recherche du vrai et du juste* (Paris: Le Seuil, 2001), p. 74.

25 Primo Levi, *The Drowned and the Saved*, trans. Raymond Rosenthal (London: Abacus, 1989), p. 58.

26 *Les Ennemis complémentaires*, in *Combats de guerre et de paix* (Paris: Le Seuil, 2007), p. 685.

27 Rousseau, *Discourse on the Origin of Inequality*, p. 53.

28 Karl Jaspers, *The Origin and Goal of History* (New York: Routledge and Kegan Paul, 1953), p. 197; quoted by E. Young-Bruehl, *Why Arendt Matters* (New Haven, CT: Yale University Press, 2006), p. 208.

29 Text in M. Danner (ed.), *Torture and Truth* (New York: New York Review of Books, 2004); or in K. Greenberg and J. L. Dratel (eds), *The Torture Papers* (New Haven, CT: Yale University Press, 2006), p. 208.

30 *International Herald Tribune*, 6–7 October 2007; *Le Monde*, 8 February 2008.

31 S. Levinson (ed.), *Torture: A Collection* (New York and Oxford: Oxford University Press, 2004).

32 K. J. Greenberg (ed.), *The Torture Debate in America* (New York and Cambridge: Cambridge University Press, 2005).

33 P. Gourevitch and E. Morris, 'Exposure', *The New Yorker*, 24 March 2008.

34 *International Herald Tribune*, 6–7 October 2007.

35 Stephen Holmes, *The Matador's Cape*, ch. 12, 'Battling Lawlessness with Lawlessness'.

36 *The Washington Post*, 11 May 2007.

37 P. Rotman, *L'Ennemi intime* (Paris: Le Seuil, 2002), p. 231.

CHAPTER 4 STEERING BETWEEN THE REEFS

1 Ayaan Hirsi Ali, *Infidel*, p. 269.

2 Ibid., pp. 270–2.

3 Ibid., *Infidel*, p. 303.
4 Ian Buruma, *Murder in Amsterdam: The Death of Theo van Gogh and the Limits of Tolerance* (London: Atlantic Books, 2006).
5 I am taking some of the information on these events from Jeanne Favret-Saada, *Comment produire une crise mondiale* (Paris: Les Prairies ordinaires, 2007) – a work that is entirely favourable to the position of *Jyllands-Posten*.
6 *Le Monde*, 2–3 December 2007.
7 'The Sad Lessons of the Week', *New York Times*, 22 September 2006.
8 On the official Vatican site and (in French) in *La Documentation catholique*, no. 2366, 15 October 2006.
9 On this theme, see, with regard to the Pope, the book by J. Bollack, C. Jambet and A. Meddeb, *La Conférence de Ratisbonne* (Paris: Bayard, 2007).
10 Luke 14: 23.
11 Matthew 7: 3.
12 In J. Bollack et al., *La Conférence de Ratisbonne*, p. 73; this also contains a translation of the letter from the ulemas.
13 Olivier Roy, *Secularism Confronts Islam*, trans. George Holoch (New York and Chichester: Columbia University Press, 2007), p. 102.
14 *L'Islam et les fondements du pouvoir* (Paris: La Découverte, 1994), p. 76.
15 Mohamed Charfi, *Islam et liberté* (Paris: Albin Michel, 1998), p. 151.
16 M. M. Taha, *Un islam à vocation libératrice* (Paris: L'Harmattan, 2003).
17 Mohamed Charfi, *Islam et liberté*, p. 34.
18 Régis Debray, *Aveuglantes lumières* (Paris: Gallimard, 2006), pp. 80–6.

CHAPTER 5 EUROPEAN IDENTITY

1 Valéry, 'La Crise de l'esprit' and 'Note', *Variété* (Paris: Gallimard, 1924).
2 Montesquieu, *Persian Letters*, ed. Andrew Kahn, trans. Margaret Mauldon (Oxford: Oxford University Press, 2008), letter 83, p. 116.

3 Voltaire, *Philosophical Letters, or Letters Regarding the English Nation*, ed. John Leigh, trans. Prudence L. Steiner (Indianapolis, IN: Hackett; Lancaster: PA: Gazelle Drake Academic, 2007), p. 92.
4 Hume, *Essays, Moral, Political and Literary*, introduction by James Fieser (Bristol: Thoemmes, 2002), p. 123.
5 Ibid., p. 127.
6 Ibid., p.126.
7 Eric Jones, *The European Miracle* (Cambridge and New York: Cambridge University Press, 1981), pp. 111 and 112.
8 Herodotus, *History*, I.2 and IV.45.
9 Rousseau, *The Social Contract*, II.2 (p. 183).
10 Condorcet, *Rapport sur l'instruction publique* (1792), in *Écrits sur l'instruction publique*, vol. 2 (Paris: Edilig, 1989), p. 127 (190).
11 Ulrich Beck, *Cosmopolitan Europe*, p. 13.
12 Ibid., p. 15.
13 Ibid., p. 14.
14 Ibid., p. 264.

Index

221

Taha, Mahmoud
  Mohammed 162–3
Taliban 7, 206, 207
technology 2–3; and
  civilization 33, 34–9, 41, 42–3,
  45, 48, 49; conditions for future
  dialogue 199; torture 117; US
  and war in Afghanistan 208
terrorism: anti-Muslim feeling
  131, 138, 144, 146; clash of
  civilizations thesis 92–3, 95,
  97, 99; combating 6, 104–6,
  107–8, 127, 208; distinct from
  Islamism 102, 198; European
  identity 185–6, 189; fear of
  5; war in Afghanistan 208;
  see also war on terror
Tertullian 155
Thailand 116
Third World 1
Tillion, Germaine 110, 112, 133
Tocqueville, Alexis de 107
Todorov, Tzvetan 213n1
tolerance and intolerance 8, 10,
  152; collective identities 74;
  European identity 172, 174,
  180; national identity 210
Tolstoy, Leo Nikolayevich 36,
  37
torture 6, 7, 11, 14, 108, 109,
  112, 113–20, 146, 211;
  accepted forms 118–20,
  200–1; and barbarism 21,
  24, 50, 114, 126; collective
  identities 76; conditions for
  future dialogue 197; debate
  about 120–6; European
  identity 189; US and 114–26,
  200–4, 205, 207
Torture: A Collection
  (Levinson) 116
*Torture Debate in America,
  The* (Greenberg) 116
Torture Memo 115, 118,
  120

totalitarianism 6–7, 81, 99–100,
  110, 187; compared with
  Islamism 102–6; conflict with
  liberal democracy *see* Cold War;
  and torture 114, 117–18, 126
trade 34
trans-national networks, effect on
  nation-state 71–2
transport 35
travel 2–3, 29, 198
Treaty of Versailles (1919) 107
Trinquier, Roger 114, 121, 204
truth 188; war on terror 108–10
Turkey 177, 194; massacre of
  Armenians 24
Tutu, Desmond, Archbishop 62,
  112
Twenty-Four Hours (TV
  series) 121
tyranny, and barbarism 16

Ukraine 68, 194
UNESCO, Universal Declaration on
  Cultural Diversity 84
United Nations: Convention against
  torture (1984) 114, 118, 205;
  Universal Declaration of Human
  Rights (1948) 77, 114
United States: clash of civilizations
  thesis 86, 87, 90, 91, 92, 98;
  coexistence 183, 191; collective
  identities 69, 71, 78, 84–5,
  134–5; European relations
  with 187–91; Islamism and 104;
  Manicheism 99, 100; neo-
  conservatism 136; Obama
  administration and Afghanistan
  War 204–10; reaction to fear 7,
  8, 10; reaction to Regensburg
  speech of Pope Benedict
  XVI 153; resentment against 5;
  social violence 96;
  torture 114–26, 200–4, 205,
  207; war 111, 113, 189–91; war
  on terror 99, 106–10, 127